Housing the Masses

HOUSING THE MASSES

BY

CAROL ARONOVICI, Ph.D.

*Lecturer on Housing and Community Planning at
New York University and Columbia University*

NEW YORK
JOHN WILEY & SONS, Inc.
London : CHAPMAN & HALL, Limited
1939

Printed in the U. S. A.

THE HADDON CRAFTSMEN, INC.
CAMDEN, N. J.

TO THE MEMORY OF

KATE HOLLADAY CLAGHORN

I DEDICATE THIS BOOK

PREFACE

This book was conceived and written largely as a result of a long experience in teaching both housing and community planning in a variety of educational institutions. I have felt that most discussions on these subjects have been emphasizing the immediate objectives of these two important phases of individual and communal living, while the forces which have stood in the way of long-range creative effort have been neglected or overlooked in the interest of expediency. It is with the long-range aspects of housing that this book is concerned.

It will be noted that there is no discussion of the conditions of the slums and the alleged evils which they create. Nor has any serious consideration been given to European housing. The main reasons for these omissions are largely to be found in the fact that a vast literature already exists dealing with both these subjects. As for European housing, I have always felt that we ascribe entirely too much significance to the experience of countries with standards, laws, methods of living, and social attitudes which are fundamentally different from our own. We may seek inspiration in the courage and monumental achievement of Europe, but we must find our own way on our own terms if our efforts to improve housing conditions are to meet our needs and are to represent the American way of living.

CAROL ARONOVICI

Greenwich, Connecticut
  January 9, 1939

CONTENTS

CHAPTER   PAGE

Introduction   xi

I. Land   3

II. People   51

III. Money   67

IV. Earning Capacity and the Housing Market   89

V. Home Ownership   109

VI. The Law and Housing   125

VII. Urbanism and Housing   175

VIII. Architecture and Housing   197

IX. Housing Education   211

X. The Housing Survey and Housing Research   223

XI. Conclusions   271

Housing Literature   277

Index   289

INTRODUCTION

Housing as a problem of human welfare is as old as the human race itself. Although we have little idea of the manner of construction which was employed by the primitive races of the world, we are not wholly ignorant of the fact that from time to time the housing of the lower economic classes claimed the attention of the rulers. In this connection we might recall that Egyptian hieroglyphic inscriptions dating as far back as 4000 B.C. record a sit-down strike of the workers who participated in the building of the pyramids. The result was the first attempt to construct a model town in exchange for a waterproof tomb so essential to the health of the immortal souls of the Pharaohs.

Thucydides, the Greek writer, tells us that in the fourth century B.C. there was considerable concern with housing in Athens. The Spartans were slum dwellers *par excellence*. The rulers of Athens, however, met the problem of housing by passing many wise and drastic laws which set up standards of safety and sanitation under housing inspectors who had full power to demolish undesirable dwellings.

During the development of the great Byzantine Empire, a great deal was done to improve the sanitation of homes, and bathing as a sanitary and religious requirement assumed great importance. Indeed, there were more private baths in Constantinople about the middle of the eighth century A.D. than there were in New York and Boston combined in the middle of the nineteenth century.

In the United States the problem of protecting city dwellers in matters of housing evidently arose as far back as the earliest colonial times. Thus we find a New Amsterdam ordinance dated 1647 which attempted to reduce the hazard from fire, and another in 1657 forbidding the throwing of rubbish into the street and ordering that it be carted away. Subsequent early legislation dealt with sewers, water supply, and other regulations intended to protect health. If we may judge from early documents, the enforcement of these regulations was not very effective. That conditions went from bad to worse is evident from the many reports of health officers and the persistent changes and improvements in the laws regulating housing and requiring cleanliness. All these early regulations applied to New York City. It goes without saying that the whole problem of housing was dealt with as a matter of tenant-owner relationship and was not concerned with the more fundamental and far-reaching aspects of planning, taxation, land speculation, financing, costs, or building design.

Much has been written in the last four decades about the ways and means of solving the housing problem and abolishing the slums. Most of this writing has been concerned, not with the broader social and economic implications of providing good housing, but with the legal restrictions which might force owners to provide the kind of housing that would meet the minimum standards of decency. In this book I assume that sanitary regulations and minimum standards of safety and convenience, which should be provided for all the families in the United States, can without much difficulty be established by law. What is more difficult is to create conditions which would make housing embodying these standards financially practicable and accessible to all families as owners or renters. From this point of view, housing assumes a new aspect and one which implies the solution of a considerable number of social, economic, and legal problems not involved in the common practice of housing regulations. This is the approach attempted in this book. Many definitions of the housing movement have been suggested, but there has always been confusion between the objectives of housing and the methods of achieving these objectives. In a book which I published some years ago, I defined the objectives of housing as follows:

> The furnishing of healthful accommodations adequately provided with facilities for privacy and comfort, easily accessible to centers of employment, culture and amusement, accessible from the centers of distribution of the food supply, rentable at reasonable rates, and yielding a fair return on the investment.[1]

This set of objectives, I believe, has not altered since this book was written. What has changed is the outlook of those who are working toward the achievement of these ends. Their task may be defined as a movement intended to wrest from an unfavorable economy the means for adjusting the social, economic, legal, and technical factors affecting costs and fitness of housing so that the masses of the people may acquire the right to decent shelter in the same degree that they have acquired similar rights in matters of health and public education.

This new outlook has come about through the new conditions which this country has had to face. The recent economic crisis has been no small factor in bringing housing within the scope of the larger national issues and in taking it out of the realm of sentimentality and small politics.

Since the inauguration of the "New Deal" under the leadership of President Roosevelt, the housing movement has taken two distinct directions, both of which are growing in significance with the passing of

[1] Aronovici, Carol, *Housing and the Housing Problem*, McClurg, 1920; p. 7.

time and the evaluation of experience. The first of these is bringing the financing and construction of housing within the range of public service as a permanent part of the national government. The second, and in my estimation the more important, is the effort toward a restatement of the housing problem as a sociopolitical philosophy in which public action and private enterprise would be brought into effective relationship in the interest of building enterprise and particularly housing. If the second objective could be achieved, housing would pass from the field of charity and social service into a new phase of economic doctrine, and from a symptom of maladjustment of individuals and families in need of special attention into a new phase of economic reconstruction.

The housing movement has been delayed by no more effective obstacles than the failure to consider its causes and the economic resources of the slum dwellers. It seemed simpler and less disturbing to our social structure to stress the slum and the blighted district. There was more dramatic value in portraying the indescribable filth and misery of the slum dweller than in exposing the economic and business structure which made these slums possible and, in a sense, useful to the families who could afford nothing better. Land speculation, low wages, high interest rates, bad planning, banking and investment policies were too far-reaching in their effects upon the whole economic system and involved too many vested interests to be disturbed. All this is now clear to many students of housing, and even government agencies are taking a hand in revising the limits of public action in the matter of private investment and profit.

There are, of course, still those who insist that the slums must be cleared first. How this could be accomplished no one knows. The governments—federal, state, or local—could undertake this task if the question of cost were not so considerable. Indeed, many cities, with aid from the federal government, have attempted to reconstruct some of their slum areas; but the achievement to date, and the probable achievement in the future, is likely to be negligible when considered in the light of the vast slum areas which every large city contains and of the problem of absorbing, not alone the productive values of land and buildings, but also the speculative, non-realizable values which the owners of slum property insist upon turning into cash. Even if we assume that the government would eventually absorb all the slum areas for housing, and that this would be accomplished at the rate of 50,000 dwellings a year, it would take 140 years to absorb the 7,000,000 slum dwellings in the various cities of the United States—hardly an encouraging prospect for the next generation of slum dwellers.

No one is more eager to free our cities of slums than I. No one can be unaware of its blighting effects upon the welfare, not alone of its occupants, but upon the whole of the community as well. The difficulty, however, must be realized that slum clearance complicates rather than simplifies the solution of the housing problem. The real task is not the clearing of the slums and the salvaging of the values which the slums represent, but rather the salvaging of the human lives which now must live in slums. Take the people out of them, and the slums will be cleared in less time than it will take the government to clear them by subsidies. If we could forget the slums for a decade and proceed to develop housing where there is no decay and no mismanagement of investment or unwarranted speculation, we would open the road to decent housing, which the insistence upon slum clearing only delays.

Although throughout this book I have emphasized the economic aspects of housing, I am not unmindful of the fact that our methods of planning and construction need reorganization and reorientation. In the matter of productive capacity of the industry which is engaged in home building, we find that, whereas within the last decade many industries have increased their productivity per unit of work by 400 per cent, the building industry has made no perceptible progress. Prefabrication, which has been attempted by many, has remained in the experimental stage and does not promise much for the immediate future.

Mass production is coming into greater prominence, but it still has a long way to go when compared with the methods employed in England, Sweden, Germany, and other European countries. As to the design of large-scale housing and the relating of these housing projects to their neighborhood pattern, much remains to be accomplished. I am not concerned here with the vast and complex task of reorganizing the industry. This can and will be accomplished when the economic structure upon which housing depends has been built up to meet present-day conditions and has been safeguarded by legislative and administrative means so that it may yield to changing conditions and advancing standards.

We have, in this country, allegedly about 10,000,000 families living in substandard dwellings. Just where the line of demarcation between standard and substandard lies is difficult to state. The fact is that many standard houses of yesterday are substandard today, and that many of the so-called standard dwellings of today will be obsolete long before the end of their structural life. Certainly few families live in the kind of house suited to their needs or one which makes home life attractive. These houses may not be designated as substandard dwellings according to some code which is based upon the lowest common denominator of bad housing, but, from the point of view of the families which occupy

them and their individual standards, they may be classed as such. The
task of the housing movement is not alone the clearing away of slums
and replacement of legally substandard dwellings by legally minimum-
standard dwellings. The real task of the housing movement is the raising
of all housing standards to a point of efficiency as living machines and
as centers around which family life revolves that will be consistent with
the potential and actual advance in the technique of planning and construction, and with the way of living which American families can and
should have.

The poor must, of course, be provided for first, but this is not the
fundamental function of the housing movement, except as it would be
facilitated by all the instrumentalities which might be created in the
interest of better housing for all the people. If only we could be liberated
from the slum and lower-income-group complexes, we might forge ahead
in evolving a policy of housing which would affect the welfare of every
individual and family in the land, and raise standards favoring not only
the poor but likewise the masses of American people.

Land

HOUSING THE MASSES

CHAPTER I

LAND

I. LAND VALUES

In a land where populations are constantly shifting, where standards of living are fluctuating or advancing, where techniques of industry and business change with unprecedented rapidity, confusion in the physical pattern of communities and obsolescence of investment in real property are unavoidable. Indeed this obsolescence may become an index of movement and progress. Such progress does not take place by a process of rational planning but by that pioneering spirit which destroys, in the interest of today, what society may be needing tomorrow.

This form of individualistic effort in the march of American civilization is nowhere more obvious than in the manner in which we have attempted to reap the benefits from a growing population and a mounting national wealth in the exploitation of land as space for urban living.

We are not concerned in this work with the whole problem of urban land and its use, since our main interest is the relation between land and housing. It is impossible, however, to separate the land problem as it affects housing from the larger problem of community space, its distribution and use. Indeed no parcel of land can be evaluated either in economic or social terms without taking into account the relation it bears to its immediate surroundings, its neighborhood character, and its place in the community as one of particular importance to its present as well as future use. In fact, aside from agricultural values, land has no value except that which can be derived from its relation to the community, not alone as a stable commodity, but also as an entity changing in time and space at particular rates of speed. Thus land values must be based upon a four-dimensional formula, in which space, position in the community, time, and rate of change must be taken into account. The transition which urban land has undergone from pioneering days to its present exploitational phase, and the eventual social and economic obsolescence of large areas of our cities, resulted in the creation of blight and slums, which have involved both the welfare of our communities and the security of

3

investment in real property. As real estate embraces about one-fifth of our national wealth, its effect upon our national economy is bound to be far-reaching.

In order to understand the relation that land bears to the location, distribution, and cost of housing, it is important to analyze rather minutely the factors which make certain lands suitable for housing and the bases upon which values or costs are established.

Broadly speaking, the suitability of land for housing purposes depends upon the following classes of factors:

1. Natural character of raw land as building site.
2. Its geographic relation to the community.
3. Its quantitative relation to present and future needs.
4. Its stability and future possibilities.
5. Its place in the evolving community.
6. Its exposure to outer influences.
7. Available community services.
8. Its obligations as present and future investment.
9. Its capacity for economic development.
10. The relation of units of ownership to use.
11. Degree of intensity and variety of development possible.
12. Margin of profit to be derived from additional investment and management.
13. Social controls of use and their relation to stability of investment and possibility for speculation.

Raw Land

The value of raw land for housing purposes is derived from its natural character as a suitable building site. Where land presents such problems as drainage, difficulties in the construction of basements and cellars owing to rock formation or seepage, soft ground in need of piling before construction, slopes making building or access costly, values are of necessity lower. Where land is of such quality as to involve no extra effort or cost, however, and where use is not hampered by physical conditions, values are not affected.

In recent years some of the so-called natural objectionable conditions in land due to slope which make it undesirable for certain uses have been capitalized as assets, particularly in luxury housing. Cities within whose precincts the hills have been wholly undeveloped or only partly developed have now resorted to these hills as the best sites for luxury housing. This is due to the development of the automobile, for one thing, and also to a considerable amount of progress in the design of hillside homes, in which the problems of grade have been transformed into opportunities for architectural treatment affording variety, picturesqueness, and utility under otherwise difficult natural conditions. Not only have these lands become useful as residential areas, but in many cities they have attained values undreamed of before.

There are, of course, land conditions which, although quite suitable for housing purposes from the point of view of location, outlook, and environment, present structural difficulties which add to the cost of construction without adding to the use value of such construction. This is true of low or swampy lands, where buildings must be especially reinforced or piles must be driven into the ground to serve as underpinnings for buildings. A study of most city lands would easily reveal ample building areas without resort to this type of costly construction.

View may be considered as part of the value of land. Although this advantage is not an integral part of what might be called raw land, it is nevertheless inherent in the position of the site in its relations to surroundings.

GEOGRAPHIC RELATION TO THE COMMUNITY

Land economies and urban living are inseparable. Land values are part of the total residential value of the city or town in which they are situated, and their uses are a direct result of the sum total of the economic and social requirements of the whole community. This is not always a condition which may be summed up in quantitative or qualitative values, because our cities and towns are made up, not of a synchronized set of factors, but of a series of layers of conditions and demands which are superimposed upon the community over a considerable period of time, during which fluctuations in the rate of development, improvement of standards, and economic disturbances have been taking place. In addition, the accumulation of legal restrictions and controls over land uses, after some of the more desirable lands have been developed, makes a categorical evaluation of building sites in relation to the community difficult, if not impossible.

It would be clear to anyone concerned with housing that the lower East Side of New York, by virtue of its proximity to the greatest financial district of the city, its access to the water front, and its close relation to business and industry, should be the most valuable and desirable residential district of this great metropolis. However, the historic factors which have played a part in the development of this area have destroyed a good share of the values inherent in its geographic location, thus re-

sulting in the creation of slums. No one can deny that the geographic
location values are still there, but their salvaging would involve such
heavy costs as to counteract a goodly share of the possible gain.

Similar conditions exist in practically every city of the country, where
the most desirable and most accessible lands, although the first to be
developed, have now become outstanding centers of obsolescent residential districts and blighted business and industrial areas.

Again, we find districts in our cities favored from the point of view
of their relation to the rest of the community which, owing to inconsistent development, changes in standards of building and fluctuating
market demands, have become blighted by an admixture of land uses
consistent with temporary demands which now resist coordination. Thus
we find a certain portion of New York City—namely Astoria, in the
vicinity of the Fifty-Ninth Street bridge—made up of obsolete and
scattered buildings, open areas, factories, tenements, and apartment houses
comprising sufficient acreage to house a community of from 50,000 to
100,000 people; but the development of this site is at a standstill. This
failure to develop a coherent community has taken place despite proximity
to business and industrial centers, ample transit facilities, and low land
cost.

To what extent it would be possible to recapture the lost geographic
land values of our cities is a matter of conjecture. Zoning, planning, slum
clearance, street improvements, traffic orientation, and the complex machinery of technical planning and planning controls may play an important part in this process, but the time element involved will depend upon
the rate at which present improvements may be junked without upsetting
the economic structure of real-estate investment. For the moment, there
is a great deal of resistance to a proper redistribution of land uses, much
of which is due to the inherent difficulties of displacing one use of land
with another without loss of revenue to private owners, reduction in
taxable improvements, disturbance of the process of business and industrial relation, and inconvenience to the residents of the district to be sal-
vaged for its proper use.

In any analysis which may be made of a community, in order to determine its capacity for housing development and the distribution of the
various types needed to meet local needs, it would be essential to consider
all the housing factors which may lead to placing the home districts where
they would bear a proper relation to the community. These would include shopping centers, education and recreational centers, and such
amenities of environment as would give permanency to individual development and justify large-scale building investment, with ample con-

sideration, not alone for the inherent advantages which a site represents, but also for the manner in which these advantages will serve the people who are to be housed. Advantages of location in the abstract have no great bearing upon the problem. They must be related to the specific needs of the people whom they are intended to serve.

PRESENT AND FUTURE LAND NEEDS

No city of the United States suffers from a shortage of land for housing purposes. In fact, the expression "land shortage" is subject to a great variety of interpretations, and the methods of overcoming alleged shortage have created confusion in our urban land economy. Let us consider the various ways in which claims of land shortage are justified.

A reasonably fair definition of land shortage would be "the lack of adequate areas consistent with the various needs of the city—to provide for its normal functions for the present and its normal anticipated growth." It must be pointed out, however, that the potential activities and services which may be developed on a square mile of urban land in a typical old-time block in the City of Philadelphia, for example, where the single-row house prevails, creates one type of demand for land, while a Manhattan tenement-block development bears an entirely different relation to land use and the possibilities for land shortage, if we assume the same area and the same population. Indeed, it is conceivable that, under certain conditions, a high population load per land unit under proper land planning would result in more desirable living conditions than a low population load on a similar unit of land without proper land planning.

If a shortage of suitable land is claimed in a city, it may be reasonably expected that this is due to conditions which have permitted the best lands to be exploited until they have become blighted with obsolescent buildings, serving in a substandard manner the purpose for which they were originally designed.

The last quarter of a century has witnessed a flight of population from the center to the periphery of our cities. This flight has been partly due to a normal increase in the population, but its main cause has been the pressure of rising standards upon the lag of land-use adjustment.

The area of the City of New York is 190,161 acres, of which 83,000 acres were vacant in 1920. The built-up area represented a density of population of 52.7 persons per acre, or about 13 families, the population of New York at that time amounting to 5,620,000. On this basis, there was still room for an increase in population of 4,352,800 within the unbuilt area of New York City, or a total potential population of 9,972,800 people—the equivalent of the population of the entire New York region, which extends into three states and covers an area fifteen times as great as the area of the City of New York itself.

An analysis of the relation between population and area of almost any other city of the United States will reveal conditions similar to those of Greater New York. Indeed, some cities like Los Angeles have extended their municipal boundaries to cover the extent of the regional population flight that has been taking place, in order to recapture the population and taxing resources, which have been trying to escape from inefficient and uneconomical land use within the settled areas of the city.

Within the last twenty years we find cities like Detroit, Cleveland, San Francisco, Los Angeles, Chicago, and many others engaged in a process of land expansion through the development of new subdivisions sufficient to provide for a populational growth which statisticians tell us will never take place in this country, owing to the slowing up of our rate of population increase and to the practical cessation of immigration.

I have seen the development of subdivisions in one metropolitan district which would be sufficient to accommodate the population of the entire state, including its normal growth forecast for a generation. Many of these subdivisions were carved into landscapes which should have been preserved as public parks. Others were extended into fruitful agricultural lands, which were yielding handsome returns as intensively cultivated areas.

This wasteful method of land-development expansion has now come to a standstill, but its effects upon city and rural budgets are still being felt. Connection highways have been built at enormous costs only to be abandoned or to remain partly used. Streets have been constructed which have yielded to the ravages of neglect. Sewers and water systems have been provided on a scale wholly disproportionate to possible use, and, above all, investors in land or securities connected with these "improvements" have been left holding the proverbial bag.

Many of these subdivisions have now been returned, officially, to the designation of "agricultural land." This, however, is merely a device to gain the advantage of lower taxation. The subdivisions, with their abandoned and deteriorating equipment, still remain as evidence of an optimism which transcends the bounds of business sanity.

It seems obvious from what has been said that the expansion of land subdivision was due to two fundamental factors: first, the intolerable conditions of living which our modern cities have developed; and second, the high cost of land within our cities, which made it impossible to use adequate areas for good housing development. The latter is true of land

Photograph by W.P.A.—Division of Photography.

A STUDY IN CONTRASTS—SLUMS AND SKYSCRAPERS.

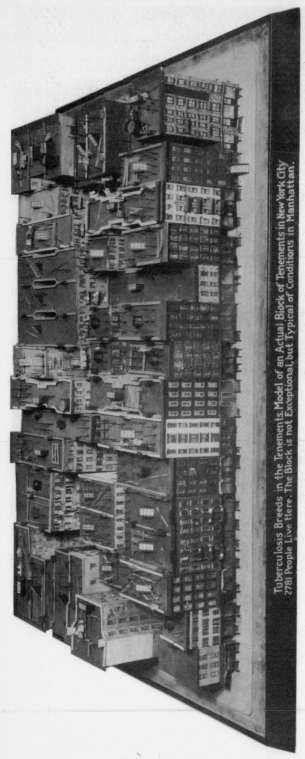

Tuberculosis Breeds in the Tenements. Model of an Actual Block of Tenements in New York City.
2781 People Live Here. The Block is not Exceptional, but Typical of Conditions in Manhattan.

Photograph by W.P.A.—Division of Photography.

THE FAMOUS LUNG BLOCK OF MANHATTAN, NEW YORK CITY.

A SLUM IN PITTSBURGH, PENNSYLVANIA.

Photograph by W.P.A.—Division of Photography.

WILLIAMSBURG HOUSING PROJECT SITE.

that is still lying idle or that has become blighted by obsolete, incoherent, or inappropriate development.

STABILITY AND FUTURE POSSIBILITIES

Stability and future possibilities in land values are almost contradictory terms, and yet much of our land-market activity depends upon alleged or actual possibilities rather than actual use. For every generation the land in our slums has maintained an almost unchanged stability as a profit-yielding power. With the deterioration of the buildings, this profit has been on the decrease rather than on the increase, but at the same time assessments on land have been advancing as building assessments have been diminishing.

Stability of revenue and its consequent stability of value depends upon conditions which protect a given investment over a considerable period of time. Zoning and deed restrictions, as applied to land subdivision and land use, tend to stabilize land values and reduce or eliminate possibilities for speculation or even gradual increases in value. Where these restrictions are lax or non-existent, the possibilities for speculation are increased, although the expected speculative price may never be realized.

In fact, much of our timid zoning effort, which has little to do with actual utility or fitness, has acted in the direction of destroying stability and raising false hopes. Out of this has grown a new kind of speculation without relation to the reality of present need or future demand. Zoning of this kind can be found in almost every city of the United States. It is a form of legalized wishful thinking that destroys the balance of community development which it is intended to encourage.

Even though it is conceivable that a rapid growth in population, a shift in the center of gravity of business, some unexpected clearing of a less intensively developed area to make way for more intensive development may enhance land values at some specific point in the community, there is no reason why such incidents in community growth should find their reflection in the speculative land values of the community as a whole. In fact, any increase in the intensity of land development in one or more areas should have exactly the contrary effect, since the larger the building load a particular area carries, the less of a load is left for the remaining areas with a given population. If an acre of land increases by twenty times its load of superficial area of office space, as a result of the building of a sixty-story building where a three-story building had stood before, it is quite obvious that, unless there is an abnormal business development, the effect upon other similar areas would be to reduce rather than enhance surrounding land values.

It may be said without fear of contradiction that, wherever symptoms of speculation in residential or other lands appear, one of two things is bound to happen. Either there will be stagnation of building enterprise, owing to the difficulty encountered in making the building absorb a heavy land cost; or the result will be land sweating, which leads to congestion on the one hand and to a reduction in the marketability of the remaining building sites on the other. A policy of reducing the possibilities for land use is therefore an advantage to landowners, although it may deprive a few individuals of unreasonable profits.

The Place of Land in an Evolving Community

There are several ways of considering the evolution of communities. One is the hit-or-miss method, which is an orderless response to growing needs or alleged needs; another, the preconceived, preplanned method, which anticipates development and makes preparations that would check evils and lead to a distribution of land uses and improvements consistent with economy and efficiency. The greatest danger to orderly development is the fluctuating land market. The hungry landowner who has held land for years, meeting heavy taxes, fighting off mortgage foreclosures, and building up hopes of large profits can not be held responsible for taking advantage of a lively land market. The real difficulty lies in the failure of the community and its governing body to anticipate during normal times the possibilities of such land-market disturbances.

By fixing the number of dwellings per acre, by prelocating the residential districts of the city, by preplanning improvements consistent with the contemplated and logical development of specific areas, and by adjusting assessment and taxes to the potentialities of residential development of the planned areas up to their capacity to yield revenue, speculation in land could be reduced to a minimum.

It has been pointed out that there is no shortage of land for housing in most normally located communities. In his studies of the City of London, Sir Raymond Unwin has made some interesting calculations of the expansion of the area of growth that can be added to a given community by increasing the radius of development by one mile.[1] This ingenious way of demonstrating the relation between orderly expansion without moving the population too far away from the center of business activity, if kept in mind when preparations are made for community expansion, will provide ample housing accommodations easily interrelated

[1] See *Housing and Town Planning*—Lectures, 1936-1937, by Sir Raymond Unwin, pp. 77-82. Published by Subcommittee on Research and Statistics, Central Housing Committee, Washington, D. C.

by traffic and transit facilities without producing either congestion, land shortage, or undue territorial expansion.

EXPOSURE TO OUTER INFLUENCES

As land for housing becomes integrated into the body of the community, it acquires a number of social values which are its qualifying characteristics as residential property. Land that is used or designed to be used for housing is dependent for its social value upon its surroundings. Every structure that is built in the vicinity of a home site has an influence upon the value of this site for residential purposes. The construction of a home whose architectural design is out of harmony with its neighboring buildings will affect land values of adjoining buildings, and the nearest building or site to such a structure would be most affected. The construction of a factory, a store, a gas station, or any other element disturbing either the harmony of the neighborhood or its quiet, peace, safety, or atmosphere, will detract from the residential value of the neighborhood and each individual site. This condition has long ago been realized, and various measures have been employed to avoid undesirable practices of this sort. Zoning, private-land restriction, architectural control, the abolition of nuisances, and other means have been used. While these methods of control have been successful in many residential areas of the more expensive type, they have been only half-heartedly applied to the less costly and less exclusive neighborhoods.

Both the restrictive regulations and the more constructive planning methods have been used in stabilizing and enhancing values. Design of buildings, skillful manipulation of masses and spaces, conservation of vistas, consideration of orientation and exposure are some of the means used in this enhancement and stabilization of values. It is quite obvious that an open lot devoted to indiscriminate dumping or even to unorganized play may be a detriment to building sites located in its vicinity. A vista that culminates in a gas tank, a tangle of railroad trucks, an abandoned factory, or a screaming advertising display would hardly enhance the residential value of a building site. Just what standard of measurement could be applied is difficult or impossible to determine. There are, however, obvious social and esthetic values which consciously or unconsciously impress themselves upon the neighborhood, as reflected in the assessment and valuation of each parcel of land.

It is true, of course, that the higher the character of the city as a planned entity and the greater the protection of amenities, the higher are the standards of the people and the more pronounced are the influences of the surroundings upon the value of the land. It is also true that the more open the development of the neighborhood, so as to make possible a closer relation between the indoor and outdoor use of the site, the greater is the influence of the environment upon land value.

More and more is this conception of the relation between the inside of the building and its surrounding areas becoming a factor in housing. The careful planning of the recent government housing enterprises, as far as the use of the site is concerned, is ample evidence of this new awareness of the relation between buildings and surroundings. In fact, given a particular standard of uniformity in the planning of apartment space, and assuming all conveniences to be the same for every apartment, rents could be based upon a differential derived entirely from the relation of the outlook to window space. The view of a garden, the long vista derived from a well planned curved street, the view of a river or fountain, the climaxing of the landscape development by focusing upon a tower, a steeple, or some monument would play an important part in determining the rental of residential quarters and would affect rental rates.

In the consideration of these so-called outer amenities, safety of children from the hazard of traffic, noises from near-by rail transportation facilities, and the prevalence of objectionable odors emanating from near-by industries play an important part in determining the market value of a site.

The importance of surroundings as a basis for the choice of residential sites will always play an important part in determining the location and development of residential districts. But, as we advance in the art of city planning and succeed in overcoming the present prevailing individualistic tendencies in the use of land, a new wealth of amenities will be afforded to residential neighborhoods which will be taken for granted, while the refinements of these amenities will take on new forms, owing to the greater skill in the use of land which city planners working under a more highly sensitized system of planning controls will be able to evolve.

COMMUNITY SERVICES

The community services distinguish, to a large extent, rural from urban housing. Water supply, sewers, street construction, drainage of surface water, street lighting, tree planting, collection of refuse, and similar communal activities, which must be shared and which at the same time are essential to all urban living, are as much a part of the land as the soil upon which a dwelling stands. In calculating land cost, these improvements play an important part, although in long-established areas where land prices are high they are commonly taken for granted and are a small financial consideration in the price of a given parcel of land.

However, where the cost of these essential improvements is a factor and where conditions make the cost prohibitive, it affects materially the base price per land unit. In many cases the cost is hidden in high water and gas rates, owing to the distance of these utilities from the center of production and other factors. The fact remains that those services must be paid for either directly through the inclusion of the costs in the price of land or by payment of taxes, special assessments, or service rates of various kinds. In the selection of sites for housing it is therefore important to examine, not alone the presence and efficiency of services essential to the normal use of such a site for residential purposes, but the costs which these services would entail. Water rates which are controlled by private corporations and which add materially to the cost of maintaining a home are as much a part of the price of the land, which must be absorbed by rents, as is the price of the land itself. Gas and electricity, garbage collection, or any other service of this kind for which charges are made according to some differential based upon zones may affect the family budget sufficiently to influence the value of a site and its desirability for residential purposes.

The services mentioned above are reasonably standardized essentials, which can be easily evaluated. There are, however, other services which do not enter into the cost of land development directly but which are, nevertheless, important. Schools are undoubtedly the *sine qua non* of residential-area development. The cost of their construction and maintenance depends upon community-wide standards, in which the neighborhood may play a part in determining the quality of the service without assuming a direct responsibility for the cost. Yet, the presence of a good school once established will affect land prices wherever transfers of land take place, and in this manner higher assessments of land may be brought about. It is not inconceivable that the promotion of high-grade schools for a special class of residents of a district may bring about changes in property values of a specific school district which would become so high as to result in a change in the character of the population. The more desirable the school, the greater is the demand for home sites, the higher the price, the higher the taxes, and the less accessible the land to people with limited means. It is only where the school system may be said to render the same standard of service throughout that it has no effect upon land assessments and values. To a lesser degree, fire and police protection have their effect upon land prices. Where fire protection is of a low standard, fire insurance rates are high, and the location of the site in its relation to such fire-protection service plays a part either in raising the cost of construction or in raising insurance rates.

Development Drifts and Obsolescence

One of the most serious difficulties in the development of services consistent with site needs is the lack of land-use control, which makes it impossible to calculate in advance the extent and character of services needed. If a standard of twelve families to the acre were established as a housing maximum, it would be possible to calculate within certain limits the services which would be needed as long as the community is expected to last. If, however, as is the case at present, the same-sized sites may vary in population load from one to a hundred families, any attempt to forecast the amount and cost of the service needed must remain in the realm of conjecture. As some sort of guess must be made as to what services to provide, it often happens that there is little relation between what is needed and what is provided. Water mains required for single-family residences may be built in expectation of greater needs which may never be realized, thus placing an unwarranted service cost upon land. On the other hand, a too conservative anticipation of population growth and increased service needs may result in inadequate services entailing costly and disturbing reconstruction. The whole process of calculation in the technique of providing services depends entirely upon the optimism or pessimism of the entrepreneur, or upon his idea of the state of development of his project when he shall have unloaded it upon his clients. In the case of schools, playgrounds, parks, and similar services, the situation is even more deplorable.

Since cities must anticipate the services needed and must incur obligations in securing land for the development of these services, it often occurs that in some sections of the city there is a superfluity of services which are not used, while other parts of the community are suffering from overcrowded schools, lack of playgrounds, and similar conditions inconsistent with local needs. Once the community has been built up beyond the capacity of the services needed, the cost of acquisition of additional land for expansion may become prohibitive. Thus a reasonably good residential area, with ample provision for services which make home life and neighborhood relations desirable, may start at first with slight increases in population, go through a period of increased land prices due to a more intensive use of the land, and end up as an obsolete district with a population load wholly out of proportion to the services provided. This form of transition is not at all uncommon, and any observant citizen may find illustrations of it around the corner from his home, if not indeed in his own neighborhood.

In fact, many neighborhoods have deteriorated, not because of the age of the buildings, but because they were too desirable in many respects and attracted population in larger numbers than its services could provide for. This can only be avoided by having regard for the proper balance between people and service, between maximum and minimum use of site, or what might be called *the relation between the elasticity of land exploitation and service expansion.*

When this relation reaches a point where land exploitation can no longer be balanced by service expansion, we begin to have slums or blighted areas, and the tide of population turns in other directions. This results in vacancies where there is not sufficient population to take the place of those who move away, or in the influx of a lower economic stratum of the population, which pays less rent and lowers the whole economic value of the neighborhood.

As no startling increases in our population are taking place and as most communities have sufficient deteriorated dwellings in which the lower-income groups may find accommodations, it often happens that these overpopulated areas with poor or insufficient services develop spots where the vacancies are so great as to require the abandoning of some of the services which were previously overtaxed. Thus we find abandoned schools in Lower Manhattan, owing to mass removals of population. The same situation often develops with respect to the various facilities for sewage disposal, water supply, police and fire protection, and so on. All of these services must be duplicated in the new settlement, regardless of whether the equipment in the abandoned areas was obsolete or not. Such mass removals of families from old to new areas entails expenditure not inherent in population growth but in the failure to keep up the standard of buildings and surroundings so that they may not become obsolete before other equipment in the district needs replacement. Failure to bring into harmony the improvement of dwellings and surroundings with the other available services leads to waste in municipal administration, a lowering of realty values, expansion of transit beyond the essential needs of the city, and an increased burden of taxation which affects the entire community.

The phrase "planned economy" has become an accepted term for discussion in matters of national concern. Again and again it has become obvious in recent years that the community-equipment economy has been of such a nature as to drive many municipalities to the brink of bankruptcy without maintaining the high standard warranted by the costs or available technical skills. They also need a "planned economy."

If the moneys invested in new schools, new roads, new sewers, extensions of water mains, transit lines, and so forth were to be applied to the improvement of blighted and partially developed areas in close proximity to the center of the city areas in which the essential services already exist, a thorough and adequate rehabilitation of these areas would be possible. The present expansion of our cities is largely the measure of our failure to use the core of the city and its improvements in the best interests of the people. The cost involved in needless expansion is a social and economic extravagance which yields no returns.

Obligations Contingent upon Investment in Land

When the cost of land has been paid for and improvements such as sewers, water, streets, and tree planting have been covered either by city expenditure or by private enterprise, the land is by no means free from contingent financial burdens.

Taxation on land and buildings has for a long time furnished municipalities with from 75 to 95 per cent of their total revenue. The taxes upon land have in most cases depended, not upon the actual or potential use to which land is or may be suitably devoted, but to the vagaries of the use to which other people in the same neighborhood may put their land. Thus the building of business structures in the vicinity of a home may force land assessments to a point where the owner would find it impossible to maintain the original use of his property because of exorbitant taxes based upon the valuation of adjoining lands due to other and at times undesirable uses. Thus tax obligations pile up where revenue can not be increased, and in many cases the assumed intensive use of the land is both socially and economically unjustified.

There are many instances of increased assessments where a small area is highly developed in a neighborhood, thus exhausting any possibilities for further similar development. Yet, the assessment by a form of "contagion" is spread over adjoining areas, regardless of the limitation of the market for such land development. This is a type of land exploitation for tax purposes in which the municipality lends itself to profiteering by taking advantage of accidental conditions which have no relevance if taxation is to be based upon a scientific evaluation of the potentialities of land development and use.

In fact, many of these unwarranted rises in assessments not only fail to bring about any realization of profit but contribute materially toward the blighting of sections which might otherwise have developed into decent residential districts with low-cost lands and low tax burdens. A scientific zoning system might prevent this type of assessment boosting and make possible a reasonably balanced relation between value, assessment, and actual or potential use.

Another contingent economic burden on land is the "special-assessment

Photograph by W.P.A.—Division of Photography.

THE ARK IN MEMPHIS, TENNESSEE.

Photograph by W.P.A.—Division of Photography.

WILLIAMSBURG HOUSING PROJECT. UNITED STATES HOUSING AUTHORITY IN COOPERATION WITH THE NEW YORK HOUSING AUTHORITY.

method" of improvement finance. In recent years, the automobile has forced cities to seek relief from traffic congestion. This has resulted in costly street plans for which the communities were not able to pay. Many of them reached their borrowing limits, while others reasoned that the "improvements" in roads should be assessed against properties benefited by such improvements. Little or no account was taken of the capacity of properties to pay for these improvements. That road building always resulted in benefits to property in the vicinity of such roads was accepted as a fact. The outcome of this practice of imposing special assessments on properties in the neighborhood of a street improvement placed a heavy burden on both used and unused land. Indeed, where the properties had already been used for residential purposes, the encouragement of streams of extraneous traffic has led to reduction in rents, a lowering of land values for residential purposes, and a slowing-up of construction of dwellings. The writer has had occasion to examine properties in several cities which carried special-assessment burdens of from 50 to 150 per cent of the actual market value of the land. In a few cases the number of special assessments on single properties ranged from 15 to 20. This was due to the practice of spreading assessments over entire neighborhoods wherever there was a suspicion that an improvement three, four, five, or ten blocks away might in the least benefit a resident of the district. That the spread of these assessments has often been used for political reasons or favoritism is quite evident from the most casual study of this practice.

While no one may quarrel with land-tax methods which prevent monopoly and force land into use, in the case of residential areas every rise in the assessment and tax burden which does not have its counterpart in production of revenue consistent with suitable use is a detriment to housing.

The Capacity of Economic Development of Land

Land prices vary with movements of population, building activities of the community, and availability of the type of land ripe for development. During the depression, when credit was scarce, building activity at a standstill, tax arrears prevalent, and, except for doubling up and flight to rural communities, population stationary, land was cheap. With changing conditions, the curve of land prices is bound to move upward again.

The question that must be asked, however, is not how land prices fluctuate but what relation these prices bear to their capacity to yield a return on the investments. Assuming an undeveloped area, properly planned, zoned, restricted against certain uses, and designed with clearly defined objectives, it would be very simple to determine the relation between projected land use and land price. For residences of the single-family type costing an average of $5,000, the reasonable land value might fluctuate between $1,000 and $1,200 per lot of 5,000 square feet, including all services. In the case of an apartment house designed to accommodate twelve families and costing $48,000, an expenditure of from $8,000 to $10,000 for land would be reasonable. Assuming, however, a developed community, with a scarcity of suitable land at desirable points and land prices doubled, the yield for each dwelling unit would either have to be reduced or rents would have to rise. Another alternative would be to use the land so intensively that the land-cost load would be chargeable to a larger number of rentable units. Thus, instead of twelve families, twenty-four families would have to be housed on the same area. The effect of the rise in land price in such an area would result in a corresponding rise in the price of all lands in their neighborhood, with an inevitable rise in assessments. Two important consequences will have to be reckoned with, first, that, as land costs increase, congestion increases; and second, that, as congestion increases, the chances for use of the remaining open areas are reduced. We know that population does not increase in proportion to the availability of land. We also know that wages and incomes do not fluctuate with investment in housing. Housing represents a long-term investment, with incomes fluctuating with the changing economic levels extending over the period of the life of the building. On the other hand, most construction takes place during times of prosperity, when land and building prices are high, while rental revenues must meet the changing levels of economic conditions. The cost of the land, therefore, often bears a closer relation to the rate at which construction is going on than it does to the revenue which a particular building is capable of yielding during its lifetime. Once a boom in the building industry has taken place and land prices have risen, their return to normal lags behind the market. This is one of the reasons for the high land prices in many of our slums which are not at present and could not in the future become productive on any basis consistent with the rent-paying resources of the tenants. Indeed, a study of land values in Manhattan slums reveals some very interesting statistical facts. The block between Third and Fourth Streets and between First Avenue and Avenue A is assessed at from $15 to $20 per square foot. Assuming the lower figure to be the actual price of the land, which covers about three acres, its total price would be $1,800,000. On such an area, 400 families might be housed at a density of 133 families to the acre. This would mean a per-family investment in land of $4,500. Calculating the gross return on the investment alone at 10 per cent, it would mean a ground rent per family of $450 a year. Such a rent can only be paid by families receiving an income of not less than $2,250, which very few, if any, of the families in that district receive. This rent would be based on the land alone, without buildings. The best that could be done for housing at this rental would be to build tents. If we add the cost of the buildings, allowing an average of four rooms per family and a maximum cost of $1,000 per room, the total rent per family would be $850, which only families with incomes of $4,250 should normally pay—and this on the basis, not of a 12 per cent, but of a ten per cent return on the investment. It is obvious that $15 a square foot for housing is out of the question for about 65 per cent of the families in the United States. The other 35 per cent of the families would certainly not choose a New York slum for their home. Indeed, if the land were given away, the present cost of buildings would make rentals in new dwellings prohibitive for a large proportion of our people.

Urban land has no revenue-producing value unless used. Unlike other non-productive investments, it must meet taxes and special assessments. When built upon, the land can not be burdened with capitalizations which make building investments prohibitive, otherwise it must be used so intensively as to reduce the chances of development for adjoining lands, thus creating islands of overdevelopment surrounded by empty spaces or spaces built up merely to produce the necessary taxes, in the expectation of a future boom.

Cities with slums and high land prices have no choice in the matter of site selection for new housing when we consider the rent-paying ability of more than three-fifths of the families, except to seek land outside the slum areas. Should this policy succeed, the owners of substandard houses standing upon high-priced land would have to choose between a drastic reduction in the capitalization of their land, in order to promote reconstruction, or a further lowering of rents resulting from competition with better housing on cheaper land. Unless reduction of land capitalization takes place first, the chance of reconstruction will be increasingly reduced.

As recently as the last weeks in 1938, there seemed to have developed a veritable propaganda in the interest of retaining the population within the precincts of the present congested and slum areas of our cities. The suggestion that peripheral housing presents many advantages for the slum dwellers in the way of cheaper land and more opportunities for providing open spaces has been met with a number of counterarguments, which may be summarized as follows:

1. The city can not afford to create a vacuum in the very center where all its business and industrial activities are located.

2. The cost of providing services and the various amenities already provided in the center of the city, so that they may fully satisfy the needs of the people, would more than absorb the excessive cost of land in the center of the community.

3. The transportation required to carry the inhabitants of the housing projects at the periphery would be a heavy burden on the city's resources.

4. The city can not afford to abandon tax values which would be destroyed by the removal of large numbers of families to outlying districts.

The particularly potent reason which is perhaps the most important factor in this propaganda is the fact that property owners in the slums and congested areas are not disposed to permit the removal of population from their homes and thus destroy the values which are or are alleged to be still remaining in substandard housing property.

If it were possible to rehabilitate these areas for the people now living in them without raising rents, there would be no justification for peripheral housing. The fact remains, however, that, even under government subsidy and mass production, the families eliminated from the cleared slums must seek housing elsewhere, as, even with subsidies, the rentals charged can not reach the lower-income families displaced.

Further consideration must also be given to the fact that any slum clearance project which does not previously make provisions for the housing of the displaced families while the slums are being cleared and reconstructed constitutes a serious hardship and expense to the families concerned.

The argument as to high cost of replacing services may or may not have any validity. Most of the old services are obsolete; schools are crowded, both as to open space and as to room accommodations, playgrounds are inadequate, and street traffic is congested. Any replacement of these services and amenities would, at least in terms of land costs, amount to considerably more than in the outlying districts; and the freedom of land use would be curtailed by the fact that the land can only be secured by the absorption of additional housing facilities, thus reducing the available accommodations for housing. The price of land in the center of the city being three or four times as high as at the periphery or in the less intensively developed areas, it would of necessity raise the cost of such facilities as might be needed or reduce their spaciousness to the detriment of the use to which they are to be put in the interests of the inhabitants. The open spaces for schools at $20,000 per acre would make possible one kind of development, as compared with similar facilities in the center of the city, where land costs per acre would amount to $400,000 per acre.

It should also be kept in mind that, as the intensity of housing concentration due to high land costs increases, the amount of open spaces for schools and parks and playgrounds in the vicinity of such housing must also be increased in proportion, to take care of the needs of the people.

If rehousing the people in the slums is to be a makeshift process, without full consideration of the needs for reorganizing and replanning slum surroundings, then the proposals made by the people interested in promoting slum rehabilitation have the better of the argument. However, if housing is to be looked upon as a problem distinct from that of the recapture of vanishing land values, and as a movement in the direction of establishing decent living conditions at a low cost, then the slum-clearance protagonists have little basis for their reasoning.

It is argued, of course, that government subsidy will continue for a long time and that thereby the slums will all eventually be cleared. At the rate at which these subsidies are being provided, however, it would take around forty centuries to accomplish this result. Assuming, however, that we speeded up the process by ten or even forty times, it would still take a century or more to clear the slums in our cities, which still contain around 7,000,000 substandard dwellings. To expect the private owners to clear slums and replace them with good housing, in the face of government-subsidized housing in the same neighborhood, is hardly consistent with business practice and good economy. In my own estimation, the more the government does in slum clearance, the less will private initiative be able to produce housing in competition with such projects and at rents consistent with the rent-paying resources of the workers.

Insofar as land values are concerned, the more subsidized housing is constructed in areas where land costs are low, the more are the chances that the slum lands will shrink in value to such an extent as to bring about conditions permitting the construction of low-rental housing. The subsidizing and absorbing of high-cost lands at high prices by government purchase for housing and open spaces only delays a process of deflation which must come if our cities are not to retain their slums in perpetuity.

There is, of course, also the possibility of reconstructing some slum areas for high-grade, high-rental residential purposes which could absorb the present land prices. As many of the slums are located in desirable areas, such opportunities for reconstruction do exist. Unfortunately, the lower-grade housing districts are too extensive to be entirely absorbed for this purpose. The use of these costly lands for other than housing purposes is hardly practical, since it is so extensive in area as to make it impossible for either business or industry to absorb it.

There is a possibility that large tracts of land might be incorporated in vast housing schemes which would include, not only low-rental housing projects, but also large community neighborhoods in which all classes and grades of rents would be made available, and where business, office space, and some forms of small industry would be provided for under one project. Under these conditions, it might be possible so to distribute the burden of land cost as to cause it to be absorbed by the various productive types of buildings, leaving the lower-rent housing to be a byproduct of the entire development.

At the present time, we count upon the provisions for business to help in the reduction of rents in housing projects. It is quite conceivable that the same principle could be applied to larger and more heterogeneous areas, so that a larger share of the land cost might be shifted to those occupants who could bear the extra burden.

The value of land, in the last analysis, is only what it can produce by way of revenue. The English method of securing land for low-rental projects is based upon the theory that the land price must be reasonable for the purpose for which the government proposes to use it. If cottages are to be built, the price of the land is calculated by assuming a reasonable rent on a given building cost, the price of the land being determined by the other two factors. In the United States, however, we begin by assuming a given land price and work backward to the rental that would have to be charged.

I am informed on good authority that the English government is now seriously considering the acquisition of all urban lands on the basis of actual revenues which these lands have been yielding in the last decades prior to acquisition. This principle was applied to the acquisition of mining lands, and the theory is that the same principle should apply to other lands as well. Whether this step will ever be taken is, of course, a matter of conjecture, but undoubtedly it is one clear way of avoiding speculation, clearing slums, and reducing the cost of housing in the future.

RELATION OF UNITS OF OWNERSHIP TO USE OF LAND

A glance of a lot subdivision map or any insurance map reveals a crazy quilt of property lines, which have little or no relation to economic land development or adequate housing standards. In many places, narrow lots 25 feet wide by 125 feet deep were the common practice. This resulted in crowded single dwellings, with narrow alleyways to the backyard which eventually became repositories of rubbish and upon which no windows could open, unless they became mere peekholes into one's neighbor's bedroom.

This kind of subdivision is no longer permitted in most states, but there are still hundreds of thousands of lots owned and undeveloped which, if ever used, will have to be built upon under these unfavorable conditions. Where tenements have been constructed on such lots, by virtue of the shape and size of the lot, they were slum dwellings, with dark or semi-dark rooms.

Excessively deep but narrow lots merely lead to a greater stringing out of buildings or waste space, which increases street lengths without providing better building conditions. It is obvious that a lot 25 by 125 feet with a 50 per cent coverage would be less desirable than a lot 40 by 80 feet with a 60 per cent coverage, although the area of the second lot is actually smaller.

We shall deal in greater detail later in this work with the whole question of subdivision of land. Here we are concerned only with the effect of subdivisions upon the economic use of land and the enhancement or restriction of use values due to the method of subdivision.

It is quite clear to anyone who may take the trouble to examine and compare buildings located on the various lot widths and depths that the same area divided into narrow strips which requires close proximity of wall spaces, does not allow for sunshine and ventilation, and interferes with the privacy of the next-door neighbor is less valuable than a lot of the same number of square feet in area, of greater width, and with an equal amount of lot coverage and building height.

I am calling the reader's attention to this very simple principle because our methods of lot subdivision in the past fixed the character of many of our buildings, the life of which ranges from two to four generations. The character of these buildings is such as to make them undesirable for decent living, although the cost per unit of construction may be the same as for buildings located on more suitably shaped lots which afford much better living conditions. Rentals in tenements built on narrow lots, imposing as they do lower standards of accommodations, would of necessity fall below rentals in buildings located on well-shaped lots which afford better living conditions.

Going a step further in the consideration of the use value of narrow lots, if we take two lots of equal depth, one 25 feet and the other 100 feet in width, we find that entranceways, halls, bulkheads, and other accessories of common use are practically the same for the requirements of buildings on both lots. Assuming 20 per cent of the building on the narrow lot to be required for approaches, a lot four times as great, with four times the living accommodations, could be provided at the same building cost, since there would be a saving of from 50 to 75 per cent in the space required for approaches, while the general layout of the apartments would be more desirable and command higher rents. So far as height of buildings is concerned, the narrowness of the lot must of necessity become a handicap in the exploitation of the land and therefore of its use value.

One need not venture into elaborate detail to emphasize the obvious fact that the parcels of land ownership in our cities can not be evaluated on a square footage basis regardless of the shapes and sizes of individual lot units. Any assessments of values which disregard the factor of lot dimension in terms of economic construction overlook economic factors which have a bearing on the whole development of the city, both as to living standards and building costs.

We hear much of land assembly for public or semi-public uses. Recent efforts at large-scale housing have necessitated the gathering under one ownership of numerous parcels of land, in order to make possible the construction of large projects. But this is only a partial and comparatively insignificant part of the larger problem of pooling property units in order to make them suitable for a high grade of dwelling construction. In fact, the reconstruction of many of our slum areas depends as much upon a new division of land in terms of construction costs and standards as it does upon legal control, finance, and other factors which may promote or force reconstruction.

Indeed, if we consider only the matter of investment, the value of each foot of ground is enhanced by the increase in the number of units of ownership of which it is a part. If assessments were to be based upon use values, the owner with a lot 25 by 100 feet should be assessed much less than the owner with a lot of 100 by 100 feet, for, aside from single-family dwellings, the use value of a building increases as the unit of ownership increases. Any slum reconstruction which may be attempted by private initiative will have to take into account existing property holding in the light of economical land development consistent with building costs and living standards.

II. LAND POLICIES

As has already been pointed out, land development and building enterprise depend upon a given condition and need at a given time. The life of the development and buildings extends over a long period of time, during which both conditions and needs may change. Social and economic demands follow a tempo different from that of physical utility. Obsolescence of the land development, buildings, and the technological utility may undergo changes at a still different tempo.

This conflict between the tempos of social and economic needs and the rate of physical and technological obsolescence creates conditions which confuse both the value and use trends of land. Conversion for purposes of replanning and modernization of use becomes more difficult and more costly. When reconstruction seems desirable, a six-story tenement area will require greater economic sacrifices than will the reclaiming and reconstruction of single- or two-family residences. Twenty-story store buildings or office buildings, once they become obsolescent, may remain idle for a long time, while business and other factors migrate to other sections of the city.

In direct line with this lack of coordination between the economic utility of a building and its physical life, we must consider the variety of intensity of development of lands with equal potentialities for residential or business purposes. Looking up and down many of our streets, we find that, given the same type of land containing approximately or actually the same area, a broad range of development is apparent. We may see a tall twenty- or thirty-story apartment house, next to it a five-story building, and bounded by two tall buildings may be found a two- or even a one-story "taxpayer."

All these buildings, located as they are on the same street, with the same traffic facilities and the same potential common services, standing in the same relation to the rest of the city, represent as many samples of development as can be found in the entire city. The personal resources of the landowner, his credit, the money-market conditions at the time of development, the renting market at the time of construction, the personal vision of the owner, and the capabilities of the architect or builder are stamped upon each building. Indeed, times of boom and prosperity, which hold out great promise of profit, when interest rates are high, building costs are rising, and population is growing, may bring into existence improvements which constitute the greatest burden upon the owners and, in the end, may be the least desirable. Thus the chaos of one period of financial optimism in the building industry may have to be paid for in times of chaos arising out of depressions, when the same improvement could be made at a lower cost of land, money, labor, and materials.

Still another factor in the consideration of land values is the improvement activities of certain owners who, with ample resources and adequate land areas, can construct buildings with capacities which transcend actual needs for a period of time, thus leaving other landowners without the possibilities of deriving enough profit from improvement of their own land to bring an equitable return on the investment. One may wander about in some of our business districts to discover that, while tall buildings are forcing assessments of land upward, they are forcing the market values of unimproved or partially improved land downward.

The greater the variants in the speed and intensity of development of land and construction of buildings, the greater is the difficulty of adjusting need, cost, service and obsolescence to the pace of social purpose and sound investment.

In the case of goods manufactured for immediate consumption, the problem is reasonably simple. Unconsumed or unconsumable goods are disposed of quickly, either by sale at a low price or by destruction. At any rate, they do not long impress themselves upon the pattern of our community life and economic recovery. Unprofitable investment is soon absorbed. New techniques and business methods create new goods in keeping with new needs and new resources. This is not true of land development and building enterprises.

We have here another case where the individual plays a sinister part in destroying values and in making harmonious development of a community difficult or impossible. City planning, through zoning in its various forms, could set the pace for a steady, profitable, and efficient development of our cities that would benefit both the landowners and the land users, but the preposterous attempts at zoning which have been attempted in the past can hardly be said to be economically sound or socially efficient.

In business and industry, the initiative of the individual and his business ventures need not be concerned with long-range objectives, except perhaps in his personal outlook. In land development, account must be taken, not only of individual investment and the chances of profit and loss, but also of the social and economic burdens which each investment places upon the community—rent payers, taxpayers, or citizens. It is for this reason that a new concept of the social economy of land use must be evolved. Zoning and city planning are thus far the only controls available. Business practice has certainly failed to show that traditional "business sense" which resents interference by government agencies.

Only recently have we realized the importance of giving consideration to the agricultural lands of our country. Overproduction and underproduction, which have created our agrarian problems, have their parallels in urban land utilization. We need a land policy in urban communities as much as in rural ones. It is not only a matter of planning and zoning, but of broad *Landwirtschaft*, or land economy in all its manifestations.

THE MANAGEMENT FACTOR IN LAND VALUES

In his discussion of land values and assessments, Rudolph Ebertadt tells the following incident bearing on land economics:

> An inn keeper had a pair of lively daughters, who helped in the dining room. Business was consequently good and showed large consumption. An assessor was ready to impose a high tax on the house, and the land upon which the inn stood was mortgaged for an unusually large sum. The liveliness of the daughters figured in the future economy as capital . . .[1]

This story may illustrate the ephemeral basis for judging values to which assessors may resort and which investors may trust. Whether it be the susceptibility of the males for the charms of a lively barmaid or the peculiar aptitude of an apartment-house manager who keeps his tenants and makes a profit, while a next-door building of similar type loses tenants and runs at a loss, the fact remains that profit and loss on the same investment may mean the difference between good management and bad management. Here the human or efficiency equation enters as a new factor which may be capitalized, assessed, taxed, mortgaged, and speculated upon, regardless of the possibilities for maintaining the standard set by individual efficiency, which may or may not be lasting. Such temporary management results, recorded by a bookkeeper, will affect the capitalization of land, which may extend over a generation or more.

In fact, this capitalization may affect neighboring lands which present the possibilities for similar uses without consideration either of the need for such use or the possibilities for similar returns. Thus through the contagion of capitalizations and taxations, investment may extend over areas which, by no stretch of the imagination, could or should be put to similar use, or produce the same returns.

The writer does not mean to imply that management is entirely a personal equation. There are, derived from long experience, principles of management which may approximate a reasonable and steady return on the investment, provided the land and buildings lend themselves to the application of these principles. Unfortunately, the manager's job begins only after the building has been completed, instead of preceding the plan of the building or even the choice of site.

The predicament in which much of our land and building investment finds itself at the present time, may prompt real-estate enterprise to conceive of housing as management translated into buildings, instead of trying

[1] Gemünd, W., *Bodenfrage und Bodenpolitik*, Berlin, 1911, p. 105.

to translate buildings into management. In the field of public housing, we are accumulating valuable experience in matters of management. Let us hope that our national housing program will yield valuable experience applicable to private enterprise.

Social Controls of Land Use and Their Effects on Values

As already pointed out, the most effective method of land-value and land-speculation control is to be found in zoning, when applied within a framework of a well conceived community planning scheme. This exercise of the police power, which is designed to prescribe the use to which land may be devoted as regards kind, bulk, height, and area of building, can be made to serve both the purpose of preventing speculation in land and, at the same time, that of bringing about such orderliness and stability of community development as to conserve real values consistent with the capacity of the people to use and pay for. Unfortunately, the methods employed in the application of zoning powers and principles have seldom brought about the desired and possible achievements in the direction of preventing speculation or stabilizing values.

It may also be assumed that many building regulations have imposed restriction of land use incident to proper lighting and ventilating of buildings, which have had some effect upon the evils of land overcrowding. These restrictions, however, were compensated for in most cases by higher rents.

The only far-reaching methods of land-speculation control and land-value stability will be found in the more recent practices of imposing restrictions upon the methods of new land subdivisions, most of which lie beyond the boundaries of the thickly settled areas, or outside the municipal limits of cities. These restrictions, regulations, and voluntary practices intended to fix land uses, both in kind and intensity, have frequently enhanced land values, without leaving room for unwarranted speculation. Land-use control has been accepted by many cities and counties of the less sparsely settled states, particularly in the North and West.

A Land Policy for Housing

We are all familiar with the many land policy movements which have motivated the shaping of national politics.

In the discussion of land policies affecting housing, we are concerned, not alone with its price, but with the effect which its use has upon the structure of the community, its functions, its rate of obsolescence, its stride toward readjustment to modern needs and the pattern which this community may assume in its relation to good, well located, accessible, and permanent development of decent housing accommodations.

It is, therefore, obvious that a land policy affecting housing must be part and parcel of the general land policies which the community may evolve for the protection of all the people. Such a land policy must include, not alone the control of evils resulting from private ownership and exploitation, but also the development of forms of public ownership consistent with public needs.

The Municipality as Landowner

In the course of our urban development, certain land policies have become established as common practices. Some of these are incidental to the carrying on of services for which there is immediate need and which local governments must provide, or services which these governments delegate by franchise to private agencies. Lands required by these services may be acquired by gift, tax-delinquency sales, or the filling in of waterways over which the governmental agency may have riparian rights.

In all these possible ways of land acquisition and ownership, there is no provision for a long-range land policy, no possible method of anticipating future needs or of accumulating land reserves which may be utilized or disposed of as necessity demands. Within the rigid framework of the exigencies of the moment, and within the limits of land prices and speculative practices, the municipality, county, state, or national governments may acquire land for immediate use.

Such acquisition of land, however, does not leave the way open for long-time planning or the contingencies of changes that may have to be met in the course of changing standards and needs. As a fundamental principle, it may be asserted without fear of contradiction that, given freedom to acquire and control land under favorable conditions, the whole problem of planning becomes essentially a matter of social and economic interpretation of the needs of the times. With a policy of easy and reasonably flexible method of land acquisition, the problems of planning and zoning, as well as the expansion of community services, must always bear the marks of the mistakes of the past, or the community must pay for them in hard cash.

Let us consider for the moment what would seem to be the most desirable program for the development of a public land policy.

What Should This Land Policy Be?

Assuming that the development of cities can only be partially anticipated and that the present use of land is in many cases inconsistent with the most pressing needs of our communities, a land-ownership and control program might be outlined somewhat as follows:

The municipal government should have the power to acquire all such available lands as may be needed for immediate use and such other lands as may be found available for future use or sale in the interest of orderly community reconstruction, development, and growth.

Such a policy would bring about a greater freedom of land use, because the land would be acquired at a time when land values are low and in parcels of sufficient size to permit comprehensive planning. The ownership of considerable land areas by the local government would prevent high prices and speculation, and could be used to establish standards of land use not generally in practice under private ownership. In the case of the resale of public lands for private use, such resales may be made contingent upon a proper development consistent with both private interest and the common good. If the cities of today were the owners of lands desirable for housing purposes, a considerable share of the difficulties encountered in securing adequate housing sites for government housing projects would have been obviated. Such was the case when certain European cities undertook to build municipal, cooperative, or subsidized housing. The City of Vienna alone owned 72,000 acres of land. By 1935, the City of Stockholm owned 25,000 acres of land or about five times the area of the city itself within a nine-mile radius from the center of the municipality. Similar conditions can be found in most German, English, and Finnish urban centers. In many cases this policy can be traced as far back as the Middle Ages. This land-ownership policy applies to areas within the municipal boundaries as well as to adjoining areas. The use of the land depends upon the requirements for local services as well as private exploitation under public control.

Objection may be raised that such land acquisition would withdraw from the tax rolls revenue-producing properties which, by the act of public acquisition, would automatically be added to the tax-exempt property list. To this objection, several answers may be given. One is the fact that, where such properties cease to produce revenue, they may be considered as insurance against later high land prices. Another answer is to be found in the fact that, while lands acquired by the municipality cease producing tax revenues, they may later, by disposal for private use under favorable conditions and controls, constitute a steady revenue, free from blighting contingent upon uncontrolled and unplanned development. It may still further be argued that the city, upon disposal of land for private use at a time when it is most needed, would make a sufficient profit to cover tax losses fully or in part. In the case of land acquisition outside of the political boundaries of municipalities, no tax losses would be sustained.

It should be mentioned in passing that the present system of municipal taxation, which places practically the full burden of municipal expenditure upon revenues from real property, needs revision. That the burden of municipal taxes often weighs heavily upon home owners goes without saying. Economists have been debating the question of land and improvement taxation for many years. The so-called "single tax," or land tax, as a means of reducing land prices by absorbing the values created by society through its activities, has been agitated for a long time. This movement has taken on various aspects in municipal taxation and has resulted in the practice of taxing land more heavily than buildings or improvements. Indeed, this practice is now so well established that most progressive cities use it as means of encouraging building enterprise. In a report issued in June, 1937, by the National Resources Committee of the federal government, entitled, *Our Cities—Their Role in the National Economy*, the following statement appears: "State and local authorities should consider the reduction of the rate of taxation on buildings and the corresponding increase of such rates on land, in order to lower the tax burden on home owners and occupants of the low rent houses, and to stimulate rehabilitation of blighted areas and slums." As an isolated remedy against land speculation and high land policies, this system of graded taxation is undoubtedly a valuable factor. However, the Pittsburgh plan, which has been in operation since January 1, 1914, and has passed through all the successive stages leading to a tax on land twice the rate imposed on buildings, has proved workable as a tax policy; but Pittsburgh slums are as bad and as extensive now as they were in 1914. It seems to me that, while land prices may be lowered because of the heavy burden of taxation which land has to carry under a land-tax system, the price can only be lowered to the point where the difference between interest and the price paid when added to the tax rate would make the same total as the interest on the investment on land at the ordinary rate of taxation. The effect upon housing might be to foster a larger amount of building enterprise and thereby bring about an improvement in the supply of houses. Unfortunately, when the houses are constructed, the capital, plus taxation carrying the charges, remains practically the same, and must play a part in the rental. It must also be recalled that the shift of taxes from building to land often has the effect of increasing taxes beyond the actual worth of the land for the purposes for which it is being used. Where land is assessed on speculative volutions, as is the case in many of our cities, the shift may bring about a higher maintenance cost, which, although it may not be reflected in the rent of the existing buildings, will have to be reflected in the rentals of future constructions. I have in mind slum areas with high assessments on land due to a possible speculative outlook. An additional tax burden on such land may result in two different lines of action: either the owner disposes of his property at a lower price—a condition which, if it becomes general, may devalue much land and reduce the revenues of the city; or, when reconstruction takes place, the necessity for absorbing a higher land tax would still not affect the general housing cost sufficiently to encourage low-rental housing.

The fact is that, whether land is forced into the market because of higher taxes or not, the rent-paying resources of the lower income groups are still too low to play any part in the land market or construction market, even if land were reduced to the lowest minimum price. There is a possibility, however, that the increase in land taxes would reduce land values so as to affect municipal revenues without affecting the housing situation in any material way. I can find no evidence to prove the contention that the graded land tax bears any relation to the supply of low-rental housing, the clearance of slums by private initiative, or any other widespread effort to promote investment in housing. The taxation of land to the point of absorbing the larger share of the values created by the community itself, without any contribution on the part of the owners, is justifiable; but whether this method of taxation will in the end produce improvements in the housing conditions of those in need of cheap accommodations remains to be seen.

It would seem that, regardless of the method of taxation which may be employed in municipalities, the demand for new and the extension of existing services warrants the conclusion that the present system of taxation of real estate is both inadequate to meet rising costs of municipal administration and too heavy a burden upon real property.

Next in importance to the right of municipalities to acquire and own land in anticipation of uses to be determined at some future time is the right to dispose of such lands according to needs and demands. In the matter of town and city expansion, much difficulty has arisen in past years through the premature development of lands not ripe for exploitation. Some of this land has been favored, not because of any inherent qualities which made it suitable for a specific use, but because the land market made it difficult to secure adequate space in areas ripe for such development. The flight from high land costs in the city has caused many of these premature developments in areas neither suited for the purpose for which they were used nor within the sphere of adequate public services which such developments demand. This has often caused new im-

Photograph by W.P.A.—Division of Photography.

HARLEM RIVER HOUSING PROJECT—HOMES FOR NEGRO FAMILIES. NEW YORK. UNITED STATES HOUSING AUTHORITY WITH THE COOPERATION OF THE NEW YORK HOUSING AUTHORITY.

Photograph by W.P.A.—Division of Photography.

KINDERGARTEN ROOM IN THE HARLEM RIVER HOUSING PROJECT, NEW YORK.

provements in public services to be undertaken prematurely and under
conditions which added to the burden of taxation of the whole municipality, while free areas ready for development and ready to yield tax revenue
have been left idle. The extension of sewers, water systems, roads, rapid
transit, and school facilities have all been made necessary by the development of unripe areas. Municipal ownership of land, with the municipal
practice of acquiring areas which need to be held in reserve and selling
them for private use when the necessity for their development arises
would obviate many difficulties and save much money which might well
be used for other more pertinent purposes.

PLANNING AND LAND DEVELOPMENT

City, county, and regional planning are practiced so generally in the
United States that one senses even in the rigid organization of the least
advanced of our communities a conscious need for a new outlook and
organized preparation for the future. Thus, literally thousands of comprehensive or partial community plans are conceived and given some
coherent form. Upon analysis, it is invariably discovered that the carrying out of these plans depends primarily upon access to land, and the
changes in present uses to some other more suitable service. If the plan
is not carried out at once, the chances are that further obstructions and
misuses of land in the path of contemplated improvements may occur.
Thus, the best of plans may become obsolete, not because of any faulty
conception, but because control of land use in the path of projected improvements is lacking.

This lack of control often causes plans to be abandoned, to the detriment of the whole development of the community. Let us assume that a
city considers a certain area suitable for residential purposes and that,
within the scope of a given plan, schools, roads, playgrounds, fire sta-
tions, and so forth, are tentatively located. In the interim, private land
owners, fully disregarding the plan, undertake developments inconsistent
with local needs and conflicting with public interest. To be sure, good
zoning might prevent a certain amount of interference with the plan, but
there is nothing in our land-control policy which would prevent an
owner from building an apartment house where a school should be, or
from creating a business center where a playground would eventually
have been of most service. Short of municipal land ownership, this could
not be prevented under our present system even if an effective zoning
scheme were in vogue.

In the case of regional planning, notably in California, a legal device
has been evolved which prevents an owner from building any structure

in the path of a contemplated public improvement recorded on a master regional plan. Should such a landowner undertake to build in the path of a projected improvement, he would either have to secure special permission from the planning authority or forego any claims for damages incident to the final acquisition of the land for public purposes. It may seem a drastic exercise of the power of land control to prevent development of private improvements prior to the carrying out of planned public improvements. In view of the fact, however, that the municipality has a joint interest with the private owners in the conservation of all community values, the prevention of blight, and economy in the cost of services incident to good or bad planning, such control does not seem a very radical step. Whatever extra costs are entailed by lack of land-use control must be met by the individual taxpayers. Whatever improvements and savings may be effected by such control reflect upon the welfare of the entire community.

As has already been repeatedly pointed out, our present-day divisions of land-ownership units make it quite difficult or impossible under private initiative to develop any considerable housing projects. The difficulties encountered by the various housing authorities in this country in assembling land for housing projects has brought this question clearly to the foreground.

THE HOLDEN PLAN

How to overcome these small landholding difficulties may well be made the subject of a special study, since it involves many aspects of the economy of construction, the advantages of good light and air distribution, so necessary in the development of plans, and the possibilities for providing adequate open spaces for common uses. Where land is not already occupied by buildings, the problem is simplified, provided the owners are willing to pool their interests. It is conceivable that a group of owners in one or several blocks with bad land subdivisions could come to some understanding as to specific uses of their holdings, and enter into an agreement regarding methods of resubdivision or adjustment which would prove beneficial to all owners concerned. Where there are buildings of various types, adjustment of equities is more difficult. In the case of open areas, two types of legal provisions might help to facilitate a redistribution of holdings or a pooling of interests. The first would be some legal provision whereby a majority of the owners might petition the corporation commission or some other properly constituted official body for the privilege of creating a temporary holding company, with powers to make adjustments through an arbiter or committee qualified to reapportion the holdings or to set up machinery for a common, cooperative use of the entire area under consideration. Another method might be to have the governing body legally empowered to take over the entire area and, after readjusting the holdings on some equitable basis, return parcels to the original owners, according to a predetermined valuation of the individual holdings. The latter method has been used in German cities, particularly in cases where both street facilities and land holdings were in need of adjustment.

Since 1933, when the housing movement began to take shape as a national concern, much emphasis was placed upon slum clearance and slum rehabilitation. Mention should be made here, of the obvious fact that, in the process of slum rehabilitation, the main stumbling blocks are the great diversity in the conditions of buildings in each block and the conflicting interests which they represent. Mr. Arthur Holden, of New York, has for several years devoted much time and energy to the task of devising a practical method of pooling ownership interests whereby it would be possible to overcome the difficulties arising from the multiplicity of individual ownership of land and buildings, with a view to arriving at a practical scheme of cooperation between individual owners for the purpose of block rehabilitation. This device finally found legal expression in a bill which is quoted and discussed in the chapter on legislation. All that need be said here is that the bill, now inoperative, contemplates the possibilities of combining a great variety of ownership of land and buildings within a given area, and the improvement of these properties so as to raise standards and reduce losses due to obsolescence by demolition of some structures, the improvement of others, and the combination of revenues according to the equity of each individual owner in the original project subjected to improvement. There are also legal means provided for overcoming difficulties that might be encountered in matters of trusteeships and ownership which may be limited by law in entering upon such cooperative enterprise.

The Holden plan is a radical step in housing legislation. If it finds favor with owners and is properly administered on a large enough scale, it may lead to the gradual rebuilding of many substandard housing areas. However, unless it can be demonstrated that this plan can be made profitable to the owners, it will remain a dead letter. In principle, the law is an expression of a widespread need.

THE PERRY PLAN

One of the most far-reaching suggestions that has been advanced recently relative to public land policy is that of Clarence A. Perry, regarding the exercise of the power of eminent domain in the interest of housing and community or neighborhood development. According to this plan, the government would take the necessary steps to assemble land for private building enterprise. In elaborating this suggestion, I wish to make it clear that the form in which it is presented may or may not be in full accord with Mr. Perry's conception of its methods and possibilities. The original suggestion, however, emanated from Mr. Perry.

There are in many of our cities areas which have been developed incoherently, without plan, without neighborhood unity, and without uniformity or standard of land division or construction. These areas constitute a sort of no man's land, where sporadic developments were started and abandoned for various reasons inherent in the lay of the land, some economic or financial accident, or a shift in the trends of city development. The result has been damage to individual properties, the development of interstitial areas without character and of slight use to the community, and land blight. Many of these areas are capable of replanning and rehabilitation. They may be transformed into desirable residential areas and, where construction has not advanced too far, into veritable garden communities in close proximity to the center of the city.

In many of these cases, land is easy to assemble and low in price. In order to achieve this end, however, it is necessary to create ways and means of using land acquisition powers which, applied according to a rehabilitation plan, could assemble the land and buildings to be found on the site, and lease or sell them to a private organization for development according to a preplanned scheme. This would, of course, involve large sums of money and efficient organization, as well as a thorough understanding of existing needs and the existing market.[2] Under such a procedure it would be possible for the municipality to reserve in advance such areas as may be needed for schools, playgrounds, parks, and so forth, and to control the method of development so that it would bear a sound relation to the services to be provided. This method of attacking the blighted areas of land, or land and buildings, might lead to further experiments in the public acquisition of land as a means of facilitating private enterprise under public control. Better neighborhood conditions and effective utilization of submarginal areas might thus be brought about.

This alluring method of rehabilitating submarginal areas is, however, beset with many difficulties inherent in the fact that the municipality would have to raise the funds for the acquisition of land and existing

[2] The Astoria Replanning Project, prepared by Aronovici, Churchill, Lescaze, and Wright, contemplated such a scheme of rehabilitation. This antedated Mr. Perry's suggestion, but did not include the possibility of government authority in land assemblage.

buildings, and also because the appraisals of private holdings may involve the local authorities in endless litigation. So far as the funds are concerned, many devices may be developed to meet specific project costs: federal, state, county, and city credit may be used separately or in combination. Federal loans or subsidies might also be secured to promote some specific enterprises of this kind. Owner participation as shareholders could also be incorporated in the general plan. The real test of the enterprise would be the adjustment of compensation for property taken. Insofar as buildings are concerned, values and prices could be determined with comparatively little difficulty. The acquisition of land, however, would involve serious problems.

To obviate the problems of land acquisition, another step must be taken in the land policy of our urban communities. It is a truism that land is only worth what it can produce under an orderly system of development. In a preplanned community, such as would be developed under the scheme of neighborhood rehabilitation, it would not be difficult to determine the use value of each parcel of land and the compensation to be paid to the owners. Recognizing the fact that land values depend upon immediate use, the municipalities should be empowered to acquire by purchase or condemnation the lands needed for a neighborhood project, and should pay compensation according to the revenue-yielding power of the use proposed, as mentioned above. This method of paying for land needed for housing purposes is in vogue in England, and has worked satisfactorily. Similar powers should be granted American municipalities.

TAX-DELINQUENT PROPERTIES

Recent years have witnessed vast accumulations of tax delinquencies on many housing properties. Many tax-delinquent dwellings represent the poorest types of construction or are actually part of slums. The present method of disposing of these properties by public sale varies in different states, but it is certain that nowhere have the cities made an effort to take advantage of these public sales for taxes to acquire and hold or to use lands thus acquired. The usual procedure is to dispose of such lands and buildings as soon as possible. Tax-delinquent properties often present rather extensive opportunities for land rehabilitation and the destruction of substandard buildings. By adopting a policy of acquiring such properties, the city would find itself in a position where it could clear out many dwellings unfit for habitation, or where the disposal of such properties under proper conditions and restrictions would result in improved housing provisions. This, in turn, would remove these properties from the

tax-delinquent list and result in buildings which would add to the supply of housing and the revenues from taxes.

The City of Milwaukee has done splendid work in acquiring tax-delinquent properties and, where justified by conditions, in clearing out slum
buildings. The policy of handling tax-delinquent properties is often
hedged in by a great maze of restrictions, which cause delay and confusion, without in the end being of great value to the owner of such
properties. A way must be found for disposing of tax-delinquent cases,
particularly where the public interest is involved.

SUBDIVISION CONTROL

The present situation in our cities regarding land subdivision and use
is due essentially to the fact that land division for building sites has continued to follow the practices required by the simpler ways of building
which prevailed up to the middle of the latter half of the last century.
Buildings were seldom more than two stories high, home ownership was
a common practice, and traffic needs were comparatively limited. It is on
this basis of land division and ownership that our "macropolis" reached
upward and outward for space. This has resulted in land sweating on the
one hand and in flight of population to the periphery of the city on the
other.

Within the built-up areas of our cities, the transition from a low to
heavy land load resulted in the confusion and blight which we now must
face. The flight from the city congestion produced radical changes in the
towns and villages in the vicinity of our cities, but mainly it resulted in a
rush to subdivide suburban and rural land into building, and especially residential sites. We have no record of the total number of lots subdivided
under this impetus. If we may judge, however, by the subdivisions around
New York, Chicago, Philadelphia, Detroit, Los Angeles, and other cities,
the number of new lots carved out of the countryside would be enough to
rehouse all the population of the country in single-family dwellings.

In the development of these subdivisions, no account was taken in most
cases of many of the factors and methods of planning which lead toward
successful land subdivision. The rush toward the less settled areas
prompted the conversion of fertile fields and fruit-producing orchards of
high quality into dismal suburban residential layouts with concrete streets,
electroliers, sewers, and other services. A monotonous street pattern is the
rule in these subdivisions, and roads devoid of proper orientation or clearly
defined objectives, surrounding lots of dimensions designed more for sale
than for home sites, characterize the vast majority of them. Millions upon
millions of dollars have been invested in these ephemeral land operations,

and high-pressure salesmen and saleswomen raided many a savings account of the lower-income families, while optimistic banks made investments which culminated in a country-wide break in our credit system.

The tragic fiasco in the land-subdivision market has brought clearly to the attention of both investors and public authorities the need for subdivision control.

As far back as 1924, it became obvious that some steps should be taken in the direction of controlling, if not curtailing, land subdivision. From the present situation and the experience of the past, it is evident that at least the following forms of control should be made the prime conditions of land subdivision:

1. All subdivisions must be designed so as to fit into the existing physical pattern of the communities to which they are related.

2. All services must be provided before building may be undertaken.

3. Provision must be made for open spaces, shopping centers, school sites, playgrounds, and the usual amenities of modern living.

4. The entire area should be zoned before the ground plan is developed.

5. Lots must be of ample size and suitable for the various types of buildings provided by zoning.

6. All public areas, such as streets, alleys, and so forth, must be dedicated to the municipality without cost, or provision should be made for adequate care of these areas by the original owners and their successors. In addition to these restrictions, private land developers should impose deed restrictions upon individual sites, which would guarantee high standards of construction and maintenance.

The study of many of the subdivision regulations reveals the fact that standards are generally low and that the need for the subdivision is seldom based upon the resources of the local market or a shortage of building sites. The overdevelopment of subdivisions has therefore resulted in an overstocked market, slow sales, blighted areas, partial occupation, and low service standards resulting from a lack of resources.

A land policy applied to subdivisions which would require the subdivider to prove the need for such a subdivision would therefore be a progressive step in the direction of protecting investors on the one hand, and of saving open areas around our cities, either for farming purposes or as park and forest reserves, on the other. If we apply restrictions upon cultivation to agriculture, there is no reason why similar restrictions should not be applied to the use of open areas around our cities.

Still another proposal must be made regarding urban land policies. It has often been found that lots intended for one purpose are used for other and less suitable purposes. A single-family residence area eventually develops into a hotel or an apartment-house district. This is frequently due to defective zoning regulations or to frequent and lax zoning amendments, which permit easy changes from one use to another without due consideration of the actual needs of the community or the land-division conditions of the district. As various types of buildings require sizes and shapes of lots consistent with their own size and use, it is essential that zoning should take account of the lot divisions, so that use and site would bear some relation to each other. Conceiving a subdivision as an integrated entity, a great deal can be anticipated regarding future development, with due regard to such an entity, by careful consideration of all social, economic, and cultural requirements. The whole problem of land subdivision and the expansion of land uses is one which must be solved, not alone for the protection of the future purchasers of lots, but in the interest of the whole community, so that there will be no waste of needed open spaces, no extravagance in the extension of services, and no blight due to partial development.

SUMMARY

This somewhat lengthy discussion of the land problem as a factor in housing is by no means as complete as it might be. We have endeavored to focus the reader's attention on the character and peculiarities of land as a commodity, which determines land assessments, land values, land prices, and land use. That a great variety of controls are needed to bring land within the reach of low-cost housing is evident. It is my conviction that, in the long run, both owners and users of land would profit from such controls.

People

CHAPTER II

PEOPLE

The whole of any social structure and its varied manifestations and functions depends upon two fundamental factors, land and people. By land, I do not mean mere ground, but the sum total of natural environmental conditions, its resources as they are suited for exploitation, control in the interest of human welfare, and the changes that land undergoes under human exploitation which affect society and the individual.

Housing has often been considered independent of land in its broadest sense. We have, of course, given much attention to the land problem, not in the sense of its natural character and resources, but as space upon which homes could be built and the various social manifestations which have interfered with the use of land for housing purposes. In this chapter we should like to consider land and people from the broader aspects of location, migrations, shifts in the centers of activity, effect of resources upon population, climate, and similar aspects of the subject. The housing problem as it appears from this point of view involves, not alone building and living standards, but also regional relationships of site and the potentialities which these regional conditions afford to permanent human settlements. Professors Odum and Moore point out that the Indians have developed housing methods consistent with the region in which each tribe lives.[1] Similar differences may be found in the construction and manner of using homes in the various regions among the white population of the country. To be sure, architectural styles and the tendency to copy from one another have somewhat beclouded the local character of construction and ways of living which regional conditions have produced. The discerning student will, however, find no difficulty in discovering prevailing and clearly regional architectural characteristics in many communities.

It has been pointed out in the course of this book that housing is built, not for short-time service, but, as implied by the economic nature of the investment and the character of the commodity, for long-time service extending from one to three generations. The character of the population has been changing in this country both because of immigration and

[1] Odum, Howard W., and Moore, Harry Estill, *American Regionalism*, 1938, p. 304.

because of the transformation which takes place in the cultural character and economic and social outlook of the generations following a
large immigration influx. Immigration in itself has ceased to be a factor
in the United States since the doors have been closed to immigrants following the events of the Great War.

The Family

According to the Census of 1930, there were 29,904,663 families in
the United States. These families were of various sizes, dependent upon
the number of children on the one hand and the number of lodgers on
the other. I am giving in the following table their percental distribution.

Families Classified by Number of Children Under 21 Years Old, by Divisions and States: 1930

DIVISION AND STATE	All Families	Per Cent of All Families							
		None	1	2	3	4	5	6 to 8	9 or More
United States..........	29,904,663	38.8	20.8	16.2	10.1	6.1	3.6	4.0	0.5
Geographic divisions:									
New England.............	1,981,499	42.1	19.7	15.5	9.7	5.8	3.3	3.5	0.5
Middle Atlantic..........	6,374,380	39.7	21.2	16.8	9.9	5.6	3.1	3.3	0.4
East North Central.......	6,362,823	40.8	21.4	16.5	9.7	5.5	3.0	3.0	0.3
West North Central.......	3,317,881	40.1	20.6	16.1	9.9	5.9	3.4	3.5	0.4
South Atlantic............	3,511,860	32.3	19.9	16.0	11.2	7.8	5.2	6.7	0.9
East South Central........	2,273,359	32.6	20.3	15.9	11.2	7.7	5.2	6.3	0.7
West South Central.......	2,868,262	33.0	21.4	16.7	11.2	7.3	4.6	5.2	0.6
Mountain................	914,408	38.3	19.6	16.0	10.4	6.7	4.1	4.5	0.5
Pacific..................	2,300,191	49.2	21.2	14.9	7.5	3.7	1.8	1.6	0.2

This above table presents a number of very interesting conditions
which, in any consideration of size of dwellings and general trends of
building enterprise, should not be overlooked. The Pacific states show
the largest number of families without children, while the South Atlantic
states have the smallest number of families without children. The most
startling fact, however, is the frequency of families without children for
the whole United States, amounting to 38.8 per cent. While these figures
may represent, not the sterility of families, but rather the tendency among
young people to maintain their own homes, still, in the general planning
for homes as units of accommodation, these figures should play an important part. Whether the general character of the home has forced
young people to undertake living in their own establishments, or whether
the spirit of independence and freedom which characterizes the modern

generation has created a demand for small dwellings for one or two persons we can not say with any certainty, as no information is given on the marital condition of the persons living in individual homes or on the relation between those occupying the homes, except where the occupants had children. The fact is that, on the Pacific Coast, families without children constitute nearly half of all the families living in that part of the country. In the New England states, the proportion of families without children to the total number of families is 42.1 per cent, also a rather large proportion. When we combine these figures with those relating to the average size of the family in the United States, we realize that a radical change has taken place. The average number of persons for every 100 families in 1900 was 430, while in 1930 it was only 407; a decrease of 23 persons for every 100 families.

That no plan for the development of housing can be made without considering this trend is obvious. But the figures which reveal the changes in the birth rate are still more significant. In 1800, the birth rate in the United States per 1,000 persons was 55. In the middle of the last century, it was only 43.3; by the end of the century, it had been reduced to 30.1; and in 1930, it was only 20.1. These figures are not only indicative of the decrease in the rate of growth of population, but also imply a change in the general composition of the families of the country which need to be housed. That this condition is not to remain stationary is recognized by students of population who are concerned with national fertility. Thompson and Whelpton, in their book *Population Trends*, calculate the "medium" birth rate for 1960 as 14.6. With a birth rate nearly one fourth of what it was at the beginning of the nineteenth century and immigration no longer a factor in the growth of population, the whole outlook has changed or should change insofar as housing is concerned. No longer can we plan on buildings being absorbed by a transient immigrant population on its way to prosperity, nor can we assume that whatever growth takes place in specific communities is due to a natural increase in the local population.

As a counterpart to the low birth rate, a very considerable change has taken place in the expectation of life in various age groups. Edgar Sydenstricker, in his chapter on "The Vitality of the American People," which forms part of the first volume of *Social Trends in the United States*, has compiled a very valuable table showing the life expectation and its evolution from 1789 to 1929. In this table we find that, for males, the life expectation of children born in 1789 was 34.5, as opposed to 46.01 years in 1901. For females, the increase of life expectancy rose from 36.5 to 49.42 for the same period in our history. From 1901 to

1928, there was a rise in the life expectancy for males from 46.01 to
58.11, while for females the rise was from 49.42 to 61.36.[2] In seventeen
years, there was a gain of nearly eleven years for males and nearly twelve
for females. This condition should, for the time being, compensate in
part for the low birth rate. As the distribution of ages advances, however,
and the number of old people increases, there is bound to be a shift
which will no longer take care of the low birth rate. The figures given
by Sydenstricker show that, after the age of sixty, the life expectation
for persons of that age is actually lower for 1928 than for any previous
period in our history.

Many of the cities of the United States, in particular the metropolitan
centers, have completely disregarded the evidence concerning the changes
which have taken place in our birth rate and the drop in the immigration
ratio. Their prognostications about population increases have at times become so fantastic as to be ridiculous. The City of New York, disregarding the actual drop in the population of Manhattan, its most densely settled area, has assumed that by 1960 the city itself will have a population
of about ten millions and the entire metropolitan region some sixteen
to twenty millions of people. The City of Chicago, in its preparation for
a regional plan, has assumed—or its planners have assumed—that, between 1930 and 1960, the population should increase from 3,376,438
to 5,100,000, while the entire metropolitan region with 5,058,147 people
will have a population of 8,738,000 in 1960. If all prognostications regarding the regional population growth in the United States were to
come true in the year 1960, according to the probable growth of population which can be reasonably expected in the country at that time, it
would take all of this country's population and the population of Canada,
Mexico, and Brazil to fulfill the prophecy of the regional planners.

It should be remembered in this connection that many of the so-called
"metropolitan regions" are merely metropolitan districts with none of
the fundamental characters of integrated regions. They are the agglomerations of population which, as a result of historical conditions and forces
and the establishment of certain industrial activities, have been thriving
and attracting more people. The natural trend of population may be in
other directions, owing to the many conditions of urban obsolescence,
changes in the character of industrial distribution, and the greater awareness throughout the country of the possibilities for a more rational distribution of people and their activities. This, however, does not seem to
have entered into the calculation of metropolitan planning. Much of

[2] For a more recent and detailed analysis of American age distribution and life span see *The
Problems of a Changing Population*, National Resources Committee, May, 1938, p. 22.

what is generally designated as "metropolitan area" is an artificial classification developed largely as a prospective shopping and business resource in relation to some central community. To all intents and purposes, many of these communities are rural or semi-rural, are rooted in their environment, and are but slightly related to the metropolis. There were 392 communities of less than 2,500 population included in the metropolitan districts of the eleven largest metropolitan centers of the country. These are certainly devoid of most of the characteristics of metropolitan districts, and serve to distort the conception of the growth and development of the metropolitan areas. It is a very simple matter to extend the boundaries or contract them according to need. In fact, there has been a great loss of vitality and individual initiative in local development of small communities taken into the fold of some specific regional calculation as a result of the pressure and control exercised over them by the metropolitan city.

There is, of course, no question of the value of the metropolitan concept as a basis for social and economic planning. The most serious danger is in the orientation given to this planning, which so often tends to converge all services and activities in the direction of the metropolitan city rather than toward the development of such services and activities for the benefit of the local community. So far as tendency affects housing, the emphasis has been on the need for rehousing in areas that have long ago outlived their usefulness and fitness for residential use. The rehabilitation of slums and the reclamation of blighted areas used for housing purposes have been constantly focused upon the fact that the vitality of the metropolitan district, as a central factor in the distribution of population and population activities, must continue to follow an outworn historical pattern.

In the course of the next few years, there is every evidence that there will have to be a good deal of housing construction. Under the pressure of an existing housing shortage and political influence of metropolitan communities, there is danger that much of this housing will be located in areas where the best conditions are difficult to attain because of the very character of these metropolitan cities. There is the danger that, although housing may be provided where it is needed at the present time, eventually there will be a shift in the industrial and general economic life of the country which will necessitate a new program of housing consistent with a new set of regional requirements. It would not be desirable to delay construction until that new regional pattern is created, but I venture the assertion that much could be forecast at the present time, and that these forecasts could be made through the elaborate and thorough studies of the National Resources Board, the Railroad Commission, the Home Loan Bank Board, and various other investigating and policy-control agencies of the country, and which could be crystallized into national policies.

RURAL AND URBAN POPULATION

While certain efforts are being made to improve housing conditions in large centers of population, the smaller communities, and particularly those classified by the Census as rural non-farm communities, which constitute nearly one-fifth of the population of the United States and nearly half of the total rural population of the country, have received no attention whatever. It would seem that the migration from rural to urban communities is not only farm population migration but also migration from rural non-farm to urban communities. These rural communities are generally small villages, many of which are devoid of most of the advantages of the larger population centers, and yet they present an important factor in the life of the nation. If we consider the non-farm rural population in its relation to the total urban population, we find that the non-farm rural population constitutes 34.5 per cent of the total population not living on farms. These people represent a very important element in the population of the country by virtue of the fact that they are potential urban dwellers and also because their lot is generally ignored in the efforts that are being made to improve national conditions of living, employment, and cultural advancement. Their housing is often of the poorest, their schools of the least desirable type, and their ways of living confined to the limits of undeveloped communities, with precarious employment conditions. This non-farm rural population is equal to the total urban population of New York, New Jersey, Pennsylvania, and Michigan, four of the most urban states in the Union. Nor should it be assumed that this is a part of the population which is on the decrease. The fact is that, between 1920 and 1930, the non-farm rural population increased by 3,615,333, or 18.06 per cent, while the total population of the country increased only at the rate of 16.1 per cent for the same period of time. If we are to recapture the rural values which still surround one-fifth of our population and reduce the tide of cityward migration, we must take into consideration the rural non-farm people, who present an important and largely unexplored field. The various advantages of urban life could be made available to these people without forcing them into the congested and obsolete precincts of our cities.

That these families are not rooted in their little communities and are just awaiting the opportunity to leave for larger cities is not wholly a

TRUMBULL PARK HOUSING PROJECT IN CHICAGO, ILLINOIS. BUILT WITH THE AID OF THE UNITED STATES HOUSING AUTHORITY.

PARKLAWN-MILWAUKEE, WISCONSIN. HOUSING PROJECT UNDERTAKEN BY THE UNITED STATES HOUSING AUTHORITY.

justified assumption, if we consider home ownership as an index of stability. The fact is that, while only 42.8 per cent of the families living in urban communities and 52.3 per cent of rural farm families own their homes, the rural non-farm families own their homes in 52.6 per cent of the cases, or more often than either the urban or rural farm population. In fact, home ownership in rural non-farm type of community has been constantly on the increase since 1890.

I am not certain that home ownership in this case is an index of stability of population settlement. There is little information on this type of settlement which would furnish us with the facts regarding the migrations of the rural non-farm population, but it is quite certain that so large a portion of our population is worth study and consideration, both as social and economic entities.

Population and Community Equipment

It has already been suggested that the birth rate in this country is decreasing and that the general distribution of ages is undergoing radical changes. These changes should have their counterpart in the manner in which housing enterprises are conceived, both as habitation and in their relation to the various services essential to the development of suitable environmental conditions. Thus schools which may have been adequate ten years ago in providing ample space and equipment for a certain distribution of age groups may become inadequate in this respect with a shift in the distribution of ages.

It has been calculated that, by 1940, there will be 1,000,000 fewer children of the ages of 9 to 16, and that quite obviously fewer children will be entering school. Insofar as the institutions for higher education are concerned, there will still be the same number of students, or an increasing number by that time, since the birth rate up to 1921 was on the increase.[3] Schooling a million children and providing the various services which they need constitute very important factors in the whole problem of bringing into proper relation housing provisions and community equipment which housing must have.

It may be said, however, that, while the birth rate has been decreasing, the urban and semi-urban population has been increasing at the same time that the rural population has been decreasing. Thus, some of the changes in the age distribution may be absorbed by the increase in population. We must bear the fact in mind, however, that, while the metropolitan cities have been increasing at a comparatively normal rate, the

[3] Thompson and Whelpton, Chapter on Population, *Social Trends*, Vol. I, p. 33; McGraw-Hill Book Co., 1933.

outlying areas of the metropolitan districts have been increasing at an abnormally rapid rate. We find, for example, that, while the metropolitan districts of cities with 2,000,000 population or more increased but 21.8 per cent between 1920 and 1930, the increase in the surrounding areas has amounted to 48.3 per cent. The metropolitan cities with from one to two million population increased but 13.1 per cent, while the outside areas increased 40.1 per cent. Without exception, all of the metropolitan districts of the country have been increasing in population more rapidly in the areas outside the boundaries of the metropolis than inside.

Another interesting and important tendency in the distribution of population has been taking place within the municipal boundaries of the metropolitan cities along the lines of pushing the population from the center to the periphery of the community. This phenomenon has particular significance from the point of view of the distribution of amenities and the necessity for reorienting the distribution of schools, playgrounds, health centers, traffic, and many other facilities which relate the newly developed areas to the municipal center. The centers of the cities are at the same time undergoing serious transformations both as to use and needs. Professor R. D. McKenzie, in his book, *The Metropolitan Community*, gives a table showing the rates of increase in population in certain zones from the centers of New York, Chicago, Cleveland, and Pittsburgh. Invariably the zones within one mile from the center of the city have decreased in population, Cleveland having lost 27 per cent, New York 25 per cent, Chicago 22 per cent, and Pittsburgh only 7 per cent. In New York, the greatest increase in population has taken place in the areas which represent a minimum distance from the center of the city of from twelve to sixteen miles, where the increase in population between 1920 and 1930 has been 278 per cent. In Chicago, the greatest increase in population has taken place in the areas between eight and ten miles from the center of the city, the percentage of increase being 112 per cent in the period between 1920 and 1930. This change in the distribution of population has its bearing upon the whole question of community equipment and its planning in relation, not only to the drift of population, but also to age composition, with all its implied requirements.

I have not attempted an elaborate study of population in relation to housing, as this would require a much longer discussion than the scope of this book warrants. All that is essential is to point out the conditions which the tendencies in the distribution and rate of increase in our population present and their relation to housing. Briefly stated, the following considerations should be taken into account in planning housing programs and projects:

1. The size of families is undergoing radical changes.

2. The age distribution in these families represents basic factors which must be taken into account in planning housing and the community equipment which must serve such housing.

3. There is being created in most large cities a no man's land, as a result of obsolescence and blight, or normal transition, in housing development. The problem of rehabilitating and reconstructing these areas and reshaping their destiny must be met, not as a resettlement question, but rather as a problem involving the future of human habitation.

4. A large proportion of the population of the United States lives in villages or rural areas in which housing conditions are often in need of attention, and there is every reason to believe that these communities represent a source of conservation of human and cultural resources at present largely neglected in our social planning.

5. The distribution of population, or rather its present redistribution, as exemplified by the larger metropolitan centers, affords an opportunity for control of densities and a balancing between density and services which would give greater stability to rapidly developing settlements and a more harmonious and efficient community integration.

6. The whole program of housing, for both the underprivileged and those with incomes sufficient to maintain decent living conditions, depends upon a careful consideration and understanding of the trends of population and the needs which these trends represent, as well as the various controls which can be attained by proper planning and zoning.

Size of Family and Ownership of Homes

In 1930, there were in the United States 17,372,524 families living in urban communities. Of this number, 7,432,554, or 42.9 per cent, owned their homes or had at least attempted to acquire ownership. Tenant families numbered 9,681,359, or 57.1 per cent. In the case of the home-owning families, the percentage of those having from three to five persons was 53.8 per cent, while in the case of tenant families, the percentage was only 50.8. On the other hand, home-owning families consisting of only one or two persons constituted 28.9 per cent, as opposed to 35.9 per cent for the tenant families. The trend in the direction of building small apartments has no doubt grown out of this demand on the part of three and a half million families of only one or two persons. The fact also that, in these families, often both members of the family are work-

ing, making possible the payment of a higher rent for smaller accommodations, has added to the impetus toward the construction or conversion
of buildings with an ample supply of small apartments.

It is a rather interesting fact that the proportion of families with six
or more persons is higher among those who lived in their own homes
than among those who lived in rented quarters. In the one case they
constituted 17.5 per cent, and in the other only 13.3 per cent, of the
total number of families in these groups. Unfortunately, we have no
figures showing the economic status of the families in each family group
or the kind of homes occupied by the larger home-owning families.

In any national program for housing, it is quite essential to develop
adequate data on the size of family and percentage of home ownership,
so that we may be able to judge as to the relation which government
aid may bear to types of families, particularly in the matter of adjusting
size of family to accommodations. In many European countries, notably
in Austria and France, a good deal has been done to help large families
with normal or low incomes to secure suitable accommodations at rentals
within their range of income.

Age of the Head of the Family

The acquisition of homes and the ability to meet the long-term obligations which such acquisition requires raises the question of the distribution of ages of the heads of families. Assuming that the highest earning
capacity is reached around the age of 45, undertaking the obligations of
home ownership must be related to the age distribution of the heads of
families. There are, of course, exceptional conditions when other members of the family contribute toward the payment for a home, but generally that is not the case.

Of the 29,904,663 families in the United States, 3,792,902 have as
head of the family a woman. Of those with a man as head of the family,
a considerable proportion is made up of persons 45 years of age and over.
Of this number, 22.0 per cent are between 45 and 54 years of age, 14.1
per cent between 55 and 64, and the remaining 9.4 per cent over 65.
In other words, 45.7 per cent of all the families are headed by persons
beyond the age of highest earning capacity. Should it be possible to eliminate the pseudofamilies of one or two persons who live, not as families,
but merely as individuals, without any intimate family ties, the proportion
would be much larger. It is unfortunate that we have no figures relating
to the urban and rural distribution of family heads according to age; but,
assuming that the distribution corresponds to the general age distribution
in these areas, we find that a very considerable proportion of the families

which do not own their homes are headed by persons who are not in a
position to become potential purchasers of homes at present costs and
under the usual methods of payment.

Housing has been preoccupying the interest of many government
agencies, both in the matter of supplying homes and in the matter of
setting up an economic structure which would make decent housing
accessible to larger numbers of our families. It would be worth while to
elaborate the census schedules for 1940, therefore, so as to contain adequate and better-focused information, not alone on existing conditions,
but also on the possibilities for providing the proper kind of homes for
the great variety of needs represented by the types of families to be
accommodated.

Money

CHAPTER III

MONEY

In the chapter on land, we pointed out the various ways in which housing is affected by the fluctuation in the values of land and the factors that bring land into play in financing housing. Here we shall consider the matter of money in its various aspects, as regards availability, cost, and liquidation of indebtedness; the relation that housing investment bears to the economic structure of the country; and the consequences involved in the relation between money and housing.

There are no figures which could be said to be dependable regarding the total investment in dwellings in the United States. Indeed, there have been such violent fluctuations in values that any estimate we might make today would hardly hold for more than a short time. In round figures, it has been estimated that the total value of dwellings in the United States is approximately one-fifth of the total wealth of the country. Assuming this wealth to be about $500,000,000,000, the value of housing real estate would be about $100,000,000,000. This would hardly correspond to the assessed values for taxation purposes, nor does it represent values which could be made the basis for estimating actual realizable investment.

While this valuation of the dwellings in the United States may be somewhere near correct under normal conditions, there is serious question whether it would hold today, after eight years of lack of replacement of old buildings and failure to meet the normal demands due to increase in population and in the number of families. It may be added that, in view of the fact that more than half the values of dwellings are mortgaged in the cities of ordinary and large size, the whole estimated valuation of the relation of homes to national wealth needs revision.

According to estimates made by the Federal Home Loan Bank Board, the total amount in home mortgage loans outstanding in 1925 was $13,-843,000,000. By 1930, the home-mortgage loans outstanding increased to $22,153,000,000, an increase of over 66.9 per cent in six years. By 1936, however, the figures had receded to $17,798,000,000, or a decline of 19.7 per cent. But if we consider the $2,763,000,000 taken over by the Home Owners Loan Corporation, the actual decline in the outstanding loans on homes in six years rose to 32.1 per cent.

I am citing these figures because they show how spasmodic the whole lending market of the country is and how rapidly it responds to changing conditions. This is true regardless of the fact that investment in housing is a long-term investment and that the payments of both capital and interest, as well as the costs, generally extend over two or more decades.

In small, stable communities, with non-fluctuating populations and well established economic resources, the valuations may remain reasonably steady for a long time. In communities like New York, Boston, or Chicago, however, which are highly sensitized to the economic changes taking place in industry and business, these values of necessity depend for their stability upon economic changes.

What we are concerned with, however, is not so much the value of existing dwellings as the investment market, which makes the providing of dwellings possible and economically practical. Long experience has established the conditions under which investment in any enterprise can depend upon the support of capital. These are:

1. Adequate return on the investment.
2. Capacity of the investment to be liquidated.
3. Continuity of productivity.
4. Safety.
5. Freedom from heavy taxation and the incidents of advancing tax burdens.
6. Large-scale investment, with reduced management responsibilities for the individual investor.

These are the essential requirements which certainly apply to housing with greater force than to any other investment venture.

Adequate Return on the Investment

We shall see that, insofar as the housing market is concerned, between one-third and one-half of the population can pay rentals so small that any heavy burden of interest would make investment in housing quite unsafe if such housing were intended for lower-income families.

The result has been that the kind of housing which found a ready money market was the type that could carry the extra charges for money costs. This is the type that, with the addition of a few luxuries, can yield luxury rents, although the total investment per unit of building cost differs only very slightly from the simpler requirements of the lower-income families. Thus, during the period of prosperity, when profits were expected to be high, there was actually more construction of a luxury type than could possibly be absorbed, although income groups capable of paying the high rentals were not numerous enough to absorb the available accommodations. In New York, Boston, Chicago, and many of the Western cities, private houses, apartment houses, and apartment hotels were built with no regard to the income distribution of the population, but only from the point of view of expected returns in rents or sales based upon calculations which completely disregarded the actual market. At the beginning of the depression, there were many more losses due to luxury-housing construction than to investment in and ownership of low-rental housing. Thus the intent to avoid the small profits to be realized in the building of lower-cost and lower-rental housing resulted in vast losses which could otherwise have been avoided and, at the same time, could have served to produce the type of house for which there was a market at a lower profit. The building boom which characterized the period of prosperity, particularly between 1926 and 1929, proved the debacle of the building industry and of building investment.

The further fact should be observed, namely, that, during the boom period, not only were large returns expected but the charges for financing and the parasitic manipulations of various aspects of building enterprise became so burdensome that the investor was left with a building in which the actual use value, after speculative values had been eliminated, was too small to produce the expected revenue. There were cases of buildings of the luxury type which, after all, except the actual cost of building had been covered, left the investors with a mere shadow of what was intended to be a source of revenue. In numerous cases, foreclosures yielded less than the first mortgage, leaving the holder of the second mortgage with the proverbial empty sack. In some cases, persons forced foreclosure on their homes, since they were aware that, in a prostrated market, they could repurchase their homes for less than the first mortgage. Where refinancing of a large housing enterprise became necessary, the risk was considered so great that from 12 to 15 per cent on the annual rate for second mortgages was not an uncommon practice.

Thus the period of great prosperity, after sowing its wild oats, left us a harvest of bankruptcies, lost property, reduced incomes from housing investment, and a building industry which, after ten years, is still trying to recover.

CAPACITY OF INVESTMENT TO BE LIQUIDATED

In most investment fields, particularly where the investment is represented by stocks and bonds, the sensitiveness of the market and the needs of the investor can be met through the flexibility of the stock market. In housing, the investment is fixed and difficult to liquidate without serious loss, except in cases where a shortage occurs or some special condition favors the investment. There is little room for speculation after the investment has been made and the rentals or prices for homes have been fixed. The investment is made, not for a year or two, but for a decade or, as is more often the case, for twenty to thirty years. The hazards entailed by such an investment are great, and the fact, as has been pointed out, that investment is made in housing at times of high prosperity and rentals, and that disposal of property generally takes place during times of depression, the hazard becomes still greater and must be compensated by high interest rates and heavy financing charges.

As housing is not a matter of large-scale investment in any single enterprise, no adequate mechanism for marketing investment shares in housing has been devised. Each individual or organization handles its own project or investment and expects to liquidate the investment as best he can. The fundamental philosophy of housing finance is therefore highly individualistic, with the promoter unloading his burden as soon as possible and leaving the financing agency to reap the results.

Continuity of Productivity

I have dealt in detail elsewhere with the many foreclosures which were brought about during and even before the depression. In addition to the various and more or less regular depressions which affect the housing market, the matter of obsolescence is seldom taken into account. We know that, in the upper brackets of rental ranges, families are always seeking to improve their housing conditions, to take advantage of every invention or new gadget that comes into use. New houses, as they are built along modern lines, therefore drain off much of the tenancy of the older houses. Rentals must be gradually reduced to compete with the newer buildings, and the anticipated income is of necessity reduced, unless allowance is made for this type of obsolescence and revenue calculated to meet these conditions.

In the many plans for housing finance that I have had the opportunity of examining in the course of the last few years, the matter of rent reduction is seldom considered. Now and again allowance is made for depreciation, but little heed is given to the fact that, in the course of time, rentals will have to be lowered.

Where mortgages are placed upon the so-called owner-occupied homes, it is taken for granted that the purchaser who assumes a mortgage obligation will always be able to meet his obligations, regardless of changing conditions. As most mortgage obligations are assumed at a time when income is steady and high, and the mortgage must be paid up mostly when times are normal or bad and earning capacity is reduced, the result can hardly be satisfactory.

The figures reported in the *Financial Survey of Urban Housing* show that, in the fifty cities in which the investigation was carried on, 58.5 per cent of the homes occupied by the owners were mortgaged, while 42.8 per cent of the rented dwellings were mortgaged. In the cities of the New England states, the proportion of mortgaged owner-occupied dwellings reached 83.6 per cent in Worcester, Massachusetts, and 81.1 per cent in Waterbury, Connecticut. We have no figures either as to the length of time that has elapsed since the mortgage obligations were contracted or of the rate at which they were being cleared up and the homes held free from debt.

We have likewise no figures relating to the relation between original investment in housing and the rents which houses yield. Nor have we any adequate figures to show the relation between value and revenue, net or gross. All we have are some fragmentary figures, reported in the above-cited survey, which relate to the average value of single-family dwellings and the rents which they yield. These figures, as of 1934, show that, for single-family dwellings, the average valuation was $3,142 and the average rent $248 per annum. This is a return of only 7.89 per cent gross, which must take care of interest on the investment, taxes, depreciation, vacancies, time lost in rerental, management, rent collection, repairs, and so on. On the other hand, the tenants in these same dwellings, although failing to pay a reasonable return on what is presumed to be a safe investment, are themselves paying an average of 24.2 per cent of their income in rent, or nearly one-fifth more than is generally assumed to be the normal proportion between rent and income. In many cities, the proportion of rent to income is even higher and the return on the value of the property lower.

It may be said that the figures relate to an abnormal period in our history, but abnormal periods have been occurring from time to time, and the investment in housing has had to meet these conditions regardless of the original investment.

Enough has been said to show that, unless the fluctuations in the productive capacity of housing as an investment can be absorbed by reduction in costs, or by high initial rents in the case of rented dwellings, or much lower financing charges where private ownership is involved, continuity of productive investment does not seem to characterize housing, or at least not without a downward trend.

Safety of Investment

The records of the banks and insurance companies could tell a very interesting, though tragic, story of the safety of investment in housing. The slums of our cities—those specifically blighted areas which held the promise of great demands for additional housing, into which vast migrations which have been brought by changes in the character of districts, or by the incidence of unemployment—are mortgaged to our various investing institutions for amounts ranging from a few hundred dollars to millions.

Some studies made by the Chamber of Commerce of the Lower East Side of Manhattan Island teach a serious lesson in investment finance, as practiced by some of the most outstanding and reliable financial institutions of New York City. The very fact that these great institutions, shrewd in their financial operations, guardians of millions of depositors' savings, could have failed to visualize the impending tragedy merely indicates either that we know little about the whole science of real-estate economics—if, indeed, it can be called a science—or that the winds of investment blow with the irregularity of our changing tides of prosperity and depression.

How much of these investments will have to be written off the books of these institutions no one can forecast, but that the chances of recovering these losses are slight, even though prosperity may return, has been already recognized by those who do not refuse to see that much fiction has been masquerading as reality.

Freedom from Heavy Taxation and the Incidence of Heavy Tax Burdens

Our municipalities have become more and more costly to service, and the burdens of taxation have been mounting at a pace that has made homeowners the victims, in many instances, of levies which they could not carry. In congested districts, tenements often bear a tax burden equivalent to 30 per cent of the gross income. In areas which are undergoing transition, the tax burden may be even higher. In new and still undeveloped communities, like those of the Far West, local improvements, as has been pointed out, reach a point, through special assessments, where the market value of property is equal to or even lower than the assessed value.

The more complex the community, the greater is the per capita cost of local government; and the greater the per capita cost, the heavier is the taxation. As from 85 to 95 per cent of all local budgets must be derived from real property, the renter or homeowner carries the burden. Some countries have relieved unoccupied dwellings of taxation. This seems to have worked rather well in Germany, where housing is taxed only on a basis of income or value for occupancy, and not on a basis of assessed value regardless of revenue. It would seem to me that, aside from the taxing of unused lands, one way of relieving housing from its present heavy taxation might be to apply the principle of taxation upon income from property rather than upon assessments, many of which, particularly in congested areas, are based upon possibilities for future use of land rather than upon actual use at the time of the assessment.

At present, there is considerable difficulty in securing capital for housing purposes where the tax levy is high and the rentals to be expected leave little margin for profit. In the security field, the hazard is often slight, as taxes on incomes are low and the chances of a sudden change in the tax rate are few. In the real-estate field standards are constantly being changed and rates are juggled to meet emergencies, regardless of revenue from rents or returns due to sale of property.

LARGE-SCALE INVESTMENT WITH REDUCED MANAGEMENT RESPONSIBILITIES FOR THE INDIVIDUAL INVESTOR

In the United States, with few outstanding exceptions, low-rental housing is undertaken as a business by small operators, who either are ready at any time to unload their buildings or must carry the property at a small return. Most of the properties are comparatively small and are occupied by families with low incomes. In recent years, only luxury housing has assumed the larger aspects of investment, but these accommodations are designed for the upper tenth of the population and not for the people with moderate or small incomes.

Sir Harold Bellman, of England, who has been responsible for some of the largest housing enterprises in his own country, referred to our method of housing production as a "shoestring industry." Under the conditions that prevail in the United States, management often absorbs from one-third to one-half the revenue, not so much because the service is of a higher grade, but because of the fact that the units of construction are small, and economical business organization for each small unit is difficult, if not impossible, under present conditions. In order to overcome this difficulty, the whole industry and the business methods under which it operates will have to be reorganized on a large scale.

Under the conditions pointed out, it is not surprising that housing finance has lagged behind the financing of many other enterprises, and that the hazards involved have tended to develop methods which have burdened housing with financing costs out of proportion with the rent-paying resources and buying power of the people.

There are no figures available which would show with any degree of accuracy the amounts which are loaned every year for housing purposes. Nor do we have available figures which would tell the story of losses sustained from investment in housing enterprise either by the banks and other investing agencies or by private individuals who lend money for housing purposes. The only figures we do have relate to foreclosures, and even here the information is neither accurate nor of a sufficiently general character to convey an idea of the conditions throughout the country. In fact, mortgage holders often defer foreclosure because of a bad market, which would make it impossible to realize from the sale even the amount of the mortgage.

The Financial Survey of Urban Housing represents a cross-section of urban community housing. The following figures apply only to owner-occupied dwellings:

OWNER-OCCUPIED RESIDENTIAL PROPERTIES: PERCENTAGE DISTRIBUTION OF AMOUNT OF FIRST MORT-
GAGE LOANS OUTSTANDING BY AGENCY HOLDING THE LOAN
(JANUARY 1, 1934)

Agency Holding Loan	Per Cent of Total
Life insurance company..........................	15.0
Building and loan association....................	13.6
Commercial bank...............................	18.5
Savings bank..................................	17.2
Mortgage company.............................	7.1
Construction company..........................	0.3
Title and trust company........................	3.2
Home Owners Loan Corporation.................	3.3
Individuals....................................	19.7
Others..	4.1
Total..	100.00

This is a rather remarkable distribution of investment, showing that the private investor plays a very small part in the whole loan market of owner-occupied dwellings. The various banking institutions are involved to the extent of 72.6 per cent of all mortgage loans on the dwellings studied in 52 cities throughout the United States. The balance is distrib-

Robert Maclean Glasgow, Photographer.

HILLSIDE HOUSING. A HOUSING PROJECT BUILT WITH THE AID OF GOVERNMENT FUNDS IN THE BOROUGH OF THE BRONX, NEW YORK. CLARENCE S. STEIN, ARCHITECT.

Photograph by Robert Maclean Glasgow.

HILLSIDE HOUSING, BOROUGH OF THE BRONX, NEW YORK.

uted among private individuals, who exceed investors not mentioned, and the Home Owners Loan Corporation, which has comparatively recently taken over some of the mortgages threatened with foreclosure. The most remarkable fact revealed by this table is that the construction companies played practically no part in the financing of their enterprises, as they held only 0.3 per cent of the mortgages. An examination of the detailed table dealing with the distribution of mortgages and mortgage-holding agencies in the 52 cities studied, shows that insurance companies carried very few mortgages in New England and Middle Atlantic cities, the percentages being 3.1 per cent and 4.6 per cent, respectively. On the other hand, they carried 31.2 per cent in South Atlantic cities and 42.1 per cent in East South Central cities. The savings banks carried the heaviest load in the New England states, where they held 44.8 per cent of the mortgages, and next in the Middle Atlantic states, where they held 42.1 per cent of the mortgages. In Worcester, Massachusetts, the savings banks held 76.8 per cent of the mortgages.

There are, no doubt, historical and legal reasons for this distribution of mortgage investment. In all probability, however, these reasons have long ago lost their justification, and there is room for a complete revamping of the legal restrictions and practices in the interest of better financing methods, in order to make housing loans more easily accessible and not subject to the risks and costs involved in transactions of this kind.

MORTGAGE DEBT AND VALUE OF PROPERTY

The *Financial Survey of Urban Housing* also presents some very interesting figures on the relation between the value of property and the amount of mortgages. In Table 111, it is shown that the average ratio of mortgage debt to the value of the property for the 52 cities included in the investigation was, as per January 1, 1934, as much as 60.4 for rental dwellings and 55.6 for owner-occupied dwellings. We, of course, do not know the age of the mortgages and can therefore not judge whether this mortgage situation was the result of unusual business depression or whether it represents normal conditions in these cities. It is an interesting fact that the ratio of rental property value to the mortgage debt is invariably higher than the debt ratio of owner-occupied dwellings. The reason for this is not available. However, there are two probabilities: either the people who invest in homes find it difficult to meet their obligations out of rents or, as in the case of many business buildings, owners use money secured on mortgages for business purposes because of the quick turnover in business which they can not find in property ownership.

INTEREST RATES

It has been alleged that the interest rate in the United States is very high. In view of the fact that the ultimate cost of a house includes not only its construction investment and other charges inherent in ownership but also the rate at which money can be obtained in the market. This rate is an important factor in housing costs. They affect the whole economic status of housing, both in owner-occupied dwellings and in rental property. It is quite impossible to ascertain what the actual rates of interest are, because the picture is often befogged by all sorts of charges intended to conceal the rate of interest. This is more frequently done by including a heavy financing charge in the loan, upon which interest must be paid throughout the life of the loan. Thus, it is impossible to ascertain the actual amount of money borrowed and, therefore, the actual interest rate exacted.

The only first-hand statistical information we have regarding the prevailing interest rates on loans which may be considered reliable is again to be found in the *Financial Survey of Urban Housing*. These figures, as all others quoted in this work, relate to 52 cities of this country. The average interest rate reported was $6.18 per $100, on the basis of the contract rate (weighted), and the effective rate averaged $6.54 per $100 in owner-occupied homes. The rates for owned dwellings were $6.25 and those for rented dwellings were $6.75. The rate for rented dwellings, probably because of their speculative nature, was higher. As far as the figures show, the fluctuation in the rates of interest ranges from $5.40 in Syracuse, New York, to $8.71 in Butte, Montana. The general average, however, is a very high rate, and of course it affects both rents and capacity to carry mortgage obligations.

I have always been impressed with the sanctimoniousness of the limited-dividend enterprises which have set, as their goal, a maximum of 6 per cent on the investment. This is entirely too high a rate and is in no material way a departure from normal investment return which commercial institutions expect to derive from such investments.

In looking over some figures on loans made in France by the most important lending institutions of the country, *La Société Centrale de Crédit Immobilier,* I found that the government had, by a decree issued in August 1937, permitted this organization to charge as high as 2.75 per cent on housing loans. The organization, however, did not take advantage of this privilege except in certain cases, and established a graduated scale of interest rates on the following basis:

2.75% on loans to families with one child
2.50% on loans to families with two children
2.25% on loans to families with three children
2.00% on loans to families with four children

Here is a new approach to the dwelling-house financing problem which takes into account differences in the economic burden which families must carry and the effect upon the resources which are left for housing purposes. To be sure, the difference in the interest rate is not material, but the principle is sound. When we compare our idea of "6 per cent and philanthropy" with the rates charged by the French institution, we are not so sure that there is any valid reason for granting tax immunities and other privileges where the interest rate is higher than 3 per cent. So far as I know, money for housing can now be obtained at less than 5 per cent in any part of the country, even through private institutions, whether its mortgages are government-insured or not.

Sir Harold Bellman, in an article published in the *Journal of Land and Public Utilities Economics* for May 1938, has this to say about interest rates charged here and in England as they affect housing loans: "We have devised a technique for making the borrower's burden as bearable as possible, which is in turn rendered practicable by the high average standard of borrowers' integrity and a relatively stable level of property values."

It is not difficult to realize that rental rates or the ability to acquire and pay for a home is, in large measure, determined by the cost that must be charged up against interest. *Rent Tables*, published in February 1937 by the Technical Division of the New York City Housing Authority, are significant in this connection.[1]

This important document is divided into two parts. The first part deals with rentals under stipulated amortization periods with government capital subsidies, while the second deals with the same housing costs without such subsidies. In each case, variants in interest rates are used as a basis in calculating rents.

Assuming a period of amortization of 40 years, and also taking it for granted that a housing project of any magnitude would derive some benefit from the rental of stores, which would help to reduce residence rentals, we find the following variability in rents dependent upon the interest rates:

[1] Uhl, Charles H., *Rent Tables*, New York City Housing Authority, United States Works Progress Administration, revised February 1, 1938.

(Cost per room, $1,200)

Interest Rate	Rent per Month per Room
No interest......................	$ 6.96
1 %	7.73
1½%	7.84
2 %	8.17
2½%	8.52
3 %	8.88
3½%	9.25
4 %	9.64
4½%	10.04
5 %	10.46

Each room is reduced in rent by $.50, which is expected to be derived from business rentals as part of the project. So far, this expectation has not been justified by the experience of recent projects.

The calculations have not been carried beyond the 5 per cent basis, on the assumption that most public enterprise will not have to pay more than this interest rate. However, when we consider the major activities in housing for which money costs 6 per cent or more, it is obvious that rentals would have to be proportionately higher. Admitting, however, that some means might be found of providing money at a rate of 5 per cent for all housing enterprises, if we consider the difference between such a rate and that charged in France averaging 2½ per cent, the effect on the rentals is quite significant. At 2½ per cent, the rent per room would be $8.52, as compared with $10.46 for the same room if the interest rate were 5 per cent. This makes a difference of nearly two dollars per month per room, and, for a four-room dwelling, it would mean nearly eight dollars per month. If we accept the usual standard of one fifth of one's income for rent, we must recognize that a different income group could occupy the same houses under a 2½ per cent interest rate than under a 5 per cent interest rate. The difference in income groups that could occupy the dwelling on the basis of the two interest rates would be about $50.00 per month, or $600 per year. It is hardly necessary here to emphasize the importance of this difference in the income groups which would be affected by such a change in the interest rate.

As it is invariably true that the interest rates charged for loans on rented houses are considerably higher than for owner-occupied homes, it is quite evident that a very considerable saving in rent from the present requirements could be effected by a reduction of the cost of money from the present figure of around 6¼ to 2½ per cent. This would mean a saving, in the average rent for rooms costing about $1,200 of about $3 per month, and would bring down the whole level of rents to income groups who can not be provided for, even by government enterprises, unless subsidies equivalent to a large proportion of the original investment are granted. There is still a large field in which the government must and probably will continue to operate, but I am strongly of the opinion that private enterprise can and should provide a large share of the housing requirements for self-supporting families, and that this should be done by providing housing credit at a cost not greater than the cost of money to the government for other enterprises.

The full story of the methods which had to be employed to reduce the outstanding home loans from 1930 to 1936 by 32.1 per cent, as pointed out at the beginning of this chapter, will perhaps not be told fully for a long time. The fact that the United States government, through the Home Owners' Loan Corporation, had to step in and take over mortgages to the amount of $3,093,459,271 affecting 1,018,171 homes by June 1, 1936, is itself an index of the serious condition into which the mortgage field had drifted by 1930. Unfortunately, there are no figures available to show how many homes were actually mortgaged when the United States government took a hand in saving homeowners from foreclosure. If, however, we accept the figures of the *Financial Survey of Urban Housing* as typical relative to the proportion of non-farm homes owner-occupied which were mortgaged in 1934, we find that the total number of such homes was 6,226,372, or 58.3 per cent of the total. On this basis, it would seem that the government had to step in to save these homes from foreclosure in 16.3 per cent of the cases. In other words, the government had to intervene and save one in every six owner-occupied homes of the non-farm type. How much of this condition was due to the heavy interest and financing rates we can not say. The government's reduction of the interest rate to 4½ per cent was a decided gain over private rates.

Before we discuss the various steps which the United States government was led to undertake in order to meet the market situation in housing and employment conditions, we are prompted to give a more general picture of the situation as it developed from 1921 to 1936. This situation is presented in a chart taken from the *Annual Report of the Home Loan Bank Board* for June 30, 1937, the last report available.

Chart I on page 82 is significant because it shows the trends in construction from 1921 to 1936, and also because it reveals the lag in rent reductions to meet the industrial situation while clearly indicating that a reduction in the construction of homes tends, even under conditions of

CHART I. SHOWING RELATIONS BETWEEN WHOLESALE COMMODITY PRICES, INDUSTRIAL PRODUCTION, HOUSING RENTALS AND RESIDENTIAL CONSTRUCTION FROM 1917 TO 1936

From the Annual Report of the Home Loan Bank Board, June 30, 1937.

CHART II. SHOWING FORECLOSURES, RENT REDUCTIONS AND RATE OF RESIDENTIAL CONSTRUCTION BETWEEN JUNE 1921 AND JUNE 1937

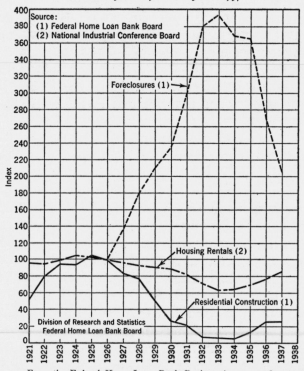

From the Federal Home Loan Bank Review, August 1938.

depression, to keep the rents at an even level. As soon, however, as there was an upward trend in employment, which took place in 1933, there was a corresponding increase in the rentals, in spite of the fact that the supply of houses was also being increased.

A reasonably clear conception of the mortgage foreclosure situation can be gleaned from Chart II, on page 82, which was taken from the *Federal Home Loan Bank Review* for August, 1938, an official publication. The curve which indicates the trend of foreclosures between 1926 and 1933 is a clear index of the situation of the real-estate market. This is particularly striking when we take into account the fact that there was little construction going on between 1929 and 1933, thus creating a shortage of housing. There is also to be considered the fact that rentals decreased only slightly during the same period of time.

The drop in all construction enterprises, the decrease in industrial production, with its consequent unemployment, the fall in commodity and security prices, and the mounting number of real-estate foreclosures, which reached an average of about 1,000 a day by 1933, were the critical factors which brought the government into the housing business. Appeals for help against foreclosures came into the national capital by the tens of thousands, and Congressmen were finally made aware of the need for action. At first, an effort was made through the Reconstruction Finance Corporation to save the banks and lending institutions from failure, or to rehabilitate those which had already failed. Later, it was found necessary to create the Federal Home Loan Bank System, with a capital of $125,000,000. It was soon obvious that this amount was insufficient to meet the needs of distressed homeowners, as well as those of the banks which had made loans.

The Home Owners' Loan Corporation was the next venture into housing of the federal government. This corporation undertook to refinance the loans of distressed homeowners to the amount of 80 per cent of the value of the property, at 5 per cent interest and repayable over a period of 15 years. The total amount made available for this purpose was at first $2,000,000,000, but was later raised to $4,750,000,000. Of this amount, $3,093,459,271 was actually used to refinance mortgages up to June 12, 1936, when operations under this appropriation were concluded.

The Federal Home Loan Bank Board, through its directors, acted as the Board of Directors of the Home Owners' Loan Corporation. In addition to the function performed by the latter organization, it was essential to bring savings accounts into some condition of safety, so as to increase the flow of thrift money into the real estate market and other enterprises. This led to the creation of means for safeguarding small deposits and encouraging thrift through federal control of the institution's resources for investment in housing. Up to June 30, 1937, 637 new federal associations had been organized and 639 other local thrift organizations had been converted from state and federal institutions. It was soon discovered, however, that control under federal regulation alone would not produce the desired results. Regulation was not enough, and, in 1934, the United States Congress finally created the Federal Savings and Loan Insurance Corporation, which created great confidence through its insurance of deposits not in excess of $5,000. Through this new device of protecting bank deposits and investments the savings of a million and a half persons in 1,756 institutions were affected up to June 30, 1937. It is interesting to note that, despite this very important step in the direction of encouraging deposits and investment, only 250,-000 dwellings were built in the United States during 1936. The actual need for absorbing the housing shortage created by the depression was between 1,500,000 and 1,750,000 dwellings, exclusive of replacements.

The question that naturally arises is why, with money available through the various banks, with ample protection for the small investor and with the federal government having absorbed a considerable share of the mortgages threatened with foreclosure, was there not a revival of construction? The answer to this question is to be found, in large part, in two fundamental difficulties. First, the market in housing of a higher price had been oversupplied during the boom period preceding the depression, and there was little opportunity for further investment in this type of dwelling. Second, although there was a great need for additional low-cost housing, the margin between the cost of money and the profit that could be derived from housing as an investment, after all other charges were met, was too small to warrant a rapid recovery of the building industry insofar as housing was concerned. At the same time, the building enterprises, upon which the federal government ventured through its various departments, particularly through the Public Works Administration, led some investors to the unjustified belief that these enterprises would reach proportions which would constitute a formidable source of competition with private investment. Unjustified though this assumption was, it nevertheless seriously affected investment.

The following are offered as the main causes of the lack of private investment in housing:

1. The interest rates at which money is obtainable from both private and public sources are too high to encourage building for the families affording the largest housing market in the United States.

2. The upper brackets of home purchasers find a saturated market

and comparatively low prices, as compared with the cost of construction and building costs, since recovery started on its upturn.

3. Banks and insurance companies have not yet unloaded all of the bad investments they made during boom times, and there is no way of unloading without writing off more than it would be safe to do in a short period of four or five years, which is the length of the present trend toward recovery.

4. Incomes have not yet become sufficiently certain and steady, or normal, to encourage investment in small homes.

5. A considerable number of workers, who, under normal conditions, would have become homeowners, have in the last nine years dropped out of the market, either because they have become dependent upon government relief or because they have become unemployable due to age, technical changes in their trades, or other conditions.

6. The hazards which characterized the real-estate business after the boom have created a psychology regarding investment in real estate which will require a much longer period of time to be forgotten than has elapsed since the last experience of that kind.

In my estimation, the efforts which the government is making to encourage housing, while certainly of great value, are still insufficient to accomplish the most important result—namely, to reduce the cost of housing by creating legal, financial, and technical conditions capable of bringing about economic construction of a decent standard within the reach of a larger number of people. To achieve this end we must have a lower interest rate, lower taxes, lower building costs, and more rational building regulations. We must also develop ownership and investment insurance at a cost sufficient to meet the hazards involved and yet low enough to keep the cost of financing within the reach of every investor.

Earning Capacity and the
Housing Market

Chapter IV

EARNING CAPACITY AND THE HOUSING MARKET

It is common belief among students of housing that, essentially, the problem depends for its solution upon the establishing of a stable relation between incomes and housing costs. How to bring these two factors into harmony is still a matter of controversy. Dr. Edith Elmer Wood, one of the outstanding figures in the movement for improving housing conditions, presents a point of view which is shared by many. While admitting in the first sentence of her book *Recent Trends in American Housing*[1] that "the crux of the housing problem is economic," she clearly rejects as impractical any adjustment of the wage scale to meet housing costs. Two paragraphs in her introduction are evidence of this point of view:

> No such simple remedy as raising wages will solve the problem. If the group involved were a small one, it might answer. But a general increase in wages for unskilled and semi-skilled labor would add to the general cost of production and, therefore, to the cost of living, which would force up salaries and the wages of skilled labor. The cost of the home would increase in the same proportion, and we should be just where we were before, on a higher price level. It is not the absolute figures that are important, but the ration between the family income and the cost of a home.
>
> It is easier in practice to lessen the cost of housing than it is to change the distribution of income in favor of the lower groups. It disturbs the existing order of things much less.

I am quite in agreement with Dr. Wood that a change in the wage scale would disturb the existing order more than subsidies and the other varieties of reforms. The difficulty with this line of argument is that it separates housing as the only problem with which we are concerned from the general condition of the underpaid workers who must face not only rent bills, but bills for food, clothing, the doctor and hospital, and for the education of their children, insurance obligations against old age, sickness and burial insurance, and a host of other obligations which stand in a similar relation to income as rent. It would therefore seem logical under this kind of *status quo* social reasoning that the responsibilities of the lower income groups, of whom there are at

[1] Wood, Edith Elmer, *Recent Trends in American Housing*, The Macmillan Company, New York, 1931, pp. 1-2.

89

least a third of the American families, should be assumed by the state, and that subsidies or other devices be evolved to meet the difference between decent living and the ability of the wage earners to pay for these necessities. Are we willing to assume this burden, and is it compatible with our democratic outlook and philosophy that one-third of our people should become in part public charges, if they are to live up to even a minimum standard of decency?

The whole theory seems to be a negation of the trends of modern times in the direction of wage increases in the interest of better living conditions for the workers. As we shall see in the course of this discussion, it is not wages alone that make housing inaccessible to the lower-income families but a host of other economic factors representing profits and services which have grown out of our complex financial structure, in which labor plays a comparatively small part.

Dr. Coleman Woodbury, in an article on "Integrating Private and Public Enterprise"[2] suggests the following guide or principle for public policy:

> Public enterprise should be limited to developments to house those families whose normal incomes do not enable them to afford the soundly constructed product of private building enterprise, meeting modern minimum standards, produced in substantial volume at prevailing wages, in localities in question.

While on the whole no one can argue that subsidies and public enterprise should be dispensed with, I seriously doubt that this guide would lead to any material changes in our housing conditions, since it would involve such vast expenditures as to make the public investment impractical, except for a very few families fortunate enough to reap the benefit of the fragmentary efforts of government housing aid. But even assuming that the government would be in a position to meet all of the present demands for better housing for those who can not meet the cost, it seems to me that we would be creating a separate class of citizenry who would become "housing wards" of the state. Such a situation is wrought with political, economic, and social dangers which I dare not contemplate.

Among those working towards improvement in housing accommodations there are sincere people who believe that the present structure of the building industry and its financing methods could be doctored up to bring about a new era in housing enterprise and a rise in standards. Among those we find people who believe that even the slums could be rehabilitated by the master hand of business organization. Mr.

[2] Woodbury, Coleman, *The Annals of the American Academy of Political and Social Science.* March, 1937, p. 171.

Arthur Holden has been the chief exponent of this movement, which contemplates the gradual reconstruction of slum blocks by a pooling of resources and real estate holdings in slum areas. The more radical group believe that housing is merely a small fraction of the larger problem of decent living, and that the present profit system must be radically altered or completely abolished in order to bring within the reach of the masses the kind of homes that modern civilization warrants.

In this connection we should not overlook the technicians who for years have been working upon the problems of mass production, simplification of production processes, reduction of essential requirements to the lowest minimum, and thus reducing costs to a point where every family would be able to secure a home.

There is, of course, no single scheme that would bring the desired results within a time that would benefit the present or the next generation of the underhoused. The problem presents too many phases and reaches too far into the social structure of our times to be solved by doctrinaire methods.

If we accept the assertion that housing is essentially an economic problem we must seek a solution in economic terms. As a commodity, housing is subject to most, if not all, of the laws of the business world and all of the conditions which control supply and demand in other business enterprises. The first consideration, therefore, is the power of consumption which business enterprise can depend upon should it be disposed to undertake the construction of minimum-standard, minimum-rent dwellings.

Let us see what the purchasing power of the families in the United States is and deduct from this the housing market which private enterprise can depend upon. Before we do this we might consider some of the peculiarities of housing production in its relation to its character as a commodity.

1. Housing is a product that remains stationary and does not have the mobility possessed by other commodities to seek the market. This involves either a highly stable community without the risk of serious changes in the character of the environment or economic conditions which would remain stationary over long periods of time.[3]

2. While housing from the point of view of rising standards may become increasingly obsolescent, its life as shelter can be prolonged for an indefinite period of time. It can always be adjusted to meet emergency needs, and there are always families who are forced to accept whatever they can secure within their means.

3. Most marketable products are purchasable in the market, are paid

[3] See Perry, Clarence Arthur, *Housing for the Machine Age*, Russell Sage Foundation, New York, 1939, p. 15.

for within a comparatively short time, and are discarded when they reach obsolescence. The renting of homes, on the other hand, is on a contract basis between the owners and the tenant. The sale of a home is seldom a cash transaction. The long-term installment method is used, and the period of payment extends over a twenty- or thirty-year period.

4. Production of housing is determined by a great variety of changing conditions which are more closely related to the ability to derive a paying rental than upon an existing shortage. In other words, the motivation of the construction industry and financing organizations is the production of the type of dwelling which is most profitable and not the one that is most in demand. The most profitable housing in the United States, when rented, is the type that will command the highest rent for the same amount of space as must be afforded for low-rental housing. In fact the hope for high rents has, in many instances, led to the overbuilding of luxury housing, when the demand was for low-rental accommodations. This has resulted in an oversupply of high-rental dwellings and an undersupply of low-rental housing.

5. Low-rental housing, while generally in demand, yields a lower return on the investment under normal economic conditions and is a serious risk in times of unemployment.

6. In most industries the relation between the supply and demand is very close as to the time element. In the case of housing, the investment in housing brought into the market during periods of prosperity must be liquidated over long periods of time, during which depressions and a lowering of the market must be accounted for. Thus while the original investment may hold the promise of profit, the final result may prove otherwise.

7. Standards of construction lasting only half a decade may become frozen into buildings from one to two generations. Obsolescence in many respects may overtake a building from six to ten times in the course of its life, both on account of changing methods of construction and because of changing standards of comfort and convenience.

8. Methods of financing are constantly changing, and the advantage of one period in which some buildings are constructed may be brought into competition with buildings of another period when conditions of construction are less advantageous. What is true of financing is true of the cost of materials and labor. It may not be out of place here to call attention to the fact that during periods when the labor and material costs might be low, and money comparatively easy of access at a low rate of interest, the financial outlook of the country would be such as to make investment slow to take up the slack of the housing shortage. Thus

Photograph by Samuel H. Gottscho.

HILLSIDE HOUSING, BOROUGH OF THE BRONX, NEW YORK.

DIXIE HOUSES, MEMPHIS, TENNESSEE. P.W.A. PROJECT.

building always booms when prosperity is in our midst, while rents must be fixed to meet the resources of the people at all times.

I have pointed out these conditions because in the end they are fundamental in controlling the supply of housing and in fixing rents. Housing costs, as can be seen from the above, can not be calculated in relation to rent in the simple manner in which the price of other commodities can be priced. There is a time element involved, and with that time element go all the changes which take place in the life of the building.

Incomes. Disregarding the original cost of a single dwelling with all of the additional investment contingent upon ownership, the housing market can count only upon rents or purchase price on the basis of income. The distribution of the incomes of American families will therefore determine the revenue that can reasonably be expected from housing.

There are a great many estimates of the income distribution among American families. Many of them have been based upon limited numbers of families in specific localities, while others have been gathered by official bodies from a great variety of sources and with very clear understanding of the difficulties involved in gathering such data.

In view of the rather detailed information which is necessary to gain a clear conception of the meaning of income and the sources from which such incomes are derived, I shall analyze at first a rather well-conceived tabulation of incomes which was presented before the United States Senate Committee in June 1935, at the time of the hearings on the Wagner Housing Bill. This bill was enacted into a law which created the United States Housing Authority. The table, prepared by Mr. Milton Lowenthal, combines the data gathered and reported by the 1934 *Monthly Labor Review*, which recorded income in 75 per cent of all industries, the balance being calculated by assuming that the ratio of employees and wages, using 1929 as a base, is the same as in the industries' record. The number of families was derived by taking account of the rate of increase that took place between 1920 and 1930. The 1929 incomes were adjusted to the 1934 dollar. While this table presents a rather circuitous way of arriving at the results, it does not seem to deviate in any substantial degree from the many other estimates of income distribution, of which we have had many and some of which we shall consider in this discussion.

This table in its detailed analysis of income groups, which are segregated into less general groups than is usual in the consideration of incomes, presents a number of interesting and valuable facts regarding the housing market. If we assume that 20 per cent of the family income is a normal expenditure for rent, we discover that 1,600,000 families are

Income per Family (Non-farm Population), 1929, Adjusted to the 1929 Purchasing Value of the Dollar, as Compared to the 1934 Purchasing Value

Income per Year	Number of Families (in thousands)									Per Cent of Total Families	Cumulative Percentage
	With 1 Worker	Per Cent	With 2 Workers	Per Cent	With 3 Workers	Per Cent	With 4 Workers	Per Cent	Total		
Unemployed..									600	2.560	2.560
Unsupported..									1,000	4.280	6.840
$670–$745....	927	100							927	3.960	10.800
$746–$820....	927	100							927	3.960	14.769
$821–$895....	998	100							998	4.270	19.030
$896–$970....	808	100							808	3.440	22.470
$971–$1,040..	2,328	100							2,328	9.950	32.420
$1,041–$1,115	375	54	316	46					691	2.945	35.365
$1,116–$1,190	1,901	86	316	14					2,217	9.465	44.830
$1,191–$1,265	1,696	100							1,696	7.220	52.050
$1,266–$1,340	944	73	340	27					1,284	5.465	57.515
$1,341–$1,415	772	74	275	26					1,047	4.470	61.985
$1,416–$1,490	244	69			108	31			352	1.500	63.485
$1,491–$1,565	46	5½	793	94½					839	3.575	67.060
$1,566–$1,640	188	45	128	30	108	25			424	1.815	68.875
$1,641–$1,715	19	100							19	.081	68.956
$1,716–$1,790	65	7½	648	73½	116	13	53	6	882	3.770	72.726
$1,791–$1,865	106	15	580	85					686	.930	75.656
$1,866–$1,940	78	45			95	55			173	.737	76.393
$1,941–$2,015	370	50	321	43			53	7	744	3.180	79.573
$2,016–$2,090	53	14	263	68	72	18			388	1.660	81.233
$2,091–$2,160	83	59					57	41	140	.595	81.828
$2,161–$2,235	75	37½	83	41	43	21½			201	.855	82.683
$2,236–$2,310			16	100					16	.068	82.781
$2,311–$2,385					221	83	46	17	267	1.128	83.879
$2,386–$2,460			64	100					64	.274	84.153
$2,461–$2,535			6	1½	198	58½	135	40	339	1.440	85.593
$2,610–$2,685			22	16½	111	83½			133	.565	86.158
$2,686–$2,760			37	64			21	36	58	.248	86.406
$2,761–$2,835					91	100			91	.388	86.794
$2,836–$2,905			26	19			110	81	136	.578	87.372
$2,906–$2,980			127	82	29	18			156	.665	88.037
$3,055–$3,130			18	15	5	4	96	81	119	.508	88.545
$3,131–$3,205			28	100					28	.119	88.664
$3,206–$3,280					22	28	55	72	77	.328	88.992
$3,281–$3,355			25	100					25	.107	89.099
$3,356–$3,430					2	100			2	.008	89.107
$3,431–$3,505							44	100	44	.196	89.303
$3,506–$3,580					8	100			8	.034	89.337
$3,581–$3,655							14	100	14	.060	89.397
$3,656–$3,730					12	100			12	.051	89.448
Over $3,730..					77	55	62	45	139	.592	90.040
Total..........									291,09		90.040
Entrepreneurs (assumed earnings over $1,700)............									2,331	9.960	100.000
Total..........									23,430	100.000	

receiving incomes so meager that, if they are to subsist, payment of rent can not be included in the budget. This represents more than one-fourteenth of all of the 23,000,000 non-farm families in the United States.

Assuming an income ranging from $670 to $1,040 per year, as indicated in the above classification of incomes table, we find that 25.58 per cent of American non-farm families belong in this group. Leaving out of consideration the factor of family size and the diversified needs for accommodations incident to various family types, the maximum rent payable by 25.58 per cent of the families would be $16.33 per month. This constitutes less than one-third of the total number of families with incomes below $1,040 per annum. To put it another way, 1,600,000 families, according to the above table, are clearly to be classed as public charges insofar as housing is concerned. An additional 3,660,-000 families could only pay from $12.85 to $16.16 a month in rent, while 2,328,000 families could pay from $16.26 to $17.33 a month in rent. In all cases, we assume that only one-fifth of the income is to be devoted to rent. It must be kept in mind, however, that the lower the income, the greater are the inroads made by rent into the family budget. A family with an income of only $670 per year would have to devote $134 per year to rent, leaving a balance of $536, or $44.66 per month, to cover the cost of food, gas, fuel, light, clothing, medical care, insurance, education, recreation, transportation to and from work, and in most cases dues to various societies whether they be fraternal orders, burial societies, unions, or churches, and so forth. On the other hand, a family with an income of $1,040 per annum, although paying a higher rent in proportion to the income, would still have nearly $25 a month more to spend on other family needs.

The important fact is that 1,600,000 families in this country are without the means of paying rent and that 5,988,000 families can pay only $17.33 or less in rent. These families are the poorest-housed group in this country, and it is here that the main problem exists. I venture to say, however, that the task of rehousing these families is far beyond the government's capacity to meet, even if the federal, state and local governments were to combine their financial forces. To be sure, the total burden of housing these families would not all fall upon the government, as some rent could be paid by these families, but under government standards of construction the investment for both paying and non-paying families would amount to about forty billion dollars, or nearly half the total value of residential property in the United States.

I have used Mr. Lowenthal's tables because of their more detailed classification of incomes. Turning to the Brookings Institution publication *America's Capacity to Consume*, prepared by Leven, Moulton, and Warburton, we find, on page 227, table 37 giving a more elaborate classification of families and a slightly different classification of family incomes. These incomes relate to 1929, when conditions were more favorable so far as wages are concerned. But although wages were undoubtedly higher, rents were also higher.

DISTRIBUTION OF FAMILIES AND SINGLE INDIVIDUALS AND OF AGGREGATE INCOME RECEIVED, BY INCOME LEVEL, 1935-36

Income Level	Families and Single Individuals			Aggregate Income		
	Number	Per Cent at Each Level	Cumulative Per Cent	Amount (in thousands)	Per Cent at Each Level	Cumulative Per Cent
Under $250.................	2,123,534	5.38	5.38	$ 294,138	0.50	0.50
$250-$500...................	4,587,377	11.63	17.01	1,767,363	2.98	3.48
$500-$750...................	5,771,960	14.63	31.64	3,615,653	6.10	9.58
$750-$1,000................	5,876,078	14.90	46.54	5,129,506	8.65	18.23
$1,000-$1,250..............	4,990,995	12.65	59.19	5,589,111	9.42	27.65
$1,250-$1,500..............	3,743,428	9.49	68.68	5,109,112	8.62	36.27
$1,500-$1,750..............	2,889,904	7.32	76.00	4,660,793	7.87	44.14
$1,750-$2,000..............	2,296,022	5.82	81.82	4,214,203	7.11	51.25
$2,000-$2,250..............	1,704,535	4.32	86.14	3,602,861	6.08	57.33
$2,250-$2,500..............	1,254,076	3.18	89.32	2,968,932	5.01	62.34
$2,500-$3,000..............	1,475,474	3.74	93.06	4,004,774	6.76	69.10
$3,000-$3,500..............	851,919	2.16	95.22	2,735,487	4.62	73.72
$3,500-$4,000..............	502,159	1.27	96.49	1,863,384	3.14	76.86
$4,000-$4,500..............	286,053	0.72	97.21	1,202,826	2.03	78.89
$4,500-$5,000..............	178,138	0.45	97.66	841,766	1.42	80.31
$5,000-$7,500..............	380,266	0.96	98.62	2,244,406	3.79	84.10
$7,500-$10,000.............	215,642	0.55	99.17	1,847,820	3.12	87.22
$10,000-$15,000............	152,682	0.39	99.56	1,746,925	2.95	90.17
$15,000-$20,000............	67,923	0.17	99.73	1,174,574	1.98	92.15
$20,000-$25,000............	39,825	0.10	99.83	889,114	1.50	93.65
$25,000-$30,000............	25,583	0.06	99.89	720,268	1.22	94.87
$30,000-$40,000............	17,959	0.05	99.94	641,272	1.08	95.95
$40,000-$50,000............	8,340	0.02	99.96	390,311	0.66	96.61
$50,000-$100,000...........	13,041	0.03	99.99	908,485	1.53	98.14
$100,000-$250,000..........	4,144	0.01	100.00	539,006	0.91	99.05
$250,000-$500,000..........	916	*	....	264,498	0.45	99.50
$500,000-$1,000,000........	240	*	....	134,803	0.23	99.73
$1,000,000 and over.........	87	*	....	157,237	0.27	100.00
All levels.................	39,458,300	100.00	....	$59,258,628	100.00	....

* Less than 0.005 per cent.

Taking the groups with income under $1,500 per year, we find that 7,484,000 non-farm families of two or more persons came within this income group. These figures are almost exactly the same as the figures found in the table by Mr. Lowenthal, if we make allowances for the cost of living index, which was 170.8 for 1929 as compared with 136.4 in 1934. It is easy to realize that while wages may have differed in the two periods, the higher wage was absorbed by the cost-of-living differential of the low periods under consideration.

The problem of providing housing accommodations affects not less than a third of the population of the United States whose incomes do not make possible payment of a business basis return on housing investment under the present system of organization of the building industry. The solution of the housing problem for this sector of our population must, therefore, be found in forms of promotion and control of the building industry and a land economy which have so far not been developed.

We have no adequate figures which would show the net incomes from rents or imputed incomes from owned non-farm homes. In a table contained in the Brookings Institution study mentioned above, the total income from rents is given as $2,825,000,000 and imputed incomes from home ownership of a non-farm character as $1,900,000,000. The combined amount is $4,725,000,000, which, if calculated in terms of a net 5 per cent on the investment or valuation, would make the total value of all non-farm homes around $95,500,000,000, or a little less than one-fifth of the national wealth. I am emphasizing this aspect of the subject because any steps that might be taken in the direction of improving housing conditions, particularly for the lower-income groups, would have to face the problem of dealing with the largest single investment in this country. This investment, as was pointed out elsewhere, involves not only the individual owners of property but the whole economic structure of the country. In stating the alleged investment represented by the dwellings of this country, I do not mean to assume that the actual value from the point of view of use can be found in these properties. Indeed, there is no question that much of this investment should be liquidated at its real value, which in many cases would replace mistaken hopes and misguided business shrewdness.

Let us turn now to a recent report issued by the Bureau of Foreign and Domestic Relations of the United States Department of Labor. This report, entitled *Financial Survey of Urban Housing*, is the best cross-section study of rents and property values we have so far made in this country. Some objections have been raised as to the accuracy of this study, but a check of the various results would seem to indicate that, while undoubtedly some errors might have crept into the count, in its essential results it may be taken as the most accurate and comprehensive in the territory covered and the most revealing study yet made in this country.

This investigation reveals the astonishing fact that the traditional one-fifth of the income for rent does not prevail except in eleven cities, where the rentals constitute from 14.7 per cent as in the case of Wichita Falls, Kansas, up to 21 per cent, as in Lansing, Michigan. One is prompted to ask a variety of questions regarding these low rents, such as the method of selecting the dwellings investigated in these communities, the preponderance of slums, the severe effects of the depression, the movement of population, the seasonal presence of people in the community, and their departure for other parts during periods of unemployment, and so on. Unfortunately, the figures are permitted to stand without any analysis of local conditions. Here and there a suggestion may be derived from such a statement as the following:

> "Among tenants, expenditures for rent required an average of about 25 per cent of the family income in most cities. Families with higher than the average income required smaller proportions for rent, while families with less than average income generally spent a substantially larger share for housing."

It would have been of the greatest value to students of housing if the study had included a compilation of facts, available on the schedules, which would have brought rents and incomes in closer correlation. As the facts stand, however, they prove clearly the contention of students of long experience that rentals go up in proportion as the incomes go down. The figures also show that, despite the low average rents in eleven cities, the total average for 1933 was 24.2 per cent, with the highest proportion of rental to income in Trenton, New Jersey, where it was found to be 30.3 per cent. In calling attention to these rental rates I am particularly eager to emphasize the importance of recognizing the local variants and of approaching the subject from the local rather than the general point of view.

Another defect of the investigation is the fact that the tables in the introductory section of the *Financial Survey of Urban Housing* fail to reveal the general classification of incomes in their relation to the assumed rental in owner-occupied homes. We have the statement of David L. Wickers, director of the survey, that: "The value of owner-occupied homes averaged from two to three times the family income in most cities. The total incomes of the families occupying their own homes averaged nearly one-third larger than for the tenants in the same city."

These assertions, if we understand correctly, mean that those who owned their homes carried a much heavier burden of financial obligation toward their homes, on the average, than families occupying rental dwellings. This being the case, it would seem that ownership of homes imposes financial costs upon occupants that are much greater than those often met by renters. It would have been of the greatest value to the study if a more detailed study of incomes in relation to the value of the owner-occupied homes had been made. Mr. Coleman Woodbury has raised the question as to the possibility which federal investigations present for error in income returns because of income tax considerations. However, in view of the fact that the investigation revealed a constantly increasing rental rate in relation to incomes for the lower income groups and a decreasing rate for the higher income families it would seem that the contention of Mr. Woodbury is without material foundation.

Should we accept the correctness of the figures showing the high proportion of assumed rent to income of home owners, it would seem obvious that home ownership is on the whole less desirable financially than renting. Whether this is due to the manner in which the financing of owner-occupied homes is carried on in this country, or whether it is due to the tendency to overreach oneself in the purchase of a home under unstable conditions of income, I am not prepared to say. It would seem, however, that, in view of the much discussed and presumably desirable social objective of "making every citizen a homeowner," much remains to be learned from the experience of the past as to desirability of this ideal state.

In connection with the ownership of homes it need not be assumed that the purchaser overreaches himself in actual accommodations, but that the whole mechanism of calculating costs is so badly encumbered by parasitic and non-creative charges that the ultimate owner becomes possessed of a dwelling which represents only in part the actual cost, the rest having been dissipated in a great variety of charges which have no relation to the cost of production. *Housing America*, written by the editors of *Fortune* in 1932, contains a significant chapter entitled "How Much Housing for a Dollar?"

In this chapter are discussed the many charges which are added on to the cost of a home built by the speculative builder. The details cited in the case of a house priced at $10,000 show that a saving of 22 per cent, or $2,200, could have been effected had the non-creative cost involved in the transaction been eliminated. This would have meant that the ultimate consumer of the house, instead of paying $10,000, would have paid only $7,800 for the same house. This means that taxes, interest, rate of amortization, and resale in case of necessity, would have been less burdensome to the owner for the same accommodations. It may be added that the interest rate, as indicated in the same chapter, increases as the investment in the home is lower. The cheaper the home, the more the excess cost above the actual building cost.[4]

What is true of the speculative construction of single-family dwellings is to a large extent true of rented buildings, whether of the single- or multiple-family types. When second mortgages are required in the financing of building transactions, the interest rates often go as high as 8 or 9 per cent.

Let us examine the housing market at the present time from a different angle. In consideration of the market, the present conditions of costs, charges, methods of construction, interest rates, taxes, amortization rates, and all the other factors which determine the rental of a home, require a gross return per annum of between 10 and 12 per cent. This return must include all of the charges which go to produce a house from commissions to the agents, to the profit on land development, and such speculative profits as can be attached to the costs. According to the 1930 Census figures compiled by the Federal Housing Administration, there are in the United States 9,805,847 families which either pay less than $30 a month rent or own homes which are valued below $3,000.

The figures can be distributed as follows:

Rents	Number Non-Farm Families
Under $10	1,563,952
$10 to $14	1,330,927
$15 to $19	1,302,387
$20 to $29	2,545,208
Total......	6,742,474

As the total number of non-farm rented homes is 12,351,549, this number of dwellings renting at less than $30 per month represents 54.6 per cent of the total rented dwellings in the United States. This is the market for low-cost housing we need to deal with, as it is assumed that families paying above that amount would under normal conditions be able to find accommodations that do not belong in the problem class. Neither is there any very great market for the rental or sale of homes

[4] See *Housing America*, by the editors of *Fortune*, New York, Harcourt, Brace and Company, 1932, pp. 67-69.

among those who already have homes, and certainly there is little possibility that the people now owning homes valued at less than $3,000 would constitute any large portion of possible rental or purchase prospects. Of the families owning homes valued at less than $3,000, there were 3,063,373, or 29.2 per cent of the total of 10,503,386 non-farm families who owned their own homes.

Assuming, as we have already said, that the home-owning families would not be prospects for new houses, except in rare instances, we have therefore to contend with the group of renters who could have some choice in the matter of housing. Dr. Edith Elmer Wood has stated repeatedly, and most authorities on the subject of housing would agree, that families paying less than $20 a month have no choice and could not undertake or should not undertake the purchase of a home. Nor could a home be built and the land paid for in most of our non-farm areas which would cost less than $2,000 and furnish any of the modern amenities or reasonably decent accommodations for normal families. The market for the lower-income families is confined, therefore, to the 2,545,208 families which pay a rental of from $20 to $30 per month or 37.6 per cent of the families paying a rent of less than $30 per month.

Another way of presenting the potentialities of the housing market, from the point of view of the lower-income families, is to consider not the whole population, but the renting population. In the release already mentioned and which was issued on June 26, 1935, by the Bureau of Foreign and Domestic Relations of the Department of Commerce, we find the following interesting table, which is part of the report *Financial Survey of Urban Housing*:

This table relates to the special study carried on by this Bureau into the financial conditions of urban housing and extended over 61 cities in every part of the United States. This study did not include cities of over a million, with the exception of Cleveland, and did include five cities of less than 25,000 population. Thus this may be a fair sampling of the normal run of urban communities, since the number of properties studied included some 300,000, or the equivalent of about two-thirds of the total number of dwellings in the City of Philadelphia.

This table shows that the average proportion of families with an income of less than $500 per year is 30 per cent, while those with an income of from $500 to $999 was 25 per cent, of the total number of families for which data was available. This means that at the time of the investigation 55 per cent of the families were receiving less than a normal subsistence wage or income. If we take the budget of the normal family which has been developed by various organizations, including the Bureau of Municipal Research of Philadelphia, we find that, assuming a $20 per month rent, there would be just enough left in the family budget of $1,000 to keep up the common obligations required for subsistence. But the vast majority of these families do not receive anywhere near the $999 per year and, indeed, more than half of them receive less than $500 per year. Can we say, therefore, that there is a market for housing in any quantity for nearly half of the population and the half that is most in need of improved living conditions?

PERCENTAGE DISTRIBUTION OF TENANTS' FAMILY INCOME BY INCOME GROUPS AND GEOGRAPHIC AREAS*

Area and number of cities:	Total Per Cent	Income Groups—Tenants					
		Under $500	$500 to $999	$1,000 to $1,499	$1,500 to $1,999	$2,000 to $2,999	$3,000 and Over
61 cities....................	100	30.8	25.4	18.4	12.4	8.6	4.4
New England—6 cities..........	100	21.1	27.3	23.0	14.2	9.3	5.1
Middle Atlantic—5 cities.........	100	31.5	27.6	18.6	11.4	7.5	3.4
East North Central—7 cities.....	100	29.8	25.3	18.6	12.1	8.9	5.3
West North Central—10 cities....	100	23.4	27.2	21.2	14.1	9.7	4.4
South Atlantic—10 cities.........	100	40.1	24.5	13.9	9.8	7.8	3.9
East South Central—4 cities......	100	49.7	21.2	12.6	8.6	5.4	2.5
West South Central—7 cities.....	100	29.4	24.0	19.5	13.1	9.6	4.4
Mountain—8 cities..............	100	30.6	24.5	18.1	13.3	8.9	4.6
Pacific—4 cities................	100	25.8	26.2	20.3	15.0	8.8	3.9

* From *Financial Survey of Urban Housing.*

The *Financial Survey of Urban Housing* presents a cross section of the individual communities. The average value placed upon the properties as of January 1, 1934, was $4,447 per owner-occupied dwelling and $3,142 for rented dwellings. If this connection of the financial value of housing is anywhere near the facts and these values represent the housing-investment capacity of these cities, the outlook is certainly not very bright insofar as the future housing market is concerned.

Rentals are fixed by incomes and not by the desire for better housing, although within certain limits each family tries to secure the best accommodations for the rent it can pay. It would be interesting to discover by a careful study of the building industry to what extent houses being built at the present time bear any relation in cost—I mean ultimate cost—to the rent-paying resources of the people in need of housing.

On page xvii, table 11 of the *Financial Survey of Urban Housing*, again, we find some extremely significant figures. An examination of the proportion of rent to income reveals that the average in the dwellings studied is not one-fifth of the family income but 24.2 per cent, or nearly one-fourth. These figures disprove the usual belief that families pay on the average 20 per cent of what they earn for rent. A further examination of the figures shows that in New England, Middle Atlantic, and East North Central cities the rents, with the sole exception of Kenosha, Wisconsin, rise in places to as high as 30 per cent of the income.

This may lead some optimists to the assumption that we need not calculate rents for the lower-income families at a rate as low as 20 per cent, but that a higher rate is actually being paid, and therefore new housing enterprise might be undertaken on that basis. While this may be true, the question still remains that many families of low income pay too much rent and that any effort to improve conditions should not be focused upon further reducing the family budget by imposing a high rental rate.

In closing this chapter I wish to call attention to the fact that when we speak of home ownership we are assuming a condition that in most cases does not exist. We shall call attention to this matter in the section dealing with financing and costs. But it is not out of place here to point out that the *Financial Survey of Urban Housing* revealed that, in 51 cities for which figures were available 55.3 per cent of the owner-occupied dwellings were mortgaged and that in New England, Middle Atlantic, and East North Central cities the proportions of mortgaged dwellings were 69.6, 66.9, and 65.3 per cent, respectively. About one-third of the dwellings in each of these sections were owned free from debt.

Throughout this chapter I have tried to show how limited the market for low-cost housing is. I have pointed out that wages and incomes, as they are distributed at the present time, suggest that any advance that might be made in the production of housing would either have to be devised to meet the needs of families with incomes above $1,000 and considerably above that figure, or else a new outlook of the whole structure of financing, taxing, building, and managing housing will have to be evolved. To try to solve the housing problem for the more than six million families of renters paying less than $30 per month within the present framework of the housing business, is a task that can not be accomplished. Subsidies would, of course, solve the problem in part, but I venture the assertion that, if such a possibility existed and government action were to be accelerated so as to bring about a major improvement, the rise in the cost of construction, the rise in the price of materials, and the taxes required to meet the cost would soon absorb whatever the government might be prepared to provide by way of subsidies.

The whole answer to the question as to what is the market for low-cost housing rests on a revision of the whole economic, technical, and legal structure under which housing is produced and marketed, and nowhere else.

Home Ownership

CHAPTER V

HOME OWNERSHIP

Home ownership is associated in our minds with so many social fixations and traditional ways of thinking that any sane consideration of the subject is likely to call forth attacks from all sorts and conditions of men. The real-estate board, the speculative builder, the investment corporation, the chamber of commerce, the respectable church warden, the preacher, the building material trade, and the recovery optimist, all will raise their voices in a babel of protest that lack of faith in the beneficent influences of home ownership is heresy, economic heresy, social heresy, spiritual heresy. Indeed, the recently amended United States Housing Act is designed to foster and promote through many devices an increase in home ownership, by making possible the acquisition of a home on a first payment of 10 per cent of the total purchase price or cost of such a home.

Home ownership would be justified on the following bases:

1. If income were steady, so that the payments on the home might be met promptly and the danger of foreclosure practically eliminated.

2. If it could be assumed that there would be no considerable need for a change in the standard of the home for a period at least as long as it would take to pay for the building.

3. If obsolescence of the various common uses of the building would not antedate the payment.

4. If there were no losses in the values of the neighborhood character, which would make continuance of occupancy undesirable or impossible.

5. If the market could easily absorb the home, in case of removal to some other community, and if this absorption could take place without serious loss of equity.

6. If the municipal and other tax burdens would not be such as to add so great a sum to the maintenance cost as to make occupancy impossible.

7. If the original investment under particular economic and market conditions did not entail price deterioration in times of depression, and if the owner could count on disposal of his property at a reasonable price at all times.

It is, of course, not intended that all home ownership should be looked

109

upon as dangerous, or that all the various questions raised could be answered in any prophetic manner. It is essential, however, that some rational consideration be given to these questions, even by the various agencies promoting home ownership, if the tradition of the value of home ownership is not to be completely destroyed and the market is to be protected.

The seven bases on which the owning of a home is justified, as here set forth, were derived from an analysis of past experiences, particularly the experience of the last ten years, which has brought into relief the situation regarding home ownership in a manner that has probably never been experienced in the history of real estate with the same degree of intensity. We shall now discuss each of these bases in greater detail.

Steady Income. We have no adequate information regarding the employment of home owners, nor is there any statistical evidence of the ranges of income among home owners. All we have is the frequency of home ownership in the cities of the United States, and a considerable amount of evidence that this ownership is not as certain as might be desired. The most valuable facts that have been gathered regarding home ownership and incomes have been published by the Bureau of Foreign and Domestic Commerce of the Department of Commerce under date of June 26, 1935.

The field covered by this study extended over 61 cities, and included, as described on page 103, reports on 300,000 dwellings.

I am quoting this table in full so as to give, not alone the classification of income changes, but also their distribution throughout the various sections of the country.

This table shows clearly how drastic the decline in incomes was during a period of four years. The more interesting fact is that this decline was more rapid in respect to home owners than tenants. This may be due to the fact that tenants were more foot-loose, and able to leave their communities in search for employment, or perhaps it may be attributed to the fact that larger incomes suffered a greater decline. The obvious fact is that steadiness of income is not of necessity characteristic of home-owning families. While the average decline of incomes in tenant families was 30 per cent, in the home-owning families the decrease was 35 per cent. The ranges of these declines, as stated in the above-mentioned release, from 1929 to 1933, were 17 per cent in Binghamton, New York, to 55 per cent in Racine, Wisconsin. On the other hand, the decline in incomes for tenant families was from 15 per cent in Richmond, Virginia, to 47 per cent in Racine, Wisconsin.

The largest average decline took place in the East North Central sec-

CHATAM VILLAGE. FINANCED AND BUILT BY THE BUHL FOUNDATION IN PITTSBURGH, PENNSYLVANIA.

Photograph by S. J. Link.

CHATAM VILLAGE. FINANCED AND BUILT BY THE BUHL FOUNDATION IN PITTSBURGH, PENNSYLVANIA.

AVERAGE FAMILY INCOME—HOME OWNERS AND TENANTS

Area and Number of Cities	Home Owners			Tenants		
	Yearly* Average Income		Decline from 1929 Per Cent	Yearly* Average Income		Decline from 1929 Per Cent
	1929	1933		1929	1933	
Average—52 cities.....................	2,269	1,478	35	1,512	1,052	30
New England—4 cities..................	2,746	1,857	32	1,701	1,217	28
Middle Atlantic—4 cities...............	2,183	1,445	34	1,556	1,079	31
East North Central—6 cities............	2,251	1,291	43	1,657	1,027	38
West North Central—10 cities...........	2,152	1,436	33	1,580	1,132	28
South Atlantic—9 cities................	2,275	1,619	29	1,218	924	24
East South Central—3 cities............	2,212	1,351	39	1,218	783	36
West South Central—6 cities............	2,444	1,591	35	1,543	1,091	29
Mountain—6 cities.....................	2,142	1,300	39	1,561	1,045	33
Pacific—4 cities.......................	2,157	1,395	35	1,648	1,142	31

* An arithmetic average of the averages for individual cities has been used to minimize the effect of variations in size of sample.

tion of the country, where it reached 43 per cent for home-owning families, and 38 per cent for tenant families. This is the section which included such cities as Cleveland, Indianapolis, Peoria, Lansing, Kenosha and Racine. In Table IV of the same release we find some additional information regarding the range of incomes of home owners:

PERCENTAGE DISTRIBUTION OF HOME OWNERS' FAMILY INCOME BY INCOME GROUPS AND GEOGRAPHIC AREAS

Area and Number of Cities	Total Per Cent	Income Groups—Home Owners					
		Under $500	$500 to $999	$1,000 to $1,499	$1,500 to $1,999	$2,000 to $2,999	$3,000 and Over
61 cities............................	100	25.0	21.5	17.7	14.1	12.3	9.4
New England—6 cities.............	100	18.8	19.2	19.4	14.7	15.0	12.9
Middle Atlantic—5 cities...........	100	28.2	24.3	18.5	11.8	10.0	7.2
East North Central—7 cities.......	100	28.7	22.7	16.8	12.4	10.8	8.6
West North Central—10 cities......	100	21.0	22.4	19.5	15.5	12.8	8.8
South Atlantic—10 cities...........	100	22.3	19.4	16.8	13.5	14.4	12.6
East South Central—4 cities........	100	31.9	19.7	15.9	13.7	11.3	7.5
West South Central—7 cities........	100	22.3	19.3	16.3	15.0	14.5	12.6
Mountain—8 cities.................	100	27.2	21.4	17.1	14.3	11.6	8.4
Pacific—4 cities...................	100	24.7	21.2	18.2	15.8	12.4	7.7

It is significant that of the home-owning families studied in 61 cities, 25 per cent of the families received an income which was far below the level of subsistence, while 21 per cent of the families received between $500 and $999 per annum, or what would be considered a low margin of subsistence.

Now let us see what took place regarding the ownership of these homes during the period of income decline. The Federal Home Loan Bank Board revealed the following situation regarding mortgage foreclosures:

RATIO OF MORTGAGE FORECLOSURES FROM 1926 TO 1937

Year	Ratio	Year	Ratio
1926	100	1932	389
1927	137	1933	395
1928	180	1934	370
1929	212	1935	366
1930	235	1936	274
1931	300	1937	207

The year 1926 was taken as the normal year, and the other years calculated from this normal basis. Whether 1926 was the normal year of foreclosures might be questioned, in view of the situation in Philadelphia, where between 1920 and 1926 there was an increase in foreclosures from 738 to 4,656, or 630 per cent. However, if we accept the figures of the Federal Home Loan Bank Board, the fourfold increase in foreclosures in 1933 is sufficient evidence of the precarious situation which home owners must face when our economic system gets out of balance.

We have no accurate figures regarding the total number of foreclosures throughout the country. Estimates for the period of eleven years between 1926 and 1937, regarding the number of foreclosures, range from 1,600,000 to 1,700,000. This does not include the number of dwellings which were saved from the disaster of foreclosures by the Home Owners Loan Corporation. These amount to over a million dwellings, and may cause the United States Government to become one of the largest home-owning organizations in the world.

This large number of foreclosed mortgages has a serious bearing upon the whole economy of many of the families affected. If in Philadelphia, since 1920, 170,000 houses out of a total of 433,140 residential structures went through foreclosure proceedings, it is obvious that even in "The City of Homes," where mass production of housing has been the general practice for many years, and where home ownership has prevailed more commonly than in any other large city, the security in ownership is very low. It almost seems as if the actual foreclosure of the mortgage would be a relief to the ex-owners, who may now be free to move to places where they could secure employment, and cease to cheat the family larder in order to save the equity in the home. This is especially true during periods of depression, when repairs can not be made, and the deterioration of the dwellings goes to lower and lower levels, while mortgage obligations and tax arrears mount.

The figures cited above show a steady decrease in foreclosures since 1933, the peak year. But it may well be asked: "How many of the home owners have been saved from foreclosure by the Home Owners Loan Corporation, only to be foreclosed later, and how many holders of mortgages are postponing action till such time as the market for resale improves?" It is not a financial secret that many foreclosures resulted in sales which did not cover the mortgage, and that millions of equities vanished. An interesting study would be to delve into the subject of losses sustained by families that started with home ownership, and lost their homes and the whole or a major part of their equity. So far as I am aware, no such a study has ever been made. It would tell a tragic story of blasted hopes, and the breaking up of neighborhoods which once were designed to furnish utopian surroundings for families seeking decent living conditions. Perhaps the most outstanding example of such a neighborhood community is Sunnyside, Long Island. This was conceived under the most favorable conditions, without any speculative intent, and designed by far-seeing experts in the fields of site and building plans; and the houses were sold to solid citizens with incomes averaging about $350 per month. Nothing could have been more auspicious, more full of promise. Yet, as a result of the economic crisis, even this ideal community experienced losses, bitter feeling, and the complete collapse of an ideal setup.[1]

There is every evidence of an accumulated shortage of housing during the period following the end of the year 1929. The National Housing Committee, in its pamphlet *The Housing Market*, estimates that two million dwellings were necessary to meet the housing needs of 1930. It is also asserted that, to keep up with the growth of population and its housing needs, an additional 485,000 dwellings should have been built in each subsequent year. Assuming that this could have been accomplished, the question as to the kind of dwellings that could be absorbed by the existing market still remains to be answered. It is alleged by the National Housing Committee that 80 per cent of the dwellings needed could not rent or be sold on a basis that would require more than a

[1] See Lasker, Loula D., "Sunnyside Up and Down," and "Sunnyside Back and Forth," in *Survey Graphic*, July 1936 and August 1936, respectively.

monthly payment of $30, and in most instances much less. A monthly payment on a home, whether as rental or payment on a mortgage, assumes an income of not less than $150 per month, or $1,800 per year. About 72 per cent of urban families do not receive that amount of annual income. As we have already pointed out, some of the families that do receive such an income are not always certain that it will continue during the life of the mortgage.

Taking the census figures for 1930 we find that, of the 22,854,935 families living in non-farm dwellings, 9,805,847, or 49.9 per cent, either pay less than $30 per month or their dwellings are valued at less than $3,000. Only 30 per cent of these families own their homes, and 70 per cent are renters. As incomes increase, the frequency of home ownership increases.[2]

It is obvious that the values of homes, as recorded in the United States Census, are not reproduction values but are values based either upon assessments or market value at the time the enumeration was made. When we propose new dwellings to make up the existing shortage, we must also keep in mind that, for the amount now being paid in rent, or the amount which represents the present value of the dwelling, the same accommodations could not be duplicated in new housing.

In considering the housing market from the point of view of the purchaser, it must also be borne in mind that, even if the purchaser were disposed to secure a new dwelling on the basis of his present income, if the dwelling comes within the bracket below $30 per month or is the equivalent of a home now valued at less than $3,000, it would of necessity be of a less commodious and less desirable type, unless some way is found to replace the old house with a newer and better building, at the same or at a lower cost. This is hardly possible under present conditions.

Changing Home Standards. Assuming that a mortgage on a home extends over a period from twenty-five to thirty years, the question must be asked: What are the possible changes that may take place in the life of the family, which would create a hazard in ownership, or disqualify the home as a suitable abode for the family?

The purchase of a home generally takes place in the middle thirties of the breadwinner of the family. In all probability, he is near the peak of his earning capacity, and the home represents an investment on the basis of normal income. Also, most purchases are made, not during periods of depression, but during the spells of high prosperity, when earnings are normal, or above normal, and chances for unemployment

---

[2] See *United States Home Market, Housing Statistics and Market Quotas*, Federal Housing Administration, May, 1935.

slight. The standard of the home purchased bears all the earmarks of an optimistic outlook in a period of optimism and high prices.

Among the wage earners with incomes of less than $1,500 per year, the period of highest efficiency begins to wane toward the early forties, and when a worker reaches forty-five his chances for steady and well-paid employment are diminishing. In the last two years we have had a very painful demonstration of discrimination against older workers, and even the daily press has appealed in their interest. The fact remains that the better the pay during the period of highest efficiency, the greater the discrimination against those who are trained only in limited spheres of industry, which require the type of physical exertion that advancing age can not meet. The payments on the home, nevertheless, continue on the basis of the highest earning capacity, over a period of a quarter of a century or more, and soon there are difficulties in meeting payments, meeting taxes, and in keeping up the building so that it may retain at least part of its original value.

The house is generally purchased when children are small and are easily housed within a certain space and number of rooms. Soon their needs become inconsistent with the original accommodations, and either an addition is needed or the little house that was once the dream of the family becomes cramped. Obsolescence in design and amenities often contributes to making the home inadequate.

Assuming that the period during which the family needs change is bridged over, and that the children grow up and leave the home, the parents are then faced with the problem of meeting the financial outlay for housing at a time when there is a shrinkage in resources, diminishing ability to care for the home, and reduced requirements as to space. By this time the home has deteriorated, so that it needs a good deal of renovation to make it marketable, and the market itself has shifted to a new type of construction which the old building can hardly meet.

I have in mind a particularly interesting example of this type of shift in the needs and outlook of a community. About thirty years ago in the vicinity of Yonkers, New York, an enterprising real-estate organization bought up a tract of land and undertook to build a very well-planned neighborhood community. Families with young children were quick to see the advantages of a good school, ample playgrounds, large yards, and a general atmosphere of contentment and comfort. During the first decade the families bent every effort to make the schools as suitable to their needs as possible, the park and playgrounds were kept up by the payment of a special tax, and community activities were back of every improvement that the residents felt would enhance their home life and

neighborhood relations. After thirty years the schools are no longer used
to full capacity, because the children have grown up and left, the playgrounds are no longer of any value except for open spaces, and the
families are carrying heavy investments in homes which are too large for
them, while the community is carrying heavy tax burdens for the maintenance of improvements no longer in full use. This is not a unique situation. It is a very common condition, and the only reason why it has not
taken place quite to the same degree in some less costly districts, is the
fact that foreclosures have often shifted the population, so that younger
families followed older ones which had failed to meet the payments on
their homes.

Rate of Obsolescence. Obsolescence is the change in the standard of
the family, owing to improved resources, changes in its standard of living,
change in taste, or the desire for better or more suitable facilities for the
family needs. Often under pressure of salesmanship, or because of a
shortage of housing, a purchase is made which is quite out of keeping with
the needs of the family. In the case of families with higher incomes, the
margin between the minimum requirement is not so narrow as in the
case of the lower-income families, and adjustments can easily be made by
adding a room, or making radical changes in the character of the building.
Working on a small margin, and within limited possibilities of reconstruction, this is practically impossible without outlays greater than the family
can afford. In the case of rentals, the family finds itself free to respond
to its needs, and may move when the home no longer meets its requirements. Under ownership such a situation presents a serious economic
problem, that can only be met by incurring financial losses which the
budget seldom permits.

Changing Neighborhoods. The shift in ownership due to frequent
foreclosures, the lack of care which results from a change in either the
character of the tenancy or the ownership, the constant encroachments
of business and small industries where zoning is inadequate—all these
conspire to accelerate deterioration in realty values and neighborhood
character. Unless a more consistent method of creating permanent neighborhood conditions is resorted to by the builders and developers, and
unless the cities take a hand in making their contribution toward the
adequate protection of the small investor, we have no justification for
encouraging the ownership of low-cost homes, even assuming that all
other conditions are favorable.

Absorption Capacity of the Housing Market. Industrial conditions in
the United States are constantly fluctuating. These fluctuations seriously
affect the incomes and employment of many workers. Where employ-

ment depends upon industrial changes the purchase of a home means investment, which, unless it can be made liquid within a reasonable time, ties the owner to his abode and makes removal to another community impossible except with serious financial risk. In a town where a single industry predominates, or where the industries are free to make important changes in their base of operations by moving from one city to another, few workers can afford to risk home ownership. The experience of the workers in the cotton and the shoe industries in the New England states, where removal of entire plants has taken place without regard to the thousands of workers and home owners who have invested their life's savings in a place to live, is one of the saddest chapters in the history of home ownership. Not only is employment lost, but the greater the effect of industrial migration upon a community, the lower is the value of the low-cost home in the communtiy.

In the case of strikes or lockouts, where large industries with vast resources are involved, an industry may pick up its machinery and move to safer grounds of operation, where labor is less organized and more willing to accept low wages. In the anthracite coal regions, and in communities where the resources of the soil or subsoil are being exploited, where there is a shift in production or a cessation of market demand for the product, home owners are stranded with a valueless investment on their hands and with no opportunities for employment. In such cases mobility is the only solution, and mobility is most difficult to face when even a small equity, ephemeral though it may be, is at stake.

Municipal and Other Taxes. In growing communities the taxes and tax rates are constantly increasing. These include general taxes, school taxes, county taxes, and special assessment. These often become so burdensome that when they are added to interest on investment and amortization there is little, if any, difference between renting a good home and the ownership of a modest dwelling.

In my experience in community planning, where I have had occasion to examine assessment districts for various improvements, I have had occasion to find special assessments ranging from one-half to two-thirds of the original cost of the house and lot. Indeed, in a number of instances in California cities, I have found districts so heavily burdened with special assessments that their totals amounted to more than the actual cost of the home. Some of these assessments are for improvements intended to assist in solving traffic problems, the location of a park at some distance from the home, or some other improvement that may or may not help to raise the value of such a home. In many cases the so-called improvement may actually lower values. The method of assessment which creates districts of large areas for the purpose of raising funds for some special improvement is particularly vicious, if we consider the small investor who calculates in pennies when it comes to payment for a home, and never anticipates new burdens which he can not meet.

There is no expedient way of preventing this type of assessment unless the community is carefully preplanned and the improvements are made only when general bond issues can be secured, or unless a pay-as-you-go method of financing public improvements is followed. Even in this case taxes are likely to be increased, laying another burden on the small home owner.

Original Cost and Market Changes. As has already been pointed out, home purchasing takes place generally in times of prosperity. At such a time, the cost of labor and materials is high, speculative building is at its peak, interest rates are high, and liberal profits are expected by the developers of low-cost housing projects. Indeed, as soon as there is any activity in the building industry, prices of building materials at once go up, as if it were intended to slow up the process of business activity. The result is that these short periods of booming building business accumulate overcharges entirely out of proportion to the cost of a similar home during normal or depression times. The payments for these homes extend over long periods of time, carrying through two or three depression periods, with their usual problems of unemployment, low wages, and poor credit conditions. The small investor therefore makes his purchase at the high tide of prices. If he has to dispose of his home, he must do so at the time when prices are low.

Much sentimentality has been developed around the idea of home ownership. Civic virtue, the sanctity of the family, the spiritual influence of the old homestead, the lasting value of the family council held around the fireside, seem to be the exclusive privilege of the home owner. Nothing is said by political orators, preachers, and crooners about the tragedy of mortgage foreclosures or overdue tax bills. Neither are the renters given a proper place on the roster of the solid citizenry, despite the fact that the majority of our people live in rented houses, while two-thirds of the alleged owners are merely custodians of other people's investments. The tenacity of the superstitions which have been built up around the "ideals" of home ownership passes understanding. If home ownership is to be encouraged among our wage earners, we must first liberate it from the hazards and tragedies which characterize it today.

This is essentially a problem of bringing into some harmony the changing employment conditions, advancing age, industrial efficiency and earning capacity, work migrations, transitions in the character, size and

needs of the family, with the cost of ownership. If this can be done, ownership should become desirable. As long, however, as society takes no
responsibility for these changes, and is not concerned with the incidents
and tragedies of workers with uncertain incomes and without economic
security, home ownership should be avoided as a social obligation.

The time may come when provisions will be made to meet all these
contingencies, when cooperative housing will mean flexibility and security, when unemployment insurance and old-age pensions will be adequate to meet home ownership obligations, and when taxation will be
shifted to the sources where it most logically belongs. When this is
achieved we shall have no concern with the problems of home ownership.
Until that time comes, the agencies which conspire to encourage and
promote home ownership are a menace to the economic structure of the
country. They are leeches sucking the lifeblood of the workers and their
families.

The Law and Housing

CHAPTER VI

THE LAW AND HOUSING

In attempting to discuss housing legislation, I am aware that there already is much law upon our statute books which not only is unenforceable but is in conflict with the very purpose which the law is intended to achieve. Thus we have laws regulating the standards of tenement construction which, by their very extravagant nature, prevent the construction of housing needed by those whom the laws are intended to protect. Again, we find many health and building regulations which, when enforced, place an added rental burden upon those who occupy the houses. I know, and everyone at all familiar with present-day housing knows, that the law has sunk down in a morass of conflicting factors which make housing for the lower-income families unattainable and investment in such housing unremunerative.

The newer outlook points to a housing economy which will harmonize the requirements of the technique of construction for a decent living standard with a planned housing economy, through which the conflict between standards and costs to the consumer will be eliminated to the full extent consistent with our economic system. The critics will raise their voices in protests against such a compromise with an outward social and economic order. To them I will say that I am not averse to any new and workable system which they can devise and impose upon this country; but this book is written on the assumption that, even under our present system, the use of technique, laws and economic organization capable of improving the housing conditions of the country are within our reach and could be used to revolutionize our methods of dealing with this problem to an extent undreamed of even by the utopians.

In achieving this end, law is of extreme importance. The law I have in mind, however, is not a set of rules applicable to methods of construction. Rather is this law a system of controls which is intended to bring into the business and industry concerned with home building a type of social symmetry which will bring into harmony social objectives, technical skills, and economic resources with a view to leveling private privilege to a point where it would not conflict with suitable housing standards for the mass of our population. There is no heresy in this point of view, and it has been common practice in this country to strive toward this end. In the name of the common good, we have deprived whole industries of the prerogative of what is called freedom of contract. Under the mistaken hope of making this a temperate nation we destroyed, without compensation, the whole liquor industry; under the pressure of economic emergencies, we forced the raising of wages and the lowering of profits. This was achieved, not by a revolution which changed our fundamental law, but often by reading it in the light of changing conditions and by shifting the accent of constitutional guarantees from privilege to common welfare.

Within the span of six years, from 1932 to 1938, the history of American legislation in a great variety of fields presents the most enlightening lesson in the sensitiveness of fundamental law to public opinion. There has been no amendment to the Constitution and there have been no radical changes in the established order of fundamental institutions, but the emphasis has been shifted from property rights to human rights. Whether the Supreme Court of the United States has gone so far as to accept the dictum enunciated by Charles Benoist that "against life there can be no principles," or whether the exigencies of the moment have temporarily injected into the judicial mind the necessity for easing the pressure out of which revolutions are born, is of little consequence. The fact is that, within less than a decade, the law and its enforcement have assumed aspects which, if utilized in the interest of housing, would bring the problem within the bounds of practical solution.

In formulating this legislation and setting up the administrative machinery for its enforcement, there is no need of abstract, philosophic speculation. The stream of experience, the clear social purpose involved, point the way toward a possible balance between legal control and individual initiative that would change our present fragmentary efforts at reform into a system of housing economy capable of wiping out most of our slums and rehabilitating the economically blighted sphere of housing investment and its blighting effects on home life.

What shape this legislation should take must depend upon the clarification of the objectives we wish to attain and the art of translating these objectives into workable legislation. We no longer think of social institutions or cultural patterns as phenomena capable of isolation from the whole structure of society. Housing legislation not only must bring into perspective the many forces which shape the character of the house and control its environment, but must take account of the social and economic forces woven into the pattern of life, so that there would be no lags and no compromises with fundamentals.

The spectacle of housing legislation and the bickering legislative debates, with their partisanship, hypocritical phrases, and bad intentions, should not continue. The average legislator is not equipped to clarify the many phases of housing legislation, so that it would stand out clearly and without those obscure phrasings which conceal purpose or leave their interpretation to the courts. Housing legislation must become simple and direct; these attributes should be reflected in the logical organization of the mechanics of realization.

Law as applied to housing is a very confusing term, since many of the acts of our legislative bodies and the machinery for their enforcement or execution do not involve the ordinary restrictive regulations associated with legislation. They transcend this method of social control and reach out into a great variety of legislative and administrative acts involving policies as well as laws, and are affected by the range of business, financial, social, and administrative policies. They relate to housing only insofar as housing must conform to these laws, acts, and policies, in order to come within the framework of our social and economic system.

It is erroneous, therefore, to speak of housing legislation as a system of coherent laws which apply to housing alone. To avoid confusion and to give housing as a public concern the broadest possible interpretation, the Germans have used the term *Wohnungspolitik*, implying all government activity which influences housing. It is from this point of view that we shall deal with housing in its relation to government action, and not from the more restricted angle with which housing reformers have been familiar up to comparatively recent time.

The public policy in housing is twofold. The first phase is the establishing of minimum standards, and the other is the creation of conditions which would make these standards attainable. As housing involves both the individual building and the environment in which the buildings must remain for the period consistent with its usefulness, housing policies must be developed in harmony with both building standards and community-planning objectives. Thus planning becomes inseparable from housing, and housing an integral part of planning. Any attempt, therefore, to develop a public policy on housing must go hand in hand with a planning policy consistent with housing needs. It is idle, therefore, to consider housing legislation without planning legislation, and to consider the technical requirements for minimum building standards without minimum requirements of community planning, such as zoning, transportation, recreation facilities, market provisions, sanitation, water supply, and so forth. True, these are essentially technical problems, but their solution depends upon such legal powers and public policies as the community affords and dares to apply.

For the sake of clarity and convenience, let us classify the various forms of public action which directly or indirectly affect housing. Generally speaking, the function of public action may be divided into three distinct ways of affecting housing:

> Restrictive legislation
> Protective legislation
> Promotive legislation

RESTRICTIVE LEGISLATION

Under restrictive legislation must be included all effort toward restraining owners, builders, and tenants in their rights to use property and to exploit it. This type of control may be said to represent a clear interference with property rights consistent with public interest, even though in so doing the public control reduces the productive value of such property without providing adequate compensation. This form of control is exercised under what is known as the "police power." The history of the expansion of the police power which the states may exercise reveals an interesting evolution of legal interpretation of the meaning of property rights, "due process of law," and, in the taking of property, the provision "without just compensation." The various controls which have been developed in the last century clearly indicate that the rights to property and the limitations of its use, even where there is a loss to be sustained by the owner, have been modified in the interest of the common good. Thus the police power *is becoming a device whereby the guarantees granted the individual by a written constitution may be socialized*. This mechanism, which is intended to control and adjust the rights of the individual to the needs of the group, is the most sensitive means for taking account of human progress and for injecting into fundamental law the newer elements which grow out of evolving social and economic relations. In achieving this end the courts have played a major part. They have sensed the need for change and have socialized the letter of the law by taking account of the broader social objectives, and by disregarding many of the traditional individualistic interpretations which interfere with the spirit of the times and the demands of the newer concepts of social justice. As far back as 1895, judges of the Supreme Court of the State of California expressed this concept in a decision regulating the location of business buildings: "If he [the owner of the property] suffers injury . . . he is compensated for it by sharing in the general benefits which the regulations are intended or calculated to secure."

Photograph by Kodatone.

CHATAM VILLAGE, A TYPICAL UNIT. FINANCED AND BUILT BY THE BUHL FOUNDATION IN PITTSBURGH, PENNSYLVANIA.

CARL MACKLEY HOUSES, PHILADELPHIA, PENNSYLVANIA. A LIMITED DIVIDEND
LABOR UNDERTAKING.

Technique of Construction. Under this type of regulation, the owner or builder is expected to comply with a certain set of rules and regulations which insure a minimum of safety, proper protection against fire, adequate considerations of the various services such as water, sewers, street access, reasonable provisions for decent family relations, and facilities for carrying on the normal processes of home life.

In discussing this type of restriction we need not deal with the details of the regulations. Standards have been set up by various cities which, if carried out, might bring about a fair amount of decent living conditions. There might be some differences of opinion as to sizes of windows, orientations of buildings, sizes of courts, sizes of rooms, amount of storage space, amount of open space around buildings, and a variety of other factors which raise the standard of living and create possibilities for making the home a more suitable center around which family life may revolve. There is no scientific minimum or maximum which may be used as a basis for this type of regulation.

A recent bulletin published by the American Public Health Association has presented an admirable set of standards which, if applied to housing legislation, would leave little to be desired. In fact I believe, after an experience of over a quarter of a century, that these standards are in some respects too high for the less costly dwellings intended for the majority of the wage-earning families. They are possible of attainment, only, if the present structure of our housing economy is fundamentally revised.

In connection with these standards I should like to raise my voice in protest against another and more dangerous trend in housing legislation and, in particular, in the planning of low-rental homes. A recent housing enterprise, sponsored by the United States government under the pressure of reducing costs to within the range of the legal provisions of the Wagner Act, was faced with the necessity of eliminating certain essentials in order to carry out the project within the allotted appropriation. Suggestions were made to eliminate doors to closets, to lower ceilings, and to reduce the sizes of rooms. The suggestions, while helpful in increasing the number of housing units for a given sum of money, would tend to lower standards of living, reduce the comfort of the families, and lay the foundation for the kind of obsolescence that even private enterprise would not countenance. No one is in favor of extravagance in low-rental housing, but if the United States government is to stoop to a recognition of standards lower than common decency dictates, it had best retire from the field and let private owners carry on the task of housing reform. If the cost of building a decent dwelling is too high for the government, there is either a serious defect in the law or in the economic structure which the government must utilize in its housing efforts.

Housing lasts at least a generation and, if we examine the present housing facilities of our cities and even of the countryside, we find that the life of a home—barring changes in the pattern of the community—is more likely to extend over two or three generations.[1] It is obvious, therefore, that unless housing legislation dealing with standards of construction takes a forward view, we shall be imposing on the innocent generations of the future the mistaken standards of a past generation.

I would not have the reader assume that standards of construction once established guarantee the construction of high-grade dwellings for those who need them. On the contrary, the stricter the legal structural requirements, the fewer are the chances for such construction. The New York Tenement House Act and its successor, the Dwelling House Act, have worked against the increase in decent dwellings for those who are most in need of them. This condition has prevailed in every city of the United States where good intentions directed toward raising the legal standards have shifted the emphasis from low-rental to high-rental dwellings. I am inclined to the belief that the slum dwellers have profited least from the laws which were intended to benefit them most.

The large number of housing laws, which reach back to the beginnings of the last century and which have become increasingly complex and exacting, are in their effect the best demonstration of the fact that so important a factor in our national life can not be dealt with by isolationist laws. Home building, which constitutes so fundamental a basis of our civilization and which represents a synthesis of so many factors of our economic, governmental, and cultural life, can not be affected by the waving of the necromancer's legislative wand. Legislative action which is confined to building regulations may become worse than useless, unless regulations are made to bear a fundamental relation to the background which must condition these regulations.

It must be admitted, however, that housing regulations for those who are able to pay have benefited by the new restrictions. Many of the old mansions were constructed without regard to either sanitation or decent human relations. The expensive apartment buildings of the era which preceded housing legislation are monuments to the disregard for decency and ignorance of essential human needs. The instance of the architect who designed the "dumb-bell tenement" and received a prize for his inventiveness is ample evidence of the need for the establishment of legal

[1] See Base Maps, New York City Board of Estimate and Apportionment, 1933.

standards of construction having for their object improved living conditions. We must, however, differentiate between the requirements which are intended to overcome ignorance and lack of technical skill and those requirements which add to the burden of cost, which can be met only by the few and removes the possibilities of benefiting the many.

Old Dwellings. In the older cities such as New York, Chicago, and Philadelphia, the vast majority of the homes are more than a generation old and some are as old as two and three generations. These buildings still yield some revenue and are occupied by families with incomes so low that rent makes serious inroads into the standard of living. These are the dwellings which make up our slums and blighted districts; these are the dwellings against which the housing movement is primarily directed.

In dealing with this type of housing and the regulations which should result in improvement of conditions, most communities have resorted to a certain minimum legal requirement involving additional expense and consequent increases in rents. As the rental for these dwellings is paid by families with low incomes, any addition to the rent would result either in loss of tenancy or a drain upon the family budget, and that drain on a low income is undesirable or impossible. Many of the dwellings still in use are so far below standard and structurally so obsolete as to make improvements required by law uneconomical, even under conditions where a slight increase in rents might be contemplated without serious strain on the family budget. The community is therefore confronted with the dilemma as to whether the enforcement of legislation affecting old buildings would not lower the standard of living of the tenants or permit violations of the law out of consideration for the economic interest of the owner and the tenant.

The whole problem of legislating for the improvement and control of conditions that prevail in the substandard housing of this country revolves around the question as to whether the regulations which the law may provide are enforceable, and, if so, whether they should be enforced as a matter of public policy. Some 63,000 old-law tenements of New York City, which violate most of the provisions of the present regulations in one way or another, have been under the jurisdiction of both the Tenement and Health Departments of the city for over a generation. That no progress has been made to meet legal requirements is sufficient evidence that such legislation is difficult or even impossible to enforce. Whether this is due to a recognition of the economic factors involved in forcing the improvement of dwellings which do not produce an adequate revenue to warrant such improvements, or whether it is due to the strong opposition of tenement owners and their lobby activities, is of comparatively little importance. The fact remains that at the rate at which improvements in old-law dwellings in New York have taken place it would require six generations to achieve the complete compliance with the present law. The life of the buildings now violating the law will have expired long before the local authorities come to the end of their legally assigned task.

We may therefore ask with full justification, What is the course that should be followed to obtain the best results and within a time limit that would benefit the present generation? The answer must be in terms of law, as we are discussing legislation and not general reform.

It must be admitted at the outset that the dwellings represent investment, the accumulated assets of years of saving, and the collateral for loans made by banks, mortgage companies, insurance companies, and other investing gencies. They are the security which financial institutions of every type hold for moneys which belong to a vast number of people, mostly small investors who are neither extortionists or capitalists with large resources. Can and should the police power be applied to these obsolete dwellings to the point of either imposing costly improvements or destroying them as we destroy tainted meat or infected milk? The reformer will say, "Yes." The financier and economist will say, "Let us protect investment before all else. The change must be gradual."

This is the reason for the many efforts to postpone the enforcement of many legal provisions which involve heavy costs. In the last two years there has been a continuous struggle going on between the people who desire to secure a reasonable improvement of living conditions in old dwellings and the owners of these dwellings. Moratorium after moratorium has been granted, and in every way the laws have been modified to gain time and avoid expense on buildings which have for years proved incapable of yielding a revenue on moneys tied up in their financial setup.

Under these conditions, there are certain ways of meeting the problem from a legal point of view. All buildings which are structurally efficient, sound, and capable of being brought within a reasonable standard of decency should be improved at once, either by the owners or by a special local authority made up of technicians familiar with the requirements and methods of reconstruction applicable to such buildings. This way of dealing with the problem has already found expression in the New York State law, which requires that if the owners fail to make necessary improvements, such improvements may be made by the community and the cost be charged up as a lien against the property. This law will prove to be another statutory provision which was a dead letter from the day it was enacted.

The New York State law unfortunately fails to make adequate provisions to establish measurable standards which would act as a guide in determining the rehabilitating character of a structure. Also, the law does not set up adequate machinery for carrying out the work in a manner that would guarantee good and low-cost improvements, consistent with the ability of the building to meet them through rentals. The law is a worthy step in the right direction, but, like many such laws, fails to embody a mechanism of enforcement that will insure results.

One feature of such a law which would prove a dynamic factor in its enforcement would be a provision placing, upon the owner and the public authority entrusted with these improvements, the responsibility for any injury which may result from the failure to bring about the improvements and changes provided by law. The many deaths which have occurred in the last three years in New York tenements because of failure to provide adequate protection against the hazards of fire are grim testimony of the need for such legislation. We hold railroads and other public service agencies responsible for any injury they might inflict upon their patrons through negligence, and there is no reason why the same principle should not apply to houses.

Another method of dealing with obsolete districts is to make possible the pooling of resources among owners, with a view to improving given groups of buildings which bear some relation to each other. This would result in the reduction of costs and the elimination of risks inherent in the improvement of single buildings in a locality where other buildings tend to keep rents low because of neighborhood conditions. It is quite obvious that the drag upon a particular property of reasonable or good character, which results from undesirable surroundings, is little encouragement to the owner who wishes to meet the requirements of the law in surroundings which flagrantly violate its most elementary requirements.

In certain areas some buildings might be capable of improvement without seriously affecting rents, while other adjoining buildings are so obsolescent that by no effort or investment could they be made livable or be brought within the requirements of the law. In some cases the demolition of the obsolete buildings would bring about a rise in the general tone of the block or neighborhood and encourage improvement of the better types of structures. The difficulties that arise are mostly due to the great variety of ownerships, which range from complicated estate situations to trusteeships, guardianships, mortgage-holding-corporation ownerships, and ownership by individuals who have small holdings and neither credit resources nor sufficient borrowing margin on their properties.

These conditions create at least three distinct problems:

1. The various ownerships are limited in their capacity to cooperate or pool their resources with other ownerships in the neighborhood or block.

2. Many housing units are so small that their operation, from the point of view of either economy of space or management, can not be handled economically because of the prevailing low rents. It is quite obvious, as was brought out in an earlier part of this book, that small units in housing can not be made as profitable as large units.

3. The third problem that arises in connection with neighborhood improvements is the fact that the subdivision of land is often so erratic as to bear all the marks of a crazy-quilt pattern. This condition often makes any rebuilding of a given housing district impossible without a readjustment of the boundary lines of individual holdings.

Arthur Holden, an architect of wide repute and a devoted worker in the cause of housing, has evolved a method of overcoming these difficulties. His efforts, extending over a period of four or five years, finally resulted in the enactment by the New York State Legislature of a bill which I shall quote in full:

AN ACT

To amend the real property law, in relation to authorizing the sale and exchange of certain real property or mortgage investments therein

The People of the State of New York, represented in Senate and Assembly, do enact as follows:

1. Section 1. Chapter fifty-two of the laws of nineteen hundred, entitled "An act relating to real property constituting chapter fifty of the consolidated laws," is hereby amended by inserting therein a new section, to be section two hundred seventy-eight-a, to read as follows:

278-a. Sale or exchange of certain real property or mortgage investments therein authorized. Trustees, executors, administrators, guardians, committees and all other persons or corporations holding trust funds or acting in a fiduciary capacity, corporations and private bankers organized under or subject to the provisions of the banking law, the superintendent of banks as conservator, liquidator or rehabilitator of any such corporation or private banker organized under and subject to the provisions of the banking law, persons, partnerships and corporations organized under or subject to the provisions of the insurance law, the superintendent of insurance as conservator, liquidator or rehabilitator of any such person, partnership or corporation organized under or subject to the provisions of the insurance law who or which own any property on which there is a building defined in the multiple dwelling law as an old law tenement or who or which hold a mortgage or other lien on such property, may sell such property, mortgage or lien, and may, notwithstanding any other provision of law, receive and hold in exchange therefor securities issued by a corporation owning or acquiring title to such property, if such corporation shall agree in writing at the time of such sale, to reconstruct, improve, alter, repair or demolish such building or to construct a new building on such property, or on such property and on any contiguous property owned or to be acquired by such corporation.

2. This act shall take effect immediately.

This bill met with the same misfortune that befalls so many other well-intended legislative acts. While it represented the instrumentality through which some progress in local district improvements might be brought about, the legislature at the same time passed other legislation which granted a variety of moratoria on compliance with the Dwelling House Act of New York. Thus the legislature took away with one hand what it granted with the other.

The act just quoted is defective in many respects, but, if intelligently used, might have marked the beginnings of economic slum rehabilitation in the interest of both tenants and owners.

The obsolete dwelling, whether a single-family building or a multiple building, presents the most difficult legislative problem, since it represents according to various estimates from 25 to 30 per cent of the dwellings of the United States and since it is inextricably entangled in a maze of economic, legislative, and planning problems which must be solved at the same time in order to achieve tangible results.

The following are the lines of legislative action which are immediately needed in order to lay the foundation for far-reaching results:

1. All buildings declared unfit for habitation according to law should be demolished as soon as due notice requirements are complied with. This practice is neither radical nor new. In ancient Athens, provisions were made for demolition of all buildings unsafe for occupancy. If a building is unfit for habitation, there is no justification for its continued existence to the detriment of the neighborhood. The damage that such buildings do to the neighborhood is both social and economic. Under zoning we do not permit the mixing of uses which might be detrimental, either to the living conditions or to the general tone of the neighborhood and the security of investment on the part of other owners. The practices which have made zoning an instrument for safeguarding the neighborhood are no less drastic than the requirement that an owner shall not maintain buildings in a condition which would do similar damage to the neighborhood.

The procedure suggested with regard to buildings unfit for habitation would accomplish several objectives. In the first place, it would relieve the neighborhood of the blight which results from the presence of undesirable buildings. The second advantage would be in the creation of open spaces, which might add to the light and air of adjoining buildings. And, finally, the owners would be more likely to improve their properties when the character of the district is no longer marred by the presence of undesirable buildings.

2. All moratoria granted to property owners should not be based upon a blanket legislative enactment which affects all properties violating the law. Instead, a commission should be established to consider each case on application by the owners or their representatives. The commission should grant a moratorium on the following conditions only:

(*a*) The building is capable of improvement to meet the requirements of the law without undue expenditure that would make such improvement uneconomical.

(*b*) The owner files a bond of compliance within a reasonable time consistent with the need.

(*c*) If the building is unsuitable for rehabilitation, notice of demolition should be served and a time for such demolition fixed by the commission.

(*d*) Not more than one extension of a moratorium should be permitted for any one building.

(*e*) The granting of a moratorium should be based upon specified improvements to be made within certain periods of time. These improvements should be agreed upon beforehand and be based upon adequate plans, to be submitted by the applicant and in conformity with the requirements of the law regarding existing violations.

(*f*) No moratorium should extend over a period of more than two years.

(*g*) At the expiration of such a moratorium the commission should proceed toward making the improvement of the building, the cost to be met by the owner. In cases where owners fail to meet the demands, the community should meet them and place a prior lien on the property for the amount involved.

New York State already has a law providing for the improvement of properties where the owners fail to comply with the provisions of the housing requirements for old-law tenements. This, however, has not been put into operation, and the machinery for its enforcement is ineffective.

3. Referring again to the act which provides for the pooling of holdings in housing, it would seem, in order to make such a law operative, that it is not enough to make it permissive, but it must be made compulsory where there is a concerted effort on the part of a substantial ownership interested in bringing about a general improvement in the block or neighborhood. In order to lend force to such an effort it is essential that the following legal provisions be enacted:

(*a*) Where 60 per cent or more of the land within a certain area is held by property owners desiring to pool their interests, the remainder of the ownership should be included in the proposed improvement project.

(*b*) Where such owners refuse to participate or where they set the value of their property too high, there should be some method provided for arbitration which would fix the property values, and the method adopted should be based upon assessments one year prior to the time the project is conceived or application for incorporation made.

(*c*) Any group of owners may initiate pooling proceedings, provided the total ownership represented is not less than one-third of the superficial area contained in the proposed project.

(*d*) Where the owner refuses to participate, condemnation proceedings shall be initiated by the municipality on the same basis as any proceedings for a public improvement.

(*e*) The municipality may acquire such areas as may seem desirable for road improvement, open spaces, public buildings, parks, recreation centers, or other public uses.

(*f*) Where conditions justify financial participation on the part of the local government, loans should be provided by the municipality at a rate of interest not to exceed the rate of interest paid by it on loans for public improvements, and the amount so loaned should constitute a prior lien against the improved properties.

(*g*) The municipality should have the power to borrow money by issuing bonds for the purpose of furnishing loans for rehabilitations of properties. These bonds should not be counted as part of the indebtedness of the municipality and its statutory limitations.

It should be understood, of course, that any improvements projected under legislation permitting the pooling of interests should be in harmony with the existing legal requirements for construction, and that they should follow a plan of land utilization and building development consistent with modern standards. Planning commissions, housing authorities, and building departments should play a part in determining the economic and social feasibility of each project.

Land Replanning. Attention has already been called to the many cases of irregularly shaped divisions, the bad street arrangement, and the lack of open spaces in many of the older and built-up areas of our cities. Slum clearance, as such, is not always desirable or economical. It is often desirable, however, to replan a district in order to improve its ground plan and secure other desirable and necessary improvements by way of roads, adequate and economical building sites, recreation fields, school sites, and so on. Where such conditions exist, the municipality should have the power to step into the breach and assist in creating a more orderly development. This can be accomplished by the use of the municipal corporation, which could act as the repository of all of the properties to be replotted. To achieve this end, the planning body, in cooperation with any existing official housing authority, might select a particular section of the community for replanning and replotting. Once such an area is selected, the authority, planning commission, or other special official agency could proceed to examine the resources and potentialities of the district in light of local needs and its relation to the community.

These facts and possibilities having been established and a plan of development evolved, the official body could proceed in one of several ways:

1. It could take over the whole area and assume full responsibility for its redevelopment, with the understanding that each property owner would have restored to him either the amount of land taken or land equivalent to it in value. Lands used for public purposes would be paid for at a fair rate consistent with values which prevailed prior to the undertaking of project.

When property owners reject participation in the proposed replanning or desire to dispose of their land prior to the consummation of the project, the municipality should have the power to acquire the property and to dispose of such portions as might not be needed for public use. This latter procedure is more or less in line with the process of excess condemnation or marginal eminent domain, which has been made possible by constitutional amendments in about twelve states of the Union.

2. Private action could be legalized along the same line by giving corporations or other legally authorized bodies the power to organize such improvement projects. These bodies would have the power to utilize the powers of the municipality in the acquisition of land, adjustment or restitution of lands, and the payment of compensation for properties taken over, and would exercise through municipal authority the right

of eminent domain for purposes of condemnation of lands and buildings which are needed for the replanning and reconstruction of the area. Mr. Clarence S. Perry has suggested, in a modified form, this method of handling replotting problems. I am inclined to the belief that Mr. Perry's suggestion relates rather to a general undertaking of housing on a large scale than to the problem of replotting and redeveloping existing and fully built-up areas.

There is no reason why both of these methods should not be used in the same community and for the same purposes.

I have elaborated rather fully the various legislative acts and possible administrative procedures which might be evolved for the removal and control of substandard housing, because, in my estimation, the old house still remains the most difficult and most important problem in housing. Many of the new buildings have at least some of the advantages of recent advance in standards of construction and care. The old dwelling stands in the way of new development, and it houses the people who are least able to meet the cost of the higher standards required by law and new techniques of construction.

Building Sites in Builtup Areas. We should deal with land use for specific buildings first. The relation of a particular building to its site must be considered from the point of view of available light, hours of sunshine per day in the course of changing seasons, the space available for recreation, landscaping, the conservation of vistas from the various windows, and so on. It is therefore of importance to control each individual site according to its own peculiar conditions and surroundings. This means a careful consideration of the site in its relation to its own capacity for development and in its relation to other buildings and sites in the same general area. We can easily conceive of a building complying with all of the existing regulations but falling quite far below a reasonable standard, if its surroundings are such as to make the legal standard inadequate for the peculiar condition and location of the building site. A very tall building in a given neighborhood may effect adversely large numbers of blocks insofar as sunshine is concerned. An overcrowded lot adjoining a proposed building site may nullify the original intent of modern legislation. This situation presents a problem in legislation which has so far escaped attention in this country. In view of the fact that our cities are developed by degrees and that building enterprise is spasmodic and sporadic, there is frequently a juxtaposition of buildings varying in standard according to the legislative requirement of various times. Most of the residential buildings in our cities are a generation or more old. Their construction is therefore of an obsolete type in most cases, insofar as existing law is concerned. A new building in an old neighborhood, although fully complying with the law, would be affected materially by the adjoining structures as to light, vistas, open space.

Under these conditions existing laws, while reasonably adequate to meet modern needs where all buildings meet the same requirements, may be inadequate when viewed in the light of the adjoining development. This condition suggests two important points:

1. Where an admixture of building standards exists, each building should be dealt with in the light of its immediate surroundings, and a building authority of some kind should be set up with power to pass upon plans on an individual basis and with power to require modification and increases in the minimum standards required by law.

2. New construction should be encouraged on sites in areas which are either undeveloped or where the magnitude of the enterprises would be sufficient to transcend the limitations caused by undesirable neighboring land use.

Lot-Use Restrictions. There are no suitable rules or practices for meeting the various types of uses which can be applied to the subdivision of land into building sites. The usual subdivision is standard, and each lot is about the same size as any other lot regardless of the type of building to be accommodated. Thus a single-family dwelling will have a site similar to that of a small apartment of four or six stories. Where buildings exceed the requirements of a standard lot it is frequently necessary to resort to a combination of lots which very likely do not meet the best planning requirements. This often results in building designs which fail to meet the functional purpose for which they are intended in an endeavor to fit structural forms into site dimensions which have no relation to the proposed use of the building.

This standardization of lot sizes has been one of the most serious difficulties in the way of proper site planning for buildings and has been developed with complete disregard for land-use economy which might be derived from a more flexible system of land subdivision. In considering such flexibility it should be remembered that light and sunshine depend both upon the orientation of the street system and upon the fact that northern climates demand a greater distance between buildings for light and sunshine than the temperate zones. Where great heat is a factor other considerations should guide the land subdivision requirements. Regulations which would meet the conditions in one community could hardly be copied without consideration of local conditions in other communities.

The various housing authorities, the Federal Housing Administration, and the United States Housing Authority have developed standards which, under present-day conditions, are satisfactory for most purposes. It must be admitted that there is no absolute and immutable standard established by science as to what is the best and most consistently scientific standard. Within certain ranges of maximum and minimum requirement, experience has shown that the standards established by these agencies are reasonably adequate for all purposes. The real difficulty arises not so much in the fixing of standards of adequate land coverage and building location, as in the fact that there is a great deal of fluctuation in land values to which the standards of site use often are subordinated.

It seems obvious that congested areas are more in need of open spaces and proper protection of the light, air, and ventilation requirements than the less congested areas. Indeed, the more recent zoning provisions of many of our cities have added to the restrictions of use, height, bulk and area specific limitations as to number of families per acre. The most effective way of meeting the problem of land sweating and the trends toward congestion is to incorporate into the building codes certain regulations affecting population or family unit capacity and make the building department responsible for their enforcement. I know it will be argued that this is an encroachment on the zoning regulations. It must be remembered, however, that zoning regulations are often very general and are established prior to the actual use of a particular site, while the building inspector faces the reality of actual use and has at his disposal all of the plans and specifications necessary to formulate a judgment of the suitability of the building to the site and its surroundings.

It is not inconceivable that the future restrictions regarding the use of land will be based not alone on specific regulations relating to the use of the site, but on the relation that this site bears to community facilities which would make its use consistent with these facilities.

The fact that a particular area has been zoned for apartment purposes would not justify the development of such a site so as to intensify the congestion on a street adequate for a less intensive use. Neither is it reasonable to assume that an apartment zone which provides no play or recreation facilities, should be heavily congested with families whose children would have only the streets and limited backyard space as playgrounds.

Such considerations may sound utopian at this moment, but the trend in this direction has been clearly established and there is no longer any serious doubt as to the relation that each home or apartment should bear to the human needs, the business activities, and the services which are part and parcel of the whole process of living. The time must come when in matters of building regulations we shall have to particularize, more minutely, the use of each parcel of land in an endeavor to bring construction restrictions into greater harmony with the peculiar character of each building site as part of the community pattern.

I am aware that these norms still remain to be developed and that the mechanics of control of land use through legislation are still in the crudest state. There is also no doubt that the manner in which housing investment and development is tied up with the necessity for encouraging private enterprise presents serious obstacles in the way of a socialized formula for land control and land use. Nevertheless, my experience of more than two decades in zoning and planning work has proved that many of the good intentions which zoning represents are destroyed by a limited conception of the fundamental intent of zoning—namely, the creation of the orderly use of land as a part of an orderly community.

Land Subdivision. In recent years, owing to the fabulously rapid subdivisions of raw land intended to cater to the exodus from the centers of our cities, a great expansion of residential territory has taken place. At the present time the total land subdivision in the vicinity of cities is sufficient to rehouse all of the people of the United States.

This excessive development of new lands has, in some cases, been carried out without the supervision of legally constituted authorities, and where such authority did exist, the standards accepted were often on so low a level as to lay the foundation for new slums.

Overexpansion has not been motivated by a need to accommodate new population or to meet the shortage of housing. Most of it was intended to provide suburban residential areas for families with large incomes who were anxious to improve their environment by a flight from the conditions of urban communities, or who felt the need for having homes in both urban and rural surroundings and were therefore willing to assume the additional cost of a rural home. The laws need to be concerned very little with this type of development, as they are luxury undertakings in connection with which entrepreneurs followed the dictates of demand and for which the market afforded ample compensation.

Within the last two decades, however, there has been an unprecedented development of subdivisions which were essentially motivated by speculative opportunities for exploiting the prevailing movement of population from the cities to less congested areas. Most of these have been badly planned, inadequately serviced, and in some instances located in areas undesirable for subdivision purposes.

Much of this land subdivision has taken place in outlying areas and outside municipal boundaries. The latter subdivisions are due largely to a desire to escape the more exacting regulations of our cities. It has generally been assumed that our cities are already overbuilt and that there are no open areas available for new developments. The fact is that there is ample open space in our cities, many of which still contain thousands of acres of undeveloped land. New York City still has about 85,000 acres of open land and is less densely settled than London, Paris, or Berlin. The real problem in land subdivision is economy and social purpose. The millions of building sites created by the land-development booms of past years have often failed to meet both these requirements. The subdivisions which were created in unincorporated areas frequently had for their main objectives avoidance of municipal taxation, escape from the stricter city regulations, and development costs required in incorporated and settled areas.

But while the subdivision developments often escape the higher requirements of the city by creating settlements in the open country, the cities must face many obligations which these settlements entail. Thus, in the past, additional highways had to be built, resulting in the increased requirements and decreased convenience of transit facilities. These land developments have in most cases failed to reduce the cost of living, seldom improved standards, and disorganized the balance of community services upon which the economic structure of the city was based.

To avoid the conditions which have prevailed in the past, legislative enactment seems desirable. All subdivisions outside incorporated areas should first be approved by both state and county planning commissions. The following questions are involved in such approval.

1. Is the land suitable for the type of subdivision proposed?

2. Is there a market for this type of subdivision?

3. What additional burden will the community have to carry in order to make such a subdivision meet the standards of decent living conditions and adequate services, such as schools, playgrounds, sewers, water, roads, and so forth?

4. Would the additional burden be justified from the point of view of the future population, tax resources, the trends of general community growth?

5. What effect would such land subdivision have upon the larger community?

6. Are the resources of the sponsoring organization sufficient to insure reasonably complete development, so that purchasers may take no undue risks?

7. Is the standard of construction to be used adequate to insure protection against deterioration and eventual slum development?

8. Will the revenue from taxes insure a self-sustaining community which would meet the essential requirements of community living and its continued existence and development?

9. Should the community fail, are there any provisions for the salvaging of the individual investments on an equitable basis?

The answers to these questions depend upon careful examination of the local situation and a knowledge of the conditions in the local community regarding the need for such developments and their ultimate value to the individual investor as well as the community as a whole. At the present time, even though there may be adequate evidence that there is no need for further land subdivision, the cities, townships, or counties have not the power to prevent their development. It is the creation of legislation making this power available that will help to safeguard overdevelopment of land subdivisions. Such restrictions are at present in vogue in Germany. What is needed is not subdivision laws in the ordinary sense of the word, but regulations such as are often imposed on corporations which sell stocks or bonds in the market and must satisfy some official body as to the purpose of the corporation and its justification as a matter of policy. The granting of permission to develop unsubdivided lands is not unlike the granting of a public service franchise.

LIMITS OF SUBDIVISION REGULATIONS

While there is great variation in subdivision regulations they are on the whole limited to specific restrictions which, in view of the fact that the final development can only be inferred rather than predetermined, must of necessity remain very general in character. Lot subdivision, zoning, and the provision of various services are included in greater or lesser degrees in the restrictions and regulations affecting land subdivision. New York State has recently enacted constructive legislation dealing with the whole problem of land subdivision, and other states have made similar efforts in the direction of developing methods of control. The conflict between private property interests before subdivision, and the individual lot ownership after subdivision, coupled with the problems of overcoming the uncertainties of future development, make this type of legislative control quite difficult.

Reference has already been made to the matter of lot subdivision, which is quite difficult to harmonize with the eventual needs of the new community in view of the almost prophetic knowledge that is required to anticipate in detail the location and type of development that will take

HILLCREST, MEADVILLE, PENNSYLVANIA. FINANCED BY THE PENNSYLVANIA STATE WORKMEN'S INSURANCE BOARD.

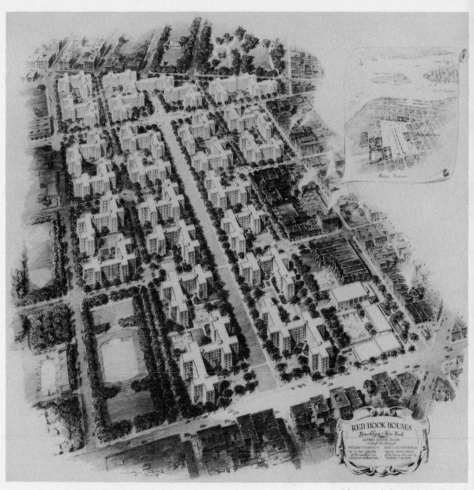

Photograph by Louis H. Dreyer.

RED HOOK HOUSES, BROOKLYN, NEW YORK. UNITED STATES HOUSING AUTHORITY
IN COOPERATION WITH THE NEW YORK HOUSING AUTHORITY.

place in a subdivision. Predetermination of the development of a new subdivision can be made effective only when and where the demand for the land is immediate and the use coordinated on lines consistent with a corporate organization the purpose of which is not immediate profit but long-term investment.

As the whole problem of subdivision is dependent upon future use of land, subdivision must follow a carefully conceived zoning scheme, rather than zoning following subdivision. This is seldom the practice except in rare instances of enlightened development and without the compulsion of the law. In my estimation no subdivision which fails to comply with strict and detailed zoning plan requirements can be designed with due regard to the interest of future property owners and the requirements of buildings according to their particular purpose and use.

This is not the place for a full discussion of subdivision regulations. The aspect of the problem with which we are essentially concerned is that there should be an adequate planning commission organized in each governmental unit in which a subdivision is to be undertaken, and that its jurisdiction should be of sufficiently wide scope to cover large areas, including the cities, so that localized interests would not override the interests of the larger community. The other important consideration is the need for wide powers of subdivision control, so that the supply of such subdivisions may bear some relation to the existing market.

ZONING

Zoning and housing. The whole field of housing has been brought within the control of zoning, at least in the urban communities of the United States. Unfortunately, the application of zoning as a factor in establishing policies of land-use control and of developing an orderly geographic classification of community functions, has been realized only in part, and in the smaller rather than the larger communities.

A discussion of the many advantages to be gained through zoning does not belong in this book. However, from the legislative point of view, the power to zone has been so well established by a generation of masterly court decisions that its full import as a means of controlling community development should have been realized long before this time. The failure to realize this is due to a mistaken conception of the advantages that may be gained from the crowding of land as against reasonable control, which would make land use correspond to community needs and the continuity of their social value.

Another consideration which has interfered with a more workable symmetry between physical plan and zoning has been the expectation that population increases would continue indefinitely either through inter-migrations between communities or immigration from abroad. Neither of these expectations has been realized. The normal increase in the population which results from an excess of births over deaths is insignificant and promises to be even less important as the time goes on. In view of these conditions it is quite obvious that zoning may follow existing trends of population increase, and may disregard booms and wishful thinking of the kind that the realty boards and chambers of commerce are publicizing in order to keep up prices and attract business. Size rather than order and stability seems to have gained the upper hand in zoning procedure.

A confidential report by the New York City Mayor's Committee on City Planning issued at the end of 1938 contains the following statement regarding present-day zoning in New York City:

> "On the other hand, within the developed residential areas 77,000,000 residents can be accommodated. If the use maps were to be brought into line with reality by greatly reducing the business areas and increasing the residential areas, some 273,000,000 residents could be accommodated without violating the zoning law."

This number of people represents more than twice the population of the United States or about a tenth of the population of the earth.

The whole legal machinery now employed in most of the larger cities in the matter of zoning is ample to bring about vastly more desirable results than have been attained in the last thirty-five years. The difficulty has been that the scientific basis for zoning has been neglected, while legal provisions have been amplified to a high degree of efficiency and legal workability.

It is not new and more stringent laws that we need, but the ability to relate zoning objectives to fact-finding technique which would make zoning not the guess work of consulting experts but the application of the science of urbanism to the orientation of community land use in the future. This means that the planning commissions must pass from the status of civic indulgence and controls, which are a blend of political pressure and good intentions, to one of integrated administrative functioning with resources and technical staff to carry on the work. This is already being done in some communities, but the whole financial set-up and administrative machinery for zoning are still in most communities a form of concession to civic pride, a conspicuous dole to the good citizen whose respectability can be used as a show-off, while the politician and land speculator run away with the spoils.

Boards of appeal. It is conceivable that, in restricting the use of land either as to type of use, height, land occupancy, or bulk, conditions arise which need individual adjustment. These adjustments are in many Eastern communities entrusted to a board of appeals. This is a body made up of another set of "prominent citizens" with a sprinkling of officials and with one member strategically placed on the board as a tie-in with the more "rational and businesslike interests." These boards consider all deviations from the strict enforcement of the zoning ordinance. I have watched the operation of these boards for nearly two decades and have come to the conclusion that many of them are usurping the functions of the zoning boards and not infrequently defeat the purposes of the zoning ordinances. The difficulty arises not from the power to vary a provision of the zoning ordinance, but from the fact that the zoning commissions or boards have, or are expected to have, a reasonably clear conception of the general scheme which is intended to be applied to the community. The boards of appeal are concerned with a particular piece of land which does not fit into the general zoning plan. I am quite ready to admit that deviations must be made from time to time, but this should be done by the same group that has developed the plan, and not by another group which acts in an independent capacity and often without full knowledge of the whole zoning scheme.

It is quite true that where a deviation is too much in conflict with the public interest, recourse can be had to the courts. It must be remembered, however, that such recourse takes money and time, and many property owners can afford neither of these. The owner who expects to gain from such zoning variations is always in a better position to state his case than the average property owner, who can not.

I have seen cases where, in anticipation of certain zoning restrictions, the board of appeals would grant a variant and make possible the construction of buildings which completely upset the general zoning plan of the district. All future legislation dealing with zoning should place in the hands of the zoning boards the power to grant variants, and the conditions for such variants should be clearly defined, so that the common interest would take full precedence over individual inconveniences. Mr. Edward M. Bassett, an outstanding authority on zoning, has been the main advocate of the boards of appeal in this country. No one can doubt the zeal and sincerity of Mr. Bassett in this matter, and his book *Zoning* gives a splendid outline of the ways in which zoning commissions and boards of appeal should operate. But I was unable to find in the book a satisfactory explanation for the division of functions between the boards of appeal and the planning boards.

Municipal Land Ownership

Lying between the type of legislation called protective which we are about to consider, and the restrictive law relating to housing which we have just discussed, is the consideration of the community as a land-owner and as a factor in permitting or restricting land use in the interest of the community and in giving a semblance of orderliness to land improvement by either public or private initiative.

The ownership of land by the community, whether this be a municipality, township, county, or state, is generally associated with ownership for public use. Indeed, it is not only ownership for public use, but for a specified use in advance of acquisition. This condition has made it impossible for communities or governmental entities to secure lands for contemplated future developments or improvements without a clearly preconceived plan. No account is taken of future contingencies, changes in the trend of community needs, or other conditions against which community land ownership might be a protection.

Land acquisition in advance of a predetermined plan for its use would be of value in the following respects:

1. The present cost of lands for preplanned purposes could be reduced sufficiently to make possible the planning of services at a land price which would make adequate space available without overtaxing the resources of the community. Thus schools, play spaces, parks, public buildings of various kinds, roads, and so on, could be planned and located at the proper time without consideration of the heavy land cost.

2. By acquiring large parcels of land the community would be in a position to plan or replan whole neighborhoods without having to resort to litigation and heavy expenses of land assembly, which have in recent years become one of the most serious obstacles to slum clearance and large-scale housing.

3. By the power to acquire and eventually resell or lease such lands for private development and use, the city, or whatever legal authority might be reselling the land, would be able under deed restrictions to establish standards of improvement and services not possible under ordinary legal regulations. This method of resale would tend to avoid irresponsible and undesirable land uses.

4. The power to acquire lands for later use would prevent extensions and other premature developments which are a detriment to the community as a whole and are bound to create substandard living conditions.

5. In the matter of locating various public open spaces, the commu-

nity could acquire lands and wait till the time when the need arises for developing them. In this manner it would be possible for the municipalities to synchronize the development of services in relation to such lands as surround these areas and to dispose of lands when they are ripe for use.

6. If any profits are to be derived from publicly owned lands, these could be applied to the cost of improvements, thus relieving taxpayers of some of their tax burdens.

7. With the power to acquire land in advance of need and to dispose of it when desirable, the community would be able, when the opportunity is afforded, to provide necessary areas for large-scale housing projects, regardless of whether these are to be undertaken by private or public agencies.

It is understood, of course, that all such land purchases should be carried out under the direction of a public agency aware of the possible advantages to be gained from each purchase, and that the body entrusted with this task would consider the needs of the community in every aspect and in relation to the general plan of development which the community is following. This does not of necessity have to be a detailed plan, but it must be based upon sound social and economic principles applicable to the community affected.

The main value of legislation which will free communities from the restrictions of land acquisition and allow them to purchase, condemn, or acquire land through gifts or tax delinquency sales, is to be found in the freedom which the community would secure in determining the land policy of its own development. To a certain extent this already exists in "excess condemnation." The power of "excess condemnation" of land, however, is tied in with preconceived improvements and does not leave the community free to expand these powers beyond a small marginal area located next to a proposed improvement. The principle is more or less the same—namely, acquisition and resale or lease—but its applicability is quite restricted in comparison with the broader policy which is suggested here.

PROTECTIVE LEGISLATION

I am aware that any law which is intended to afford protection to one party in a transaction becomes restrictive in relation to the other party against whom protection is needed. However, the classification of a law depends upon its purpose rather than upon its effects when enforced. Some of these laws are intended to protect the tenant, others the landlord, and still others the individual homeowner. All of these types of protection present peculiar problems, reaching from financial relations to the moral character of the individual inhabitant of a particular type of dwelling. We shall not take the time to deal with all of these laws. Most of them have come about because of conditions, forces, and influences which bear no special relation to the quality of habitation or to the more important tenant-owner relationships which affect housing in its stricter interpretation.

Rent Laws. These are among the most familiar and the least used of protective laws. They are intended to protect tenants from undue rent increases caused by an actual or alleged shortage of housing, as occurs after some calamity like a flood, a war, or a financial crisis, which delays the building of dwellings in keeping with need. In essence rent laws are not housing legislation in the strictest sense of the term, as they are seldom applied to protect tenants from exploitation under normal conditions. They are based not upon limitation of profits but on meeting emergencies which are common to the entire community or a considerable portion of it.

Indeed, under the present conditions when a shortage of housing has accumulated over a period of nearly a decade of the depression, no city or state has taken the initiative to prevent raises in rents because of shortage. To be sure, the tenants in the lower-income groups have on their own initiative created a surplus of housing by doubling up or leaving the more congested areas, thus keeping rentals and the supply of houses in some relation to the demand but not the need. This has kept rents from soaring despite the lag in construction enterprise.

Rent-control legislation is as important as legislation dealing with trusts and similar price-fixing private enterprises, since housing is the least flexible of marketable products and is an essential of life which every individual must have. Rent-control laws should find their justifications in shortages which may be created by other social and economic contingencies which are not an "act of God."

Rent-control legislation should be based not upon investment but upon the average return which properties yield under normal conditions. Any general increase in rents in a given district where the lower income families live, may make serious inroads on the living standard of the people.

Abatement of Violations and Rent Laws. Every city contains dwellings which violate the law to a greater or lesser extent. Many of these violations, either through neglect on the part of the authorities charged with law enforcement, or because of moratorium legislation which makes en-

forcement impossible over a given period of time, have been in existence
for long periods of time. Under the pressure of public opinion or because of some calamity, as the burning of people in tenements lacking
fire protection, there comes a time when law enforcement can no longer
be avoided. The carrying out of the provisions of the law, however,
requires additional investment of some magnitude and makes it necessary
to raise rents.

The authorities are therefore faced with the necessity either of neg-
lecting law enforcement or of protecting the tenant against rents which
he is not prepared to pay. The only other alternative is to seek another
place of habitation of lower standard. It is at this point that rent legislation might be effective. Indeed it could be made a two-way legal mechanism for the improvement of conditions. In the first instance, it is not
inconsistent with good public policy to make rent paying conditional
on compliance with the essential requirements of the law, such as fire
protection, proper repairs to avoid accidents, and minimum requirements
of sanitation regarding water supply, toilet facilities, and so on. Violations
recorded by the law-enforcing authority should be made sufficient evidence of non-compliance within a given time and should result in in-
ability to collect rents by legal means. I am aware that by this method
it would not always be possible to promote improvements, because often
the shortage of low-rental housing keeps tenants from moving even
though conditions of living are substandard. This method would bring
about a condition, however, in which the owners would at all times be
uncertain of their rents unless they comply with the law.

The other form of rent restriction is to prevent rent increases in buildings complying with the law and to fix the date before which such increases could not take place without permission from some housing
authority. This method of rent control would relieve the law-enforcing
agency of the fear that such improvements would affect the tenants un-
favorably. It would also result in closer cooperation between the authorities and the tenants. Indeed, I am looking forward to the time when the
tenants would relieve the housing reformer of his many activities in the
interest of good housing and take up the work on their own initiative
and under their own organizations. The difficulties which the tenants
have to meet in keeping rents from rising while securing some improvement of their living conditions can be partly reduced as law enforcement proceeds.

Another form of rent control is the kind imposed upon limited-
dividend housing corporations which receive tax exemption from the
municipalities for certain periods of years. It is conceivable that income-

tax exemption on investments in low-rental housing might not be out of place, provided rent controls could be coupled with such exemptions by both the state and the federal government. Such tax exemption has never been tried in this country.

Relief and Rent Control. There is one other form of rent control which could be used as a means of encouraging compliance with the law. This type of control relates to the rents paid out of relief funds. In the City of New York around $38,000,000 a year has been paid in rents for relief families. This represents a gross return on about $380,000,000. It goes without saying that the refusal to pay rents in dwellings which violate the most elementary legal requirements would result in many improvements affecting the lives of families which would otherwise have little voice in forcing these improvements. It is conceivable that relief agencies could be helpful even to the landlords by advancing money for improvements at a low rate of interest, the amount loaned to be refunded in rentals which relief families would bring and also by making provisions that, after the improvements have been made, no rent increases would take place for a reasonable period of time. This form of legislative and administrative control has never been formulated into law.

There are therefore two effective ways of using rent control, namely, to prevent a shortage of dwellings from affecting rents, and the promotion of improvements as a factor in rent collection.

Financing Laws. Building enterprise depends not so much upon the cost of construction or the maintenance charges as upon the cost of financing. The difference between a 5 per cent interest rate and a 6 per cent rate spells the difference between housing the most needy or the less needy families, if all financing costs must be reflected in rents. On the other hand, if financing is placed under restrictions that are too severe to encourage investment in housing, the supply of housing is bound to be reduced and the rents for existing houses increased. Any legislative effort in this direction must therefore guard against defeating its own purpose. Let us see in what respects these dangers can be avoided.

All loans on dwelling houses, whether for individual occupancy or for rent, should be limited to a fixed rate consistent with profitable investment so far as housing is concerned. A 4½ to 5 per cent rate should not detract from the available resources which should be directed into this channel. With government insurance of such investment at cost, the risk is reduced to a minimum. As the risk is reduced, interest rates should be reduced to a point comparable with investment in public bond issues. This method of encouragement of investment and control of profits should apply to all housing and not alone to low-cost enterprises.

It is my impression that many of the transactions of the Federal Housing Administration could reasonably apply a profit control which would greatly aid in bringing the rent of new or improved dwellings within the reach of families now living under undesirable conditions.

The cost of financing, the charges for special legal services, the recording of deeds and various other forms of procedure which are necessary as a preliminary to the undertaking of construction, should be simplified and standardized, so as to reduce all costs to a minimum consistent with the enterprise. Bond issues and the sale of stock on buildings should be made a part of the marketing methods of real estate business procedure, and the sale of such stock should be subject to the approval of a separate division of government equipped to pass upon the desirability and paying power of a particular housing enterprise. Such a procedure would protect investors and spread the housing investment load, so as to make possible large enterprises with the cooperation of a large number of small investors.

Government credit should be made available at a low rate of interest, or at an interest rate which would cover the cost of money use to the government agency plus a small service fee. The resources of the Postal Savings, which the federal government has at its disposal, and the funds which are to accumulate from the Unemployment and Disability Insurance in both federal and state treasuries, should in part be made available for housing purposes. This does not imply government housing enterprise, but the promotion of private enterprise under conditions of financing which would provide a steady flow of housing investment credit and interest rates which would reflect government credit. In other words, the public authorities should not take over the financing of housing, but should act as a balance between the charges that private investment makes and the charges which housing can carry under normal conditions of investment risk.

Other sources of housing investment are savings banks and insurance companies which have at their disposal large sums of money, a considerable portion of which is invested in real estate of some kind. These institutions make loans for profit at interest rates consistent with the money market. Under proper insurance-risk provisions, tax exemptions, and legislative enactment, these financial institutions could be required to invest a certain portion of their deposits in low-rent housing. It is a well known fact that during the periods of prosperity much building was undertaken to meet luxury needs. When the depression came, the market for luxury housing suffered, while at the same time there was and there still exists a shortage of low-rent housing. Many of these investments in luxury housing have proved unprofitable. It would not be out of keeping with public policy to legislate in the matter of insurance and savings banks investments, so that the funds of millions of small investors would be invested in low-cost, low-rent housing, at a rate consistent with the revenue-producing power of such housing. German law provided that 10 per cent of the assets of such financial institutions be invested in housing. In this country the per cent of investment in housing might remain flexible so as to meet the needs of the market in matters of money, resources, and housing needs. The authority which is to be created to determine investment validity in the issuing of stocks and bonds for housing, should have jurisdiction over insurance and savings bank investment. The function of this official agency to be established by the individual states should determine not only the validity of the investment, but also the standard and class of construction to be undertaken according to need. This may mean an elaborate organization with a research staff and expert service. In the end, however, the investor would take little risk and the home purchaser and renter would be protected against housing shortages, which result either from the building of dwellings least in demand insofar as rental ranges are concerned, or from fluctuations in the building investment market.

Mortgage Regulations. The methods of financing housing in the past have, to a large extent, been responsible for much of the survival of old buildings. The fact that most mortgages were placed upon property as a source of continuous income for a given period of time, after which the full amount borrowed was due, is responsible for a good deal of our housing problem. As the day of reckoning was far off, revenue and expenses were not based on calculations which included amortization at the expiration of the mortgage. Indeed, many loans were made on valuations which could hardly be considered as contemplating amortization. Increased land values in the course of the life of the mortgage were a consideration in the original loan. These conditions have resulted in many foreclosures in which both the owner and mortgagees were the losers. It would seem that insofar as low-cost housing is concerned, at least, mortgages should be protected by clauses which would provide for a gradual amortization of loans on housing. This would make money for housing more fluid, and at the same time it would protect both the equity of the borrower and that of the lender. There is little reason for making loans without provisions for gradual amortization. The Federal Housing Administration has set the example of gradual amortization. The present need is for legal provisions which would require all legally authorized lending institutions to make loans under conditions which provide for the amortization of the loan within a reasonable length of time. Most loans for housing are made by financial institutions under public control. Legislation requiring amortization could be made part of this control.

PROMOTIVE LEGISLATION

This type of law is intended to give aid where aid would do the most good in producing and maintaining the best housing in the interest of the people most in need of such housing. There are many forms of this type of legislation, most of which have been tried either in the United States or in some other country. I shall take them in the order of their importance.

Tax Exemption. This form of promotive legislation is planned to encourage the building of certain types of dwellings designed to meet a particular need at a particular time. When the Great War was over, many countries, including the United States, devised means for encouraging building in order to keep up with the demand and make up the deficiency caused by the construction lag during the War.

In the City of New York alone, tax-exemption legislation encouraged in the Borough of Queens a great building boom which resulted in enough construction to accumulate, to date, a deficit in uncollected taxes, because of exemptions said to amount to from $250,000,000 to $300,000,000. Had this method of promoting construction yielded an amount and quality housing equivalent to the amount sacrificed by the community in taxes, the sacrifice would have been well worth the experiment. Unfortunately the granting of tax exemption merely resulted in the construction in most instances of jerry-built dwellings which became obsolescent long before they served their purpose. Indeed, this form of tax exemption, instead of benefiting those who were to be housed, enabled the promoters to divert the benefits into their own pockets as they resold the tax-exemption privilege to the consumer. This practice has not been continued, but the lesson was well paid for by the taxpayer of New York City.

The main objective in the granting of tax exemption is the promotion of investment in low-rental housing. The policy above outlined failed to achieve this end, and the question is, should we abandon tax exemption or should it be modified in order to attain the desired results and to benefit those most in need of these benefits?

It is obvious that, if tax exemption is to be granted on individual buildings, the individual merits of each structure in relation to the benefit it will yield to the occupant should enter into consideration. No building should be tax-exempt in advance of its actual operation or occupancy by individual owners or by tenants. The rental to be charged should be fixed on the basis of the exemption so that it will become virtually a rent subsidy, rather than a tax subsidy. These subsidies should be limited strictly to habitations intended for the very lowest income group and should not reach into the higher brackets, as they so often do.

The exemption from taxation often is applied to buildings and not to the land upon which the building stands. Whether this is more or less in line with the theory that land values are public values and should meet their tax obligations as a form of repayment for values received through the development of the community, is not very certain. The fact is that it is the practice. It may also be due to the fact that as long as land values remain under the normal tax system there is an inducement to make the land productive by building upon it. After the building is constructed, however, there does not seem to be any reason for the differentiation, except that it makes the tax exemption smaller than it would otherwise be.

The whole system of tax exemption, except in the case of small single dwellings occupied by the owners, does not seem to me to be justified. If we are to consider tax exemption as a form of rent subsidy, it would seem simpler to create subsidies which would be directly beneficial to the occupants. Any roundabout way may promote construction, but it may not reach the neediest of families.

There are still other objections to tax exemptions. In cases where older buildings must compete with new and tax-exempt buildings, the disadvantage to the old buildings is far out of proportion to the difference in the character of the investment and works to the disadvantage of the older buildings. A further objection is to be found in the fact that tax exemptions, if applied on a large scale, may affect the local budget to the extent that the usual services which a community generally renders may have to be reduced to the point where an advantage gained in housing may be counteracted by a disadvantage in the lowering of the efficiency of other needed services.

In the case of limited-dividend corporations, where it is clear that all profits derived from the ownership of dwellings will be limited to a specified and reasonable yield and the rest will be used in the reduction of rents, tax exemption is justified, provided this reduction in rent affects families with low incomes and is not extended to the upper-income groups.

As has already been stated, the general practice of fixing limited dividends on housing investment at 6 per cent does not seem justified. Most of the loans on housing not favored by tax exemption privileges are made at between 6 and 7 per cent under normal money-market conditions.

There is therefore no reason for granting special privileges on any investment changing the market rate of interest.

There is one form of tax exemption which I believe would find justification when applied to housing, and that is state and federal income-tax exemption. These exemptions could be applied to owners of housing projects which have been recognized as essential to the community and which serve the lower-income groups in a manner not met by other private enterprise. There seems to be no reason for tax exemption of government bond owners, where the proceeds have been used to meet the cost of specific public services if housing, when built and maintained as a public service and at a profit as low as that derived from government bonds, is not exempt from income taxes.

Subsidies. In recent years there has been some confusion between government effort to promote housing and the more direct financial assistance which has been afforded by various government agencies in improving housing conditions for underprivileged families. It is quite obvious that any government service which has to do with the setting up of housing standards, helping in furnishing economical designs, developing site plans, and in forcing the destruction of undesirable housing, is not subsidy. It is essentially a service which the government feels called upon to render in the interest of the common welfare, and is in line with the services rendered in agriculture, mining, public health, and so forth.

Nor can it be said that legislation enacted in order to keep the cost of housing within reasonable bonds is subsidy. Legislation fixing maximum interest rates, limiting the prices of materials through control of trusts dealing in building materials, is not subsidy. It is merely the effort of the government to prevent the exploitation of the have-nots by those who have. Even where the government is directly concerned with facilitating the financing of housing enterprise, but where the government expects either to be reimbursed or merely to play the part of an intermediary between financial institutions and the borrower, there can be no question of subsidy. Such service as is being rendered by the Federal Housing Administration is not subsidy, even if the government were to meet all the expenses of its administration.

In many cases the government makes itself responsible for bonds issued for housing purposes, thus taking the risk involved in such investment, but with the expectation that the bonds would be redeemed and interest charges paid out of the revenue to be derived from the investment. This can not properly be designated as subsidy. *A subsidy is, therefore, a grant of money or other privileges and advantages which have a money value*

*intended to make possible the performance of a service or the creation
of a commodity which would not otherwise be made available.*

Capital Subsidy. This is a subsidy consisting of a given amount of
money granted to either a public or a private agency for the purpose
of securing certain results. In the case of housing there has been considerable question as to the right of specific government agencies to grant
housing subsidies. That question no longer agitates either the legal profession or the housing reformers. Subsidies have been granted and are still
to be granted under the United States Housing Administration, as provided by the Wagner Act. The original fund allocated to this arm of the
government has been and will continue to be increased. The United
States Housing Administration, in fact, promises to become a permanent
federal agency concerned with housing, just as the Housing Division of
the Ministry of Health of England has become the prime mover in all
housing activity, as to both standards and finance.

The $520,000,000 which the United States Housing Administration
was granted in the original act, however, provides that any investments
which are made should be administered by local housing authorities.
This involves additional legislation which would provide the local housing authorities with the powers to handle the properties subsidized by
the federal government, and with additional powers to expand the benefits to be derived from federal funds by supplementary resources derived
from state, county or municipal sources. By 1938, eighteen states
had enacted legislation providing for the appointment of local housing
authorities. Most of the laws were sufficiently liberal to make possible
almost any enterprise in the field of housing finance and management,
while others are more restricted. The New York State law is particularly liberal and should make it possible to surmount most difficulties
that might stand in the way of public initiative in promoting housing.
The enabling act which provides for the appointment of local housing
authorities contains provisions regarding condemnation of land, bond
issues independent of the municipal debt limit, management and rent
control, and research possibilities. The main defect in the act is to be
found in the failure to provide specifically for inclusion by the municipality of the authority's budget, so as to insure adequate staff and other
expenses.

In providing capital subsidies the tendency is to base such subsidies
on some specific percentage of the cost of the buildings, regardless of
the cost of the land, the fluctuation in the cost of materials and labor,
and the resources of the families to be served. It is quite obvious that,
where slum clearance is to be undertaken, the payment for demolition,

the coverage of the cost of the land (which has usually reached a high figure), and the resources of the families living in slums would require a much higher capital subsidy to attain the same results than could be attained in open areas, where land is cheap and the class of people to accommodate have larger resources from which rents could be paid. A dead-level standard is therefore likely to stand in the way of housing, rather than to promote it. The United States Housing Authority no longer follows this policy of fixed subsidies, and state and local governments, it is hoped, will follow the example of the federal government.

As the New York City Housing Authority has pointed out, the question in that city is how to meet the difference between $11 a month per room, which is the minimum at which housing can be provided in New York, and $6 a month per room, which is the maximum that under-housed families in New York can pay.[2] In other cities, the difference between rent that must be charged as fixed by the cost of a decent dwelling and the rent actually paid may be different, and thus the subsidy may require a different basis. Subsidy legislation should therefore be sufficiently flexible to meet all conditions, and should not be hedged in by minimum or maximum limits. If the authorities in charge of the vast sums of money required to subsidize housing can be depended upon to administer the law, they should be trusted with the task of making such adjustments as circumstances demand. These adjustments might be made to meet changes in the cost of materials, wage scales, land costs affecting total housing costs, and the regional characteristics which play a part in both standards of construction and climatic conditions.

Interest Subsidies. Rents are calculated on the basic cost of money, plus maintenance, administration costs, and amortization of capital investment. Assuming a capital investment of $1,000,000,000, a rate of interest of 5 per cent, and considering the normal costs of land and construction at an average of $5,000 per apartment, a gross return of 10 per cent on the investment would mean a rent of $500 per annum. The sum of $250 per annum would be devoted to covering the actual interest on the investment. Should the federal government, the state, and the municipality combine to meet the interest rates on such investments, the total annual cost of the interest to be met would be $50,000,000 per year, which divided by three would place a responsibility of $16,666,666.67 upon the various governmental entities assuming the responsibility for this type of subsidy. Certainly this is not a very large sum of money. Indeed, with government investment insurance and the use of government credit methods in borrowing money, the interest rate could be reduced to 3½ per cent or

[2] See *What Price Subsidy?* New York Housing Authority, 1937.

$35,000,000 per annum, an amount which the various government units could certainly carry without serious interference with budgetary balances. Whether this amount is to be included directly in the budget, as would be the case with the share of the states and federal government, or whether it is to be derived from a special tax on business buildings or other property, is a matter of detail. The fact is that rents could be reduced to one-half their present range without serious financial difficulties. As amortization progresses the contribution of the amount originally guaranteed as to interest may be applied to new housing enterprises of a similar character. By adding capital subsidies on land or buildings to the interest subsidies to the extent of the original cost of land and buildings, the amount of the subsidy covering a flat 35 per cent of the total cost, it would be possible to build $1,000,000,000 worth of dwellings, the investment from private sources being $650,000,000, on which the interest cost would be $22,250,000 per year. Is it not conceivable that this country by a combination of the various government units could meet three or four times this amount without difficulty?[3] The reduction in rents under this plan would for the first time in the history of this country come within the reach of a large number of our lower-income groups. Such a procedure would increase the supply of low rentals and afford an opportunity to reorganize the building industry, reduce costs, and raise standards. I am aware that the subsidy in capital investment would not be a full saving in rent because of maintenance requirements, but it would materially reduce rents. In this manner the $5 and $6 per room rental rate could be brought within the reach of a very large number of American families.

From a legal point of view, there are many questions to be solved in the matter of sources from which both subsidies, the direct cost subsidies and the interest subsidies, should be derived. The tax on business property which New York City has secured the right to impose through the state legislature may be practical in this great metropolitan center, but it might prove less practical in smaller cities. Consumer taxes such as have been suggested at various times can hardly be said to have the popular appeal that other forms of taxes have, if any taxation has popular appeal. But whether the funds are to be derived from taxes on sales, or from additional

[3] The New York State Legislature enacted the Occupancy Tax Bill, which permits the City of New York to impose a tax of from $2 to $6 on premises within the city, according to size, in order to provide funds for the payment of interest on bonds for low-rental housing. The act is contained in Chapter 395 of the Laws of 1938. By constitutional amendment New York State has recently made provisions for $300,000,000 to be used for housing purposes in the state. Other states will certainly follow the example of New York.

Photograph by W.P.A.—Division of Photography.

FIRST HOUSES. A RECONSTRUCTION PROJECT UNDERTAKEN BY THE NEW YORK CITY HOUSING AUTHORITY AND PARTLY FINANCED BY THE P.W.A. IT WAS A SLUM DISTRICT BEFORE RECONSTRUCTION.

Photograph by W.P.A.—Division of Photography.

FIRST HOUSING. A RECONSTRUCTION PROJECT UNDERTAKEN BY THE NEW YORK CITY HOUSING AUTHORITY AND PARTLY FINANCED BY THE W.P.A. IT WAS A SLUM DISTRICT BEFORE RECONSTRUCTION.

taxes on business property which stands to benefit from better housing and building activity, or whether it is to be an addition to the regular budget of the governmental entities concerned, will have to be settled by experience. It is certain that by a combination of federal, state, county, and municipal financing the total burden could be so distributed as to make it practical without material additions to normal tax rates. These forms of subsidy may require a considerable amount of new legislation and possibly constitutional amendments, in order to protect any enterprises of this kind against the vagaries of court litigation and court decisions. If the home is in any way a determining factor in health, family stability, safety, and so on, it is certainly entitled to play a part in the general expenditures for such purposes through the medium of housing.

Rent Subsidies. Rent subsidies have been granted for a long time in the United States, but the objectives have been rather in the direction of saving dependent families from being deprived of shelter rather than toward the promotion of better housing. The City of New York alone, during the height of the depression, paid out around $38,000,000 a year in rents, and in many instances these rents went to owners of dwellings which were violating the law in many respects and exposed the tenants to a great variety of health and accident hazards. The type of rent subsidy I have in mind, which is recognized—particularly in England—as a justified method of promoting good housing, is a rental subsidy which is intended to cover the difference between what tenants can pay or are paying in poor housing and the cost of decent dwellings.

In my own estimation, rent subsidy in the form of relief is hardly consistent with American methods of dealing with individual families which are in every way self-supporting, but which although appreciating good housing lack the revenue necessary to pay the rents required. If rent subsidies are to be made part of the program of promoting the construction of low-rental housing, it should be handled rather as a grant to the landlord covering the difference between a fixed return on the investment and the rentals that can be obtained from families living in such dwellings. Indeed, it is quite possible that certain owners would be willing to build dwellings for the low-rental families with the understanding that these rents are to be fixed by the local housing authority, which would establish a sliding scale of rents to be fixed for various income family groups, the government making up the difference between the normal rentals for the apartments and the rentals which are considered consistent with individual family incomes.

This form of subsidy would present some difficulties because of the possibilities of political influence and the necessity for making annual appropriations. However, there is no reason why the administration of such a policy of rent subsidies should be discarded simply because it has possibilities of political mismanagement. We have removed politics from many government activities in the last generation, and the transactions involved in housing-rent subsidies are not too complex to lend themselves to effective scrutiny. This form of subsidy embodies both the features of differential rents and rent subsidy. These can be applied more effectively in combination than as separate forms of subsidy.

Land Subsidies. One of the most difficult problems in the development of housing projects of any considerable magnitude is the assembling of parcels of land adequate for such projects. Indeed, the cost of the land is often greatly out of proportion to the value which such land has when used for low-rental housing. One form of subsidy which the government might undertake is the acquisition of lands in large parcels at a low price and the turning over of those lands to private enterprise for use in low-rental housing. This would make the total housing cost fit into a rental pattern consistent with the rent-paying resources of the families to be housed.

If the land policy which we suggested in another part of this book is to be carried out, many of the communities would be in a position to reduce the whole problem of land costs to a minimum, even though the charges for such land represent the actual cost to the community. It would be largely a matter of wise planning in land acquisition rather than a matter of land grants in the form of subsidies.

Improvement Subsidies. When a housing project is of sufficient magnitude to constitute a small community, more or less independent of the surrounding developments or areas, it is conceivable that the undertaking be planned jointly with the city, so that the community would meet all of the essential costs of equipping such a community and leave the actual housing to the authority or private agency undertaking the project. The cost of roads, the providing of open spaces, the acquisitions and development of parks and playgrounds, the construction of school facilities, sewers, water and fire-protection services, all might be undertaken by the municipality, the town, the county, or the state, or a combination of these. This should be done so that actual investment would be confined, insofar as the housing is concerned, to the cost of construction and to such charges for the site as might be necessary under particular circumstances.

The forms of subsidies discussed above indicate the extent to which various government agencies can serve housing through investment directly or indirectly in housing projects. Some of these investments are self-liquidating, while others represent a service which the government feels called upon to perform in order to raise the standard of housing, to promote an adequate supply of low-rental dwellings, and to bring into harmony the rent-paying resources of the people with the type of dwelling that would guarantee a reasonable standard of home life.

It has been alleged that it would be cheaper to rehabilitate slum areas which already contain within their neighborhood the various services, facilities, and improvements essential to housing development rather than to make new investment in outlying areas. Such an allegation can hardly be accepted as valid in most cases. In the slums the underground services are often obsolete and in need of replacement, and the playgrounds are inadequate or wholly lacking. The schools are often overcrowded, obsolete as to construction and educational requirements, while school building sites are without sufficient open space. If we are to think of housing not alone as a replacement of old buildings by new ones, but as a general rehabilitation of the surroundings and community amenities, it is obvious that the clearing of slum dwellings is not enough.

If we take into account high land costs and the necessity for reconstruction of services and amenities in the slum areas in order to bring about fundamental changes in the way people are served both inside their homes and in the neighborhood, a new and different set of economic considerations must be included in the calculations of the cost of slum clearance. If the same housing and neighborhood conditions can be created by slum clearance at the same cost per housing unit in the slum as in the outlying districts, no one would gainsay the advantage of clearing up our slums. If, on the other hand, the families to be rehoused under a specific appropriation are to be less numerous and the surrounding neighborhood conditions are to remain of the same low standard as before the clearing away of the old buildings, it is obvious that in the interest of the slum dwellers the peripheral development of housing would be more desirable. I am aware that this would not help to rehabilitate investments in slum buildings, but that is not a housing problem. It is a problem in private finance, in replanning for uses which would absorb present slum land values and the salvaging of investments which were not justified, and are not justified at present, in view of their failure to produce the revenues which their valuations would justify in other enterprises. The government never comes to the rescue of bad business investments in other fields; why should the burden therefore be carried by the government and the poor in salvaging bad business in housing?

It should not be assumed that these subsidies or services are a form of charity or relief to the poor. The fact is that, under our present economic system, the lower tenth of our families could never be served by any housing movement short of such free housing as was provided under the socialist regime of Vienna, where rental rates were intended merely to meet the cost of the actual care of the buildings. In my own view, housing is a public necessity, like shipping, roads, and a water-supply and waste-disposal system. The question is not who is to pay for it, but how it is to be provided. The responsibility rests with the governing bodies, and the cost should be met by the people as they meet all other necessities. This brings within the range of public service a minimum housing stand-ard for all families, and it is as essential as the minimum standards of health, education, or public safety. It may take amendments to the fed-eral and state constitution, changes in our tax system by legal enactment, laws fixing responsibilities for housing finance which would involve all forms of local, county and state administration, and possibly a new legal interpretation of property rights and property values more in keeping with the housing market and minimum housing standards.

GENERAL DISCUSSION

1. *Housing regulations.* The body of restrictive legislation which cities and towns have enacted in the last thirty-five or forty years has tended to keep costs at high levels, without bringing building technique into harmony with the advance in the manufacture of building materials. The brick manufacturers, the roofing material industry, the insurance under-writers, and others engaged in deriving profits from the building indus-try, have often combined their forces to impose legal requirements which are not essential in the construction of low-rental housing, but which have nevertheless persisted under the pressure of strong local and state lobbies. The federal government has recently made some efforts in the direction of simplifying and reorganizing building methods, but no effort has been made to apply these methods to the revision of our housing and building codes. Safety has often been overstressed to the disadvantage of living comfort, and fire hazards have been used as an excuse for imposing heavy costs upon the building industry. The stress has, however, been largely upon the protection of buildings rather than human lives.

It would be to the advantage of the whole building industry, and par-ticularly to low-cost housing, if the states or a federal commission with regional offices were to engage in the revaluation of our housing and building codes in the light of new techniques and costs, as well as in re-gard to the matter of bringing new materials into uses where such ma-terials would improve the functional value of housing, while simplify-ing, expediting construction, and reducing cost and maintenance charges. An official testing bureau at Washington with an adequate staff would be of inestimable value in keeping the construction industry in step with technological progress and national economy.

2. *Tariff laws.* There is little reason for the present fluctuations of building material prices. The cost of production may change slightly from time to time, but the changes in the prices of materials are largely due to a nervous market, which takes advantage of every increase in the demand. It would seem that as the demand increases, production also would increase to keep up with demand, thus keeping price levels steady. Unfortunately the reverse is true in this country. As soon as consumption drops, prices drop, and as soon as it increases, prices rise. The government of England has devised a method of building-material control which keeps the balance between consumption and prices. The tariff can always be adjusted to meet the increase in prices in a manner that stabilizes the market and keeps prices at an even level. It is my understanding that this device is not used, but it is an emergency tool not without value in overcoming the machinations of a controlled market. No one desires to substitute imported materials for local products, but as a means of price control in the interest of low-rental housing it is worth consideration.

Cooperatives and the Law. In this country cooperative organizations have made scant progress. The whole mechanism of our business methods has confined cooperative activity to special phases of business where the retail production of certain commodities requires assembling and servicing in order to meet the requirements of the market insofar as quantity and quality are concerned. The raisin growers' association, the orange and other fruit growers' associations, and the milk cooperatives are examples of this kind. They are essentially devices for assembling and marketing goods. In housing, cooperative activity has been very limited and has been practiced, with a few notable exceptions,[4] by the higher-income groups.

By proper legal mechanisms and financial advantages, cooperative housing for the lower-income families might be made effective. Some of these are as follows:

1. Low-interest-rate loans to cooperatives with resources ample to guarantee the safety of these loans.

2. Exemption from taxation of land and buildings where rentals are below a certain fixed maximum and where the standards are satisfactory to the government loaning agency.

3. Exemption from corporation taxes.

4. Provisions for a simple government-supervised system of insurance which would cover investment, fire, accident, and any other form of

[4] The Amalgamated Clothing Workers' Union constructed two very successful projects in New York. Also, the Full-Fashioned Hosiery Workers Union in Philadelphia has carried through a housing project with the aid of government funds.

required and beneficial insurance which could be carried on by a combination of cooperative agencies.

5. The creation through government initiative of savings bank facilities which would be directly related to housing cooperatives, wholly or in part, with the powers to raise funds for cooperative housing projects. These funds would be insured and the interest limited to a reasonable rate consistent with the productive capacity of cooperative housing. Such a banking system might be made a part of the postal savings system, thus placing the credit of the United States Government in the position of guarantor of housing funds accumulating for housing purposes of a cooperative character only.

We have had very little experience in the United States with this type of housing finance and ownership, and it is not safe to forecast the methods that should be followed. We can learn much from Scandinavian and English experience, but no doubt our mode of doing business would require many adjustments to meet our conditions. However, the cooperative presents a vast field of useful activity which would in part make the workers take the initiative in solving at least a portion of their own housing problem. Much of our housing effort has been directed by people who invested in housing as an economical venture. The cooperatives would offer the workers a chance to participate in improving their own living conditions.

Summary

The discussion regarding housing legislation which is contained in this chapter is not intended to be exhaustive. It merely indicates the variety of fronts upon which the problem must be attacked. It is not enough to play hide and seek with the interests organized to profit from the business of building and renting houses. No sooner has the reformer secured the enactment of one law than the real-estate interests, through their lobby, secure another to counteract its effects. Nor is government subsidy in its many forms enough to bring up the standard of housing to a level consistent with our civilization. The economic structure which shapes the destiny of housing is too complex and too thoroughly interwoven with a vast number of interests and institutions to be reoriented easily toward improved housing standards. A legislative program must be as comprehensive as the radius of the factors which determine its efficacy. It must extend from the simple regulations as to minimum of sanitation and safety to the credit system which makes financing possible and to the planning regulations which make investment safe and lasting. These vast ramifications of housing law I have endeavored to present as briefly as the subject permits.

Urbanism and Housing

CHAPTER VII

URBANISM AND HOUSING

Civilization is inseparable from urban living. Without cities civilization is inconceivable. All striving toward national unity, all expression of social synthesis, all the streams of creative power and the elements that transform natural resources into vital human services, must seek their full realization in urban rather than in rural communities.

The negative attitude toward our cities, which places upon them the blame for our social and economic ills, is born of our failure to realize that criminality, high mortality rates, confusion and congestion, are the byproducts rather than the fundamental characteristics of urban living. These evils, so frequently confused with city living, are essentially due to the failure of modern civilization, and indeed of the civilizations of the past, to fully evaluate the potentialities of communal living and the changing and advancing technical skill which might be applied to the transformation of urban environment, so that it might keep pace with advancing social order. The culture of cities is not to be viewed as morbid or decadent. The unreadiness of society to make the necessary sacrifices essential in the mating of new philosophies and outlooks on life with physical well-being, as expressed in a well planned and well ordered city, has stigmatized urban living as unnatural and undesirable. Indeed, the line of demarcation between urban and rural living is bound to become more and more blurred as the rural communities and their inhabitants become aware of the values inherent in the kind of intensive cultural life which the cities afford.

I do not look with apprehension upon the depopulation of rural communities. They are merely the symptoms of the desire of rural people for a fuller life, which rural communities fail to offer. When the whole of this country becomes entirely urban, not in the methods and kinds of production, but in the ways of living, we shall have achieved full civilization. For urbanism is essentially a way of life, which brings into play all of the achievements in the sciences, the arts, the skills which make life productive and safe and convenient, into a clear-visioned set of objectives, in which human life becomes sacred and human effort a contribution toward the welfare of the whole social order.

The conditions which have caused cities to become insensible to the demands of normal living may be listed as follows:

1. The incoherent growth of our cities, due to the too-rapid increase in population, and to economic activity under a laggard adjustment between physical plant and the load of human requirements which it must carry.

2. The failure to control this growth according to a predetermined concept of the essential requirements of urban living.

3. The more rapid application of technological advance to industry than to life.

4. The precedence granted to individual property rights over the right to decent living.

5. The misconception of the value of transit that produces increased transportation facilities instead of trying to reduce the need for transportation.

6. The regard for the efficiency of a particular service as a mechanical device rather than as a social tool.

7. The farming out of public services to private enterprise, such as transportation, water supply, gas, electricity, communication, and other services essential to the orderly and economical growth of communities.

8. The failure to safeguard the interests and welfare of the smaller communities, and the concentration upon the larger centers of population.

9. The lack of coherent regional planning, as opposed to the methods of metropolitan planning, which is designed to subordinate the smaller to the larger community.

10. The lag in urbanizing the rural and semi-rural communities insofar as the value of the good life is concerned. This has led to migrations from the less populous to the more populous centers.

11. The divergence in the economic conditions, technological advance, wage scales, labor-dispute control, migrations of industry, and the periodic economic changes because of the so-called business cycles, which result in shifts in population from city to city, from region to region, and from rural to urban and urban to rural areas.

12. The lack of government restraint in permitting expansion of municipal entities beyond their capacity to use the land economically and to serve it efficiently.

These, it seems to me, are the essential causes of our deplorable urban conditions and of the development of unsatisfactory and uneconomical methods of administering and serving the interest of housing and other community needs.

Rapid Increase in Population. We have already pointed out in our chapter on population that the growth of our cities has been more rapid than have been the means of absorbing that growth. In the thirty years between 1900 and 1930, the cities of the United States have added 39,-000,000 people to their population. This increase represents 80 per cent of the total increase in the population of the United States during the three decades following 1900. It must be admitted that many of these gains have been brought about by normal growth of communities which had, in the course of three decades, increased in population to justify their classification as urban communities. There were also the expansions of many cities beyond their boundaries in order to absorb urban, semi-urban, and rural population, either for the purpose of capturing additional territory for taxation purposes, or out of a desire to rise in the census classification of cities. Whatever the cause, the fact remains that 69,000,000 people live in cities, most of which have been unprepared to absorb the population which they include. To make preparations for the absorption of a population one and one-half times larger than the original number of people living in these cities during 1900, meant a task of reconstruction to which we were obviously not equal, and for which we were unprepared. This is undoubtedly the fundamental cause of much present-day confusion, and the task ahead seems almost unsurmountable. The difficulty is not so much in lack of planning ability and skill as in the vast investment which the present-day cities represent, and the vested interest created by the very fact that the faster the increase in population, the more rapid is the enhancement of the alleged values of these vested interests. The rise in the money value of these vested interests depends for its realization upon the very factor of population which was responsible for the lag in the adjustment of the physical plant to social needs.

Control of Growth and Mode of Living. The race for population increase had no corresponding counterpart in preplanning. Land could be overloaded to take care of additional population or industrial and commercial activity; residential areas could be transformed or rebuilt, or merely abandoned to more intensive uses. Not until very recently have cities made any effort in the direction of controlling these chaotic changes. Intensification of uses, and misdirected placing of certain business and industrial activities to meet the exigencies of immediate private profit, with utter disregard for the long-range interests of both public and private investment, have been common practices.

Zoning came into use in the latter part of the last decade of the nineteenth century, but its advance has been so slow and so completely at the mercy of private interests, that in many cases it became a form of real-estate racket, even while pretending to provide adequate protection for both investor and the people at large. Even to this day, zoning has not reached a point of efficiency where it can be safely counted upon to serve the best interests of the people. Every city has accepted some kind of zoning regulation, but much of this has been wholly out of harmony with actual needs, and in some instances has become merely a tool with which politicians can play at granting favors. This is true not alone of the larger cities but of smaller communities, where the honest and purposeful work of planning commissions is distorted and nullified by boards of appeal which deliberately misread the law and distort its purpose.

Where neighborhoods have gained a certain integration and developed social values consistent with the needs of the residents, again and again the pressure of population and the desire to capitalize the economic value of this pressure have destroyed the advantages inherent in such neighborhood integration.

Whatever planning has been done has been designed to alleviate problems arising out of the lack of control, rather than to anticipate problems that might arise. Thus, transit facilities had to be developed to meet existing congestion, which had no justification from the point of view of orderly settlement. Suburban development took place, not as a normal choice of a particular mode of living, but as a means of escape from intolerable conditions that had overcome the city. Playgrounds which were ample for the normal life of settled communities, with ample space, soon became necessities which had to be carved out of heavily built-up areas at enormous costs. Schools, which were originally adequate for the specific neighborhood, suddenly became inadequate, and additional space had again to be wrested from the highly commercialized and heavily taxed areas, in order to provide for the most elementary needs of the children of school age. Country once open was soon transformed into highly speculative real-estate enterprises, covered with buildings intended to derive the largest revenue from the smallest possible space. The country was pushed farther and farther out of the reach of the people, thus making additional park spaces essential. These park spaces also had to be created out of built-up areas that could only be acquired at a heavy cost, and at a sacrifice of property yielding necessary taxes to the community.

Thus the reconstruction of our cities has been going on in a fragmentary manner, and without changing the antiquated physical pattern designed to serve a simple community. A complex set of communal functions has had to be superimposed upon an outworn community structure.

Technology and Ways of Living. One of the most startling and distressing inconsistencies of modern society is the advance of technological methods and skill in the production of goods, and the contrasting lag in the application of technology to the planning, replanning, and reorganization of the ways of living. Indeed, many of our present-day ills are the result of the too-rapid application of technology to the production of goods. This has resulted in the removal from industry of ten or more million workers, victims of "too much technology." It is a strange paradox that, while the application of the most advanced knowledge and skill to the improvement of our cities would bring about a corresponding rise in the standard of living, the application of the latest techniques to industrial production tends to accelerate and improve the efficiency of the production organization, and to reduce the number of those who might benefit by this advance.

Indeed, the obsolescence of production machinery is so rapid that often a mechanism which in one season is the last word in quantity and quality production, becomes obsolete and ready for the junk pile in the next season. Not so with our homes and our communities. The more cluttered they become, the less efficiently they serve the purpose of living, the greater the number who flock to their precincts, the more slowly they lend themselves to those changes which are known to be in the interest of the inhabitants.

Modern science has let loose many forces, the uses of which are intended to serve mankind. Unfortunately these forces have been more commonly applied to the mechanics of manufacture of goods rather than to the creation of good conditions of living. R. Buckminster Fuller, in his recent book *Nine Chains to the Moon,* contributes a very interesting, though somewhat fantastic, discussion of the vast implications which science would suggest in dealing with the problem of shelter. These implications might be carried further into the field of community planning and of all the services which are required in civilized society. I wish there could be devised a numerical index of the rapidity with which technology is applied to the production of things, as compared with the application of a parallel development of technological knowledge to the welfare of the human being, and in particular in regard to the lag in its application to communal living. We know, and are continuing to explore, the ills of disorganized communal living, but the great exploration still remains to be undertaken. *This exploration lies in the field of social dynamics, which consists in the transformation of the sources of modern technology into forces intended to serve a general social purpose.*

The development of the present mechanistic and scientific age has brought about a regrettable confusion between civilization as a social achievement, and progress as an expression of the knowledge and skill to achieve results. The latter only assumes significance as its benefits can be leveled downward to the last and humblest member of society. As long as progress remains the privilege of the few and may be used as a negative force, it makes no contribution to civilization.

Property Rights and the Right to Decent Living. The most serious obstacles in the path of communal reorganization and the development of adequate living conditions are the concepts of property rights in land and buildings, franchises and special privileges, which the community, in its ignorance or lack of foresight, has allowed to fall into private hands. In the industrial and commercial sphere of enterprise a change in the demand, a new development in the method of production, a new trend in the habits or fashions of people, must be met without any claim to compensation for losses sustained. But in the matter of land or buildings, or grants of special privileges derived from the community, any new need, any change in trends, new discovery or new demand, must be met by heavy payment out of the public treasury, not alone for the new improvement, but also to cover the loss due to the obsolescence of the old ones. The line of demarcation between what constitutes a public menace, and what is merely socially obsolescent and in need of replacement, is very difficult to draw. Our legal machinery and fundamental laws are designed to protect the values that are, rather than the values that can be. The city in its struggle to emerge from its archaic state must face not alone the losses sustained through its own mistakes, but also the cost of the mistakes of the private individuals who, through their own ignorance and disregard of the public well-being, have derived an advantage which is in conflict with the public interest.

If ever a new way of living is to be evolved in our urban communities, it will be made possible only through a new concept of the privileges of real property rights, in which the common good will play at least as much of a role as the individual owner's interest. We have already made small beginnings in this direction in our zoning and, to a certain extent, in our planning laws, but these beginnings are essentially theoretical, and find little application in fact.

A New Transportation Economy. Our modern systems of transportation are perhaps the saddest of urban spectacles. We seem to accept the theory and practice that the greater the transportation facilities, the more advanced is the community. We fail to realize that transportation is essentially a makeshift, an effort to overcome confusion by carrying people and goods to and from the places where they should have been in the beginning. In New York City alone, the number of passengers carried by the various local transit systems, including the Hudson Tubes, amounted to 3,420,999,488 in 1937, which at a five-cent fare amounts to over $171,000,000, or around $24 per year for every man, woman, and child living in the city of New York. Dr. Martin Wagner, the brilliant city planner of Berlin, now teaching at Harvard University, has pointed out the grave fallacy of this great waste of investment and energy in transporting people. He designed an interesting cartoon in which he demonstrated the fallacy of providing for transportation in the morning in one direction, and in the evening in another direction, and pointed out that while the transit system must be built to carry a peak load, its service on the basis of this design is confined to perhaps two hours in the morning and two hours in the afternoon, leaving the remaining eighteen hours inactive. This condition can be verified by anyone who will take the trouble to board a subway or elevated train at any of the hours which are not heavy-load hours. Ten-car trains, carrying loads which could easily be served by two or three cars, are running on the lines, using labor and equipment which represents an annual waste—a waste which could not be justified on any business basis.

On September 14, 1938, the Board of Transportation of the City of New York submitted to the City Planning Commission a proposal or plan for the construction of additional facilities for this great metropolis, which would involve public expenditures amounting to $827,000,000. Just what this additional expenditure is to achieve in the way of improving living conditions does not seem to be stated in the proposal. It is evident from the plan that a greater centralization of traffic would become possible, and that the center of New York City would become more accessible than at the present time. The main expenditure is obviously intended to extend present lines of travel to outlying areas. Just what effect this will have upon the already overloaded land use of the center of New York is not part of the consideration of this plan. Similar projects are contemplated by other cities throughout the country, and yet there is every reason to believe that what is needed is not an increase in facilities or a cutting of the time required to reach the center of the city, but an integration of the individual areas of these cities as self-contained and functionally self-integrated communities, where travel would be reduced to a minimum and the distribution of population would be in harmony with decent working and living conditions.

Efficiency and Service. In projecting any planning scheme for a given community, the approach is generally clinical, treating of some specific problem that has arisen out of neglect, unforeseen changes, overexploitation of land, lack of public control, and similar conditions. The result has been that a great deal of modern planning has been confined, with a few notable exceptions, to the revamping and readjustment of facilities which have become unwieldy. The advance of the automobile has diverted most planning from the creation of decent living conditions to the development of streamlined traffic facilities, designed to make travel safe, to save time, and to facilitate mass movement. It has been found, however, that the more efficient these arteries of travel become, the less efficient become the city streets, which have not been designed and have never been intended to absorb more than the traffic originating in the locality. The rigidity of the urban pattern is constantly in conflict with the easy flow of outside traffic, which makes the periphery of the city accessible in the same measure as it makes the city street unbearable.

The investment in parkways and boulevards has reached a point where it is a serious question whether the cost of these boulevards can any longer be borne by those who wish to take advantage of them by moving out of the city. I have already pointed out that in Westchester County, in New York State, there has been such a heavy burden placed upon the properties that in order to justify the investment it will be necessary to raise land values to a point where there would not be enough people of sufficient means to purchase the land for housing or other purposes. The result looming upon the horizon is that people who find the areas served by these streamlined highways too costly move still further out into the country, in order to be able to acquire land outside the zone of high taxes and high land values. Thus the expenditures made by one community serve people in communities not subject to the heavy obligations.

A glance at the map of any metropolitan district will show that all, or a major share, of the modern automobile roadways are planned in direct relation to the metropolitan city, and not for the purpose of facilitating intercommunity travel within the area outside the metropolis. These roads are, of course, technically very efficient, but socially they serve the exact contrary purpose, namely, to accelerate congestion where it already exists, rather than to distribute population, and all the essentials for its independent living.

There is no doubt that the engineering skill and the vast sums of money devoted to expanding traffic facilities to the periphery of our cities have been productive of better travel, and have stimulated shifts in the population from the center of the larger urban communities. They have also brought the city population into closer contact with the open country. In many cases, communities which geographically belonged in the sphere of influence of the larger city, but which were isolated because of lack of travel facilities, have now come to be more active participants in the family of metropolitan settlements.

The question still remains, however, whether this improvement of

DUNBAR APARTMENTS, MANHATTAN, NEW YORK CITY. BUILT FOR NEGRO OCCU-
PANCY BY THE ROCKEFELLER INTERESTS.

CEDAR CENTRAL HOUSING PROJECT, CLEVELAND, OHIO. UNITED STATES HOUSING AUTHORITY.

travel will continue to present the advantages which the technicians and the planners had intended that they should afford to the population seeking a refuge in a suburban life. Already the tenement and apartment house builder has invaded the countryside, and is repeating the methods of construction and imposing the mode of life of the city, upon the suburban dweller. Again and again the land speculator and the hopeful landowners, to profit from the flight from the city, are seeking the advantage of land overcrowding in an environment which is essentially rural in character. Are the suburban communities going to have the foresight and the courage to save the heritage of rural and suburban conditions, or are they going to yield to the speculator and speculative enterprise the advantages which are the only justification for the exodus from the congestion of city life? Recent developments do not seem to justify this hope.

More and more it is found that local communities are merely stopping places in the shuttling between the bedroom and the office or factory, and are not, in the strictest sense of the word, communities or neighborhoods. This disintegration of communal life, and the consequences of divided communal interest, are leading to serious social and political difficulties, and are absorbing much of the leisure which modern methods of production and reduction in working hours have made possible.

It is my contention that we are devoting too much time and money to making transportation easy, and have done practically nothing to reduce the necessity for transportation and the integration of communal life. As long as this is the prevailing policy, housing will remain merely shelter, no matter how well planned, how sanitary, or how convenient.

Farming Out of Public Services. Rent is represented not only by the return that must be expected from an investment in buildings and grounds. Transportation to and from work, light, heat, telephone, water rates, gas—all form part of the cost of the shelter which people in all income groups must meet. The struggle to emancipate communities from the control of these services as private enterprise has been going on for a long time. In many communities it has become a corrupting influence in local, state, and national politics. Public service corporations have become notorious as stumbling blocks in public enterprises, and in many cases it has been found that the location and distribution of industrial enterprise have been controlled by power and water rates, transit costs, and similar services. This situation has worked a hardship in the free distribution of industry, and has interfered with the free distribution of population and the effort to plan for such distribution.

This is not the place to discuss in detail the policies regarding public services and their administration. The literature on the subject is rich in suggestions, and the legislative efforts to control private enterprise in public service are ample evidence of the importance of the problem and of the difficulties which stand in the way of adequate solutions. If, however, housing is to receive the full benefits which lie within the scope of broad community-planning policies, a new national approach to the financing and control of public services must be evolved.

In the matter of heat, light, and refrigeration, many studies have been carried out which would seem to indicate that by cooperative effort, or by public ownership of power, many ways could be devised whereby the production of light and power might be made to produce adequate heat as a byproduct. This would become a significant factor in reducing the cost of living and, in particular, in reducing the cost of maintaining homes, which reduction would be reflected in the rent.

Small Versus Large Communities. The present-day tendency of population movement is from the smaller to the larger centers. There is also a tendency of the population in the United States to drift from the center to the periphery of the country, in particular towards cities near the Great Lakes and the oceans.[1] As the largest opportunities and diversities of employment are centered in the larger cities, this drift of the population tends to pile up in congested areas. As agricultural unemployment increases, and the specialized small-town industrial centers lose their stability through fluctuations in employment, the people of the lower-income groups tend to go to the larger cities, while the classes with rising income tend to drift toward the outlying areas of the same centers of business and industry. The fact is that the poorer population can not afford to live in the outlying districts because they can not afford the incidental services essential to modern living. The well-to-do classes have their large incomes to pay for transportation; they have resources so that they can support private schools; they have apartments in the city where they can remain overnight in case they wish to enjoy some special entertainment or social activities; they have their own libraries and radios, their intimate friends, week-end parties, and a great many of the advantages which the poor can not pay for. Indeed, a community of workers outside of an established community would be confined to living, in the communal sense, within the level of the taxes which they can pay, in order to meet their community needs, such as schools, churches, playgrounds, hospitals and so forth. From the economic point of view it is not only impractical, but inadvisable, for the workers to migrate to com-

[1] McKenzie, R. J., *The Metropolitan Community*, McGraw-Hill Book Company, Inc., New York, 1933.

munities outside the larger agglomerations of population because, as Lewis Mumford puts it: ". . . the prime obstacle to urban decentralization is that a unit that consists of workers without the middle class and rich groups that exist in a big city, is unable to support even the elementary civic equipment of roads, sewers, fire department, police service and schools."

The whole structure of our large city civilization, despite its many shortcomings, is setting the pace for the essential community equipment which the smaller cities should have and can not afford. The small towns, unless they are made up of an admixture of a wide range of income groups, can not carry on and maintain a standard compatible with the simplest needs of community functions. The creating of workers' colonies is therefore of little value as a method of decentralization, unless such communities can be subsidized out of funds coming from taxes paid by other communities. Such a procedure would, in the nature of things, be quite inconsistent with democratic principles and difficult to carry out, because of the administrative problem of establishing minimum standards for those communities and the amounts of subsidy necessary. This method would certainly be objectionable, since it would tend to create class distinction in communities, as we now have it between individuals and local groups. Economic ghettos we have had in good measure. We need no more of them.

If anything is to be done for the smaller communities, the objectives must be built around the idea that communities can, and should, be rounded out social and economic entities, in the development of which the wealth produced and the profits made would yield adequate taxes to meet all of the requirements which a modern community needs.

Our smaller cities have suffered from a megalomania which has affected their entire outlook as to the type of development that is needed, and the controls which would bring about stability, economy, and efficient administration. The cry has been for larger and larger populations, more industries, and the capture of business. Thus the peace and orderly development of living conditions have been sacrificed to the attraction of business and industry. Subsidies, tax exemptions, prostituted zoning projects, and vast expenditures for roads have taken the place of the more important services for the protection of health, leisuretime resources, and development of an integrated community life. The larger cities have been battling with the problems arising from congestion and confusion, while the smaller cities have yielded to the hypnosis of megalopolis, only to realize confusion and lose their individuality.

Lack of Coherent Regional Planning. Under the stimulus of, and with subsidies coming from, the federal government, a good deal has been done to formulate a new policy of regional planning. Whether this effort will bring about an understanding of the relation between the open country and the communities within specific regions, remains to be seen. For the moment there seems to be a tendency to confuse the objectives of metropolitanism and metropolitan planning with those of the newer regionalism. The distinction between these two concepts might be formulated as follows:

Metropolitanism is a concept of community relations in which a specific population center controls the welfare and destiny of a group of outlying municipalities and other types of settlements.

Regionalism is a geographic concept in which a specific area is actually or potentially capable of social, economic, and cultural exploitation within the limits of our technological and cultural capacities, in the interest of human well-being, in which each community plays an independent role while contributing to the welfare of the whole.

This concept of regional development would tend to emphasize the values of each community and its possibilities as a creative and cooperative entity, rather than its subordination to the interest of a specific center of population. Indeed, the tendency of the metropolitan center, as has been pointed out, is to communicate its form and pattern to the smaller communities, rather than to encourage individuality and specialization. The distinctive community is slowly being absorbed either politically or by imitation of forms and methods into the pattern of the metropolis, while the population seeking such distinctive characters moves on. Thus we have a constant migration of people in search of an environment free from the blighting influences of the metropolis. Our metropolitan areas are replete with communities of this kind, which in their transition have taken on the antiquated pattern of the metropolis.

If housing is to become the focal point around which the community is to be planned, and the stability of settlements is to be protected against the blight, deterioration, and waste of unnecessary changes demanded by pressure from outside, there must be a greater emphasis upon the specific character of individual communities, and in particular those communities which have not become engulfed in metropolitan meshes. Instead of the dead level of the metropolitan pattern, we must begin to conserve those values and dissimilarities which, by their nature, are the justification for the existence of these communities. In the regionalism of the future the "unlike community" will play a more important part than the communities without distinction or distinctiveness. If we are to overcome the economic and cultural lag in various parts of this country, if we are to exploit rationally the resources of the vast areas of this continent, we must establish a dynamic regional symmetry in which the human values would be capitalized, and the social level of all classes would be raised.[2]

Lag in Urbanizing Rural and Semi-Urban Communities. Before we discuss the urbanization of these communities, it is essential to define what we mean by urbanization. Students of urban life in this country and elsewhere have had great difficulty in defining what an urban community means. The United States Census has changed its definition of urban communities as those which have a population of 8,000 people to those which have 2,500 people. Prof. Walter F. Willcox endeavored to evolve a new definition by basing his criterion of urbanity upon density of population. For the convenience of enumeration and classification these measurements answer the purpose. If, however, we are to consider urbanism in its true sense, we must seek the definition elsewhere.

Urban living is a way of life, not a way of being governed, not the measure of the proximity of our neighbor. There are cities in the United States which, when considered in the light of the way in which people live, belong in the primitive category of poor rural communities and backwoods areas, which have none of the advantages of living together, except in the fact that they share the same disadvantages. *"Urbanism," in the true sense of the word, characterises a cooperative aggregate of people, regardless of the distance between their homes, which enjoy insofar as possible the many amenities which modern technique and modern civilized ways of living demand.*

The proverbial red schoolhouse, the neglect of the simplest requirements for the protection of health, the absence of facilities for comfortable living and social intercourse and the creative use of leisure time, the failure to provide hospital care, the inaccessibility of cheap light and fuel, the lack of organization for the care of dependents, and the hazards of unemployment or partial employment—all are more characteristic of lack of urbanness than of density of population. While we spend millions of dollars and much effort in trying to derive some order out of the chaos of unplanned communities, and are concerned with the drift of people from the country to the city, we completely overlook the fact that the only way to stop this rural exodus is by making the rural and semi-rural communities worth inhabiting. Much of our housing problem has its origin in the movement of population to larger centers. The one way to prevent this movement is to refocus our interest and atten-

[2] Aronovici, Carol, "Regionalism, A New National Economy," in *Columbia University Quarterly*, December, 1936, pp. 268-278.

tion upon the way of life which makes this exodus necessary. The urbanization of the rural and semi-urban community is the solution.

For the present we have no way of measuring the diffusion of urban advantages in rural communities. We know that the housing of the farmers is not above reproach. We are aware of the fact that ill health receives scant care, and hospitalization is not always within the reach of large numbers of people living in rural or semi-rural communities, and that many other advantages are not available. In the next census it would certainly be desirable to incorporate in the records facts giving some measure of the disadvantages which the population living in the smaller communities, or in sparsely settled areas, must face. Such a measurement of the rate at which urban advantages are diffused among the rural and semi-rural inhabitants of the country would undoubtedly give a new vision of the problem of the rural exodus and its causes.

Employment Conditions, Migrations, and Business Cycles. Anyone familiar with recent conditions of employment in many of the industrial cities is aware that families or single individuals have been going from community to community in search of work. To be sure, the PWA and the WPA have been responsible for a certain amount of stability in communities where industry has failed to provide employment, and where the other services incident to industry have been forced to curtail activity and reduce the number employed.

In the case of many industrial plants in New England, labor conditions and the lure of cheap labor in other parts of the country have encouraged the migration of industries, leaving thousands of workers stranded in their home communities. This is particularly true in industrial towns where the migration of industry destroyed the main source of employment of the community. President Roosevelt and his New Deal may bring about adjustments in wage scales, and provide new mechanisms for the adjustment of labor relations so as to reduce the hazards of industrial migrations, but so far little has been accomplished in this direction. Housing and employment are inseparable, and any disturbance in employment opportunities must of necessity disturb the housing market. If gypsying in industry is to be tolerated on a large scale, housing will be seriously affected.

The President of the United States has recently raised his voice in the interest of the workers of the South. More than an interest in the problem is necessary to arrest the fugitive industries which are always ready to abandon one city for another in order to gain an advantage in wages and labor relations. If we disregard this fact, we can hardly expect workers to settle down and become homeowners. Neither can we expect the building and financial interests to provide decent dwellings, if the securing of tenants and the collection of rents are ephemeral hopes that can be dashed at the will of the large employers. Let us not assume that the movement of industry in recent years denotes a tendency toward decentralization, a change in the distribution of industry desired by many social reformers, but rather that the movement of industry has its roots in other than humanitarian promptings.[3]

The migrations of population have many causes. The suburban movement, the increasing rate of unemployment, the seasonal occupations of many workers, the destruction of land and other natural resources upon which employment depends—all are responsible in varying degrees for migrations which interfere with the stability of communities and aggravate the housing problem. When, during the Great War, munitions production made new opportunities for employment, the Negro population of the South sent many of its members to the great cities of the North and Northwest.

Chicago is a very interesting example of the results of this type of labor migration. The riots which followed a few years ago are symptomatic of the conditions which are brought about by these changes in the character and numbers of people demanding cheap housing and additional services. The riots which took place in New York City's large Negro district (Harlem) are typical of the conditions that arise when a low-income group, and in particular a racial group which must confine its habitat to a specific and geographically limited area, increases more rapidly than the accommodations which are available.

Migrations of people are often the result of business cycles, with their consequent demand, or reduction in the demand, for labor. When immigration into the United States was still free from the present drastic restriction, the business cycles responded to the size of the immigrating (and emigrating) groups.[4] The same conditions prevail with regard to the industrial population, which responds to the demand for labor in various parts of the country, or leaves communities which for some reason are slackening their demand for labor. The migratory labor needed in harvesting crops has created a serious housing problem which has never been met; with few exceptions, there has never been a serious effort to meet it. The one notable exception is the California Commission of Immigration and Housing, which was created as a result of riots in the hop-raising districts of the State. That conditions have not been

[3] See Greamer, Daniel B., *Industry Decentralizing*, University of Pennsylvania Press, 1935.
[4] Jerome, Harry, *Migrations and Business Cycles*, New York, National Bureau of Economic Research, 1936.

remedied, however, is evidenced by the many disturbances which have taken place recently in California, and by the medieval attitude of the farmers, who are interested in getting cheap labor and are unwilling to assume any responsibility of its welfare.

All the labor troubles in the farm areas of the San Joaquin Valley and the San Bernardino and El Centro districts are not due entirely to failure to provide decent housing for itinerant workers. Housing, however, is an important factor in the frequent labor troubles. Where seasonal workers are concerned, every device of oppression, disregard of human rights, and vigilante methods is used. The workers are homeless, voteless, and without the resources or prestige to fight their own battles. The seasonal agricultural worker everywhere, but particularly in California, is a pariah, and he receives the treatment that the pariah of ancient times received, both in housing and in his employment relations.

How any possible combination of employment of a seasonal nature could be fitted into a pattern of living which would establish a more permanent relation between the workers and their jobs, and between the families of these workers and some kind of a permanent home with a stable community relation, is difficult to determine. It is possible, however, that some combination between industry and agriculture might be evolved, and that a new way may be found to provide intermittent employment and continuous citizenship so essential to self-respect and self-protection.

Expansion of Municipal Boundaries. The nucleus of a city is, by virtue of this circulatory system, a fixed entity, insofar as its capacity to handle the movements of population, raw materials, and finished goods is concerned. Any additions to the load that might result from the acquisition of new areas, from the increase in the density of population, or from increased commercial or industrial activities, must find their counterpart in an expansion of the traffic system, either through street widenings, subways, and elevated roads, or through underground traffic arteries which are needed to supplement the street system and its capacity load.

The delay in transit, the difficulties of safe and easy access from one part of the city to the other, the problems of traffic control, and the cost entailed in such control and policing, are insuperable problems, which no city has so far been able to meet in a satisfactory manner. Traffic engineers have labored long and anxiously to make a thirty-six foot street do the work of a seventy-foot street; police officials have devised rules and regulations so strict and complex that strangers in new communities must be instructed in new ways of guarding their safety in crossing streets and in driving their cars. Budgets for traffic police have increased at such a rate that money needed for playgrounds, schools, or the protection of life and property through adequate policing, has been sacrificed to the demands for making traffic less confusing, less hazardous, and less time-consuming. The sum total of the achievement to date seems to show that the old law of not being able to have two bodies occupy the same place at the same time still holds.

In spite of these difficulties, cities are still annexing territory, are still extending their tentacles into the outlying districts, and incorporating within their municipal domains new and unnecessary areas for the mere vanity of becoming "the largest city" in the nation, the region, the state, or the county. If annexation did not interfere with the integrity of communal entities, no serious consequences would result. There might even be advantages in the larger outlook of a bigger municipality, in the form of better educational, cultural, and service possibilities. The fact is, however, that this larger view seldom, if ever, is fruitful. There is merely a new conquest, a new set of people to pay tribute to the inefficiency and heavily burdened administrative machinery of partly obsolete, confused, and highly centralized cities. The crude "shoestring" development of many of our cities is one of the most deplorable manifestations of this trend. As the radius of travel from the center to the periphery lengthens, the shadow of blight also lengthens. The newly annexed areas soon demand new roads, sewers, and transit facilities which must be provided.

No one can object to the expansion of cities. There are advantages in large cities. The measure of these advantages is not, however, in their size, but in the manner in which they can function as places in which to live, work, and play with comfort, convenience, and safety.

The last generation has witnessed a widespread movement for city planning intended to recapture the economic and social values lost because of new conditions, and the failure to conserve what was valuable in the old communities. The main difficulty with the replanning of these communities has been not so much a lack of technical skill, or an unwillingness to spend vast amounts of money in order to make the needed changes. The real difficulty has been the fact that we have never evolved a philosophy of urban planning consistent with modern needs. Whether we accept the modern trend toward a *megalopolis* or whether we are inclined to encourage decentralization of population and its activities is of comparatively little importance. We must realise, however, that communities are essentially mechanisms intended to facilitate civilized living.

Housing reform begins and ends with the interpretation of life that finds civilization in the pattern of the community, its capacity to function in rhythm with the modern life, and is sensitive to changes brought about by new ways of living, working, and sharing in social achievements. Without community planning, city, county, state and regional, designed to implement modern ways of living and to be adjustable to desirable changes, the housing problem can not be permanently solved.

Architecture and Housing

Chapter VIII

ARCHITECTURE AND HOUSING

Perhaps it should be assumed that a book on housing should not venture into the difficult and illusive question as to the place of the architect in this field. From time immemorial the architect has been building monuments, churches, palaces, and, occasionally, homes for the leisure classes. Some of these homes are still occupied by their original owners, while others have been handed down to families for whom no one can build with profit. In fact, until very recently, the architect has had little to do with the housing of the workers. His was a luxury profession. In the building of the cheaper dwellings the jerry-builder, the small contractor, and the developer played the major part.

But conditions are changing, and the architect is beginning to play an important part in shaping the destiny of housing. It is upon him that the evolving of a technique, consistent with a modern philosophy of housing, depends. On the whole, he is not prepared for the task. This fact is easily ascertainable by an examination of the many abortive efforts which, in recent years, have afforded the architect opportunities to prove his worth as a designer of workers' homes.

Recently I visited a new large-scale housing project. In size the project is sufficient to accommodate the population of a fairly large Western town. In design, however, its sinister monotony gave the impression of a well proportioned set of warehouses. It was an orderly set of masses and spaces, free from ornamentation, adequate as a "living machine" but devoid of any vestige of the poetry of living. No one could take exception to the general plan. It was a solution, but it obviously was not *the* solution that satisfied the normal human desires for "belonging," the craving to escape regimentation and the rigidity of pattern which our cities have accepted as standard. As a warehouse for human beings it was safe but not soul-satisfying.

It is for this reason that I am venturing upon a discussion of the role the architect and his professional and artistic skill must play in giving to the means of living, vital expression consistent with our civilization. For the present it must be admitted that the confusion of purpose in housing has been more serious in its accumulated achievement than the previous failures to find the means for achieving the purpose.

The enemies of modern architecture are the three most hackneyed expressions of modern building. Functionalism has so overwhelmed the architect that he has mistaken the forms that look like function for the ability to perform these functions. We all have seen homes which are so "functional" in structure that one feels that the architect was concerned more with the aseptic and mechanistic character of his creation than with the more subtle and diversified demands for individualized life. Indeed, this complete yielding to mechanistic forms, whether efficient or not, has led to the consideration of housing as essentially a mathematical and engineering problem. The conservation of what is best in human behavior and in the highest sense humanly functional has been overlooked. This is why the engineer has usurped the architect's prerogatives as a builder.

Another difficulty has arisen from the acceptance by the architects of the doctrine of international architecture. I can not see what international architecture actually means, unless it is the license to abandon all sense of accumulated native culture and to translate all design into simple and often monotonous lines, which free the architect from any obligation to interpret the spirit of his people. On the outskirts of the City of Vienna about ten years ago several so-called international architects were given the opportunity to build a group of dwellings. Each architect followed his own fancy in designing the building assigned to him. It was the most disheartening illustration of the desire to differentiate international architecture. The result was an agglomeration of ingenious but uncoordinated admixtures of structural types, which bore witness to the flexibility and vast possibilities of engineering skill, but had no relation to the spirit of community life and its integration as a living unit. There is no "international architecture" just as there is no "international" folklore or "international" pattern of human behavior. There are, of course, expressions common to all mankind, but that does not mean that a nation does not require and maintain standards of comfort, convenience, sense of space, sense of ways of living, that are its own. To assume that there is an international architecture that serves all purpose is like assuming that there is an international way of living to which all peoples are ready and willing to fit their own individual and group behavior.

This leads us to the next aspect of architectural endeavor: the mechanistic method of design which gives precedence to mechanistic methods of producing shelter which disregards the mechanics of advancing civilization. Buckminster-Fuller's Dymaxian house is the most striking illustration of this trend. Here we have a very ingenious engineering device for living whereby the machine is given the place as a guide for life, instead of making life the guide for the machine.

The main objective in housing is not to simplify life, but to reduce the mechanics of living to the simplest and easiest terms, so that life may become richer, more complex, and more in harmony with its purpose. It is not the function of the architect to confine human experience to an architectural mold. Rather is it the function of the architect to free and broaden the possibilities for human experience, by making his task conform to the trends and craving for human experience. Any hard and fast device, therefore, whether in the manner of using space or in the manner of imposing devices, which would tend to force mathematical formulas and technological devices which tend to fit life into a mechanistic pattern, is not architecture but a utopia of forms rather than a utopia of life.

Camille Mauclaire, in *L'Architecture va-t-elle mourir*, gives a hint of this kind of thinking in relation to modern ways of building: "There is no worse barbarism than that which believes itself scientifically right." No one would ignore what modern mechanics has given to the comforts and conveniences of living, but no one can claim that these mechanical devices have made any great contribution to civilization, unless they have served to release the forces and potentialities of man so that he may enhance his own place in society and devote himself to those tasks that will bring in their wake new values to life itself.

If the architect is to recapture from the engineer his place as a builder of homes, he must prove that this place rightfully belongs to him, not because of some artificial division of labor which has grown out of a tradition, but because he has a contribution to make which is peculiarly inherent in his training, experience, vision, leadership, and because he has a capacity to interpret human life in ways which the exactness of engineering can not grasp or use.

Already the universities and colleges which afford training in architecture are seeking new methods and new outlooks in the architectural profession. Courses in housing, city planning, site planning, slum rehabilitation, regional development, community rehabilitation and reconstruction, and a great variety of other lines of study, have been introduced into institutions which for years had guarded their *beaux-arts* traditions with dogged tenacity and contempt for the vulgarities of common requirements of everyday living. The plaster casts which had been so conspicuous in the halls of architectural learning have found their way into hospitable ash cans, and the competitive efforts of the students to design tombs or copy freak buildings have been abandoned. New moti-

vations, new outlooks, new philosophies, are finding their way into curricula which were believed to be immutable and final.

I have before me a special issue of the *Architectural Record*, one of
the most progressive monthly publications devoted to architecture in
this country, and one of the most enterprising. This issue, which ap-
peared in September 1936, contains a series of articles, reports, and
opinions, and some interpretations of the modern way of teaching architecture. The most striking part of this special issue consists of opinions
given by deans of schools of architecture regarding the new ways of
teaching and the new problems which architecture must face in this
teaching. I shall pick at random a few of these pronunciamentos, as
indicative both of the resistance to the new trends and the willingness of
many to meet conditions with new ways of training.

Dean George S. Koyl, of the School of Fine Arts of the University of
Pennsylvania, writes:

> While new problems influenced by current economic and social conditions
> enter the present-day practice of architecture, such problems do not merit
> drastic changes in the educational policy at this time. . . . The architect has
> at his disposal an assortment of servants to do his bidding such as never before,
> so much so, that if not properly trained he may lose sight of their relative
> importance and be carried away with their novelty.

Dean E. R. Bossange, of the New York University School of Architecture and Allied Arts, says:

> He [the architect] must be more conscious of community requirements and
> social conditions, of problems of transportation and circulation. But, above all,
> he must be capable of sensing and idealizing the human need.

I can not refrain from quoting in part the statement by Dean Hudnut,
of Harvard University, in which he says:

> If the business of an architect is to discover some attributes of beauty in the
> life of his time and to express this beauty by a harmony between his con-
> structed forms and the life that flows through them, then it is reasonable to
> expect that every student of architecture shall attain so far as it is possible a
> clear and objective view of the world around him; of the structure of society
> and the intellectual currents that determine that structure.

One only wishes that the aspirations of the last two writers quoted
could in some way permeate not only the curricular set-up of our schools
of architecture, but the spirit in which the student approaches his new
training and, after training, his professional responsibilities.

It is generally agreed that while there are still many schools which
devote a great deal of time to the Five Orders as compiled by Vignola
from the work of Vitruvius, the impact of modern industrial and eco-

Colonial Village
Arlington County, Virginia

First large-scale housing project
built and financed with an
FHA insured mortgage

COLONIAL VILLAGE, ARLINGTON COUNTY, VIRGINIA. AN INSURED PROJECT UNDER THE FEDERAL HOUSING ADMINISTRATION.

TECHWOOD HOUSING PROJECT, ATLANTA, GEORGIA. A W.P.A. ENTERPRISE.

nomic changes has had the effect of reorienting much of the educational trend in the training of architects.

We are concerned here mainly with housing and with the methods of approach which the architect must employ in order to bring his work as a builder into harmony with his objectives as a creator of conditions of living which would be in tune with the times, both as to social fitness and as to economic reality.

We have analyzed the housing market from the point of view of the ultimate consumer. Let us for the moment analyze the market for architectural service. There are in the United States today approximately 24,000,000 non-farm dwellings. Most of these are in cities and towns. If we consider their obsolescence at the rate of 2 per cent per year, thus calculating the average life of every dwelling at about 50 years, we shall have to replace about 480,000 dwellings each year. This in itself is a task worthy of any profession to consider as a service worthy of specialization. Assuming the investment in each house at about $4,000, we have a source of architectural employment of $1,720,000,000. If to this we add the number of dwellings needed to take care of the annual increase in the number of families, at least another 480,000 dwellings would have to be added each year.

With nearly a million homes needed every year, the field of architectural service should not go begging. Needless to say, much of this construction will be carried on for some time to come by jerry-builders and speculators, without benefit of architecture. However, there is still a vast field of service to be rendered and, the greater the development of sound economic principles of housing finance, the broader will be the conception of neighborhood life and community coordination, and the more likely we are to have need for socialized architectural practice.

To bring about a coherence between the objectives of housing in its broadest implications and the architectural profession, two lines of endeavor must be developed. The first is the evolving of a clearly defined professional attitude toward housing as a specialty, which must carry with it a full appreciation of the social import of housing architecture and the relation that this architecture must bear to the whole fabric of community activities and services, in the light of the limits and potentialities of technological skill and sound economic principles. This is not easy to achieve. Indeed much research is still necessary in order to develop a set of principles, standards, and practices which would place housing architecture in its proper relation to the scope of its service and to the social philosophy which every profession should formulate as a basis for its function in the framework of the social order.

The second task for the architectural profession is to undertake active participation in creating conditions of law, economy, and standards compatible with their technical capacity to plan and build. This, it may be said, is in the province of politics and propaganda. I readily admit this to be the case, but we do find the medical, engineering, and legal professions taking an active part in molding the structure of society, so that professional efficiency and progress may be attained in the interest not alone of the practitioner of these professions, but of society which they serve. Indeed, some of the publications which have met with the greatest success among the architectural periodicals, have already opened the way for such activity, but more than publications is needed. The architect must become a militant factor in all movements which may contribute toward his prestige as a creative force in improving home and living standards and in making the application of these standards as widespread as possible.

The setting up of standards must follow a logical sequence of both reasoning and activity.

The Social Motive. Le Corbusier, in one of his aphoristic outbursts, says: "The modern home is nothing else but walls with storage space on the one hand, chairs and table on the other. The rest is encumbrance." Thus have many of the modern architects tried to reduce the home to its simplest terms. The European countries have traveled a long way from this oversimplification of the task of designing and building homes. Indeed the walls and chairs and tables are the last and the least important aspect of architecture. It is their relation to the whole complex process of living that determines whether they are architecture or merely building.

In analyzing many of the housing projects which have been created in the United States and in Europe in the last generation, I find myself asking the question, "What are the problems which the architect has to solve and in what way has he solved them?" As there is seldom a sense of finality about the answer one finds in great works of art, I am led to the belief that the question has never been stated and, therefore, there has been no answer in the work of the architect. Looking upon the architect not only as a creative artist, but one whose creative ability, more than in any other art, must reflect a clearly definable purpose, it seems to me that architecture must begin with the ability, the skill, and the knowledge required in defining this purpose. There are three fundamental elements that the architect must face in stating his problem, and this is particularly true of housing. These elements are people, space, and time.

People. We assume that the architect will take some account of the number of people who are to be housed and the make-up of the families. But when I speak of people, I have in mind a broad interpretation of the meaning of the word. The people, as numbers, have long ago been a factor in planning, but their way of living, their needs in relation to the labor they are engaged in, and the implementing of a well understood and clearly creative leisure, have seldom been given full consideration. We have of course considered health and transportation to and from work, as well as playgrounds for children and open spaces for adults. But these do not begin to convey the meaning of the term. The place where one lives must afford not only the simple essentials connected with life, labor, and leisure. It must understand and interpret the more subtle human relations, the vast differentiations in behavior, the important sources of harmony or conflict in neighborhood contacts, the varieties of resources which could be utilized, the many conditions which lead to waste or conservation of energy, cooperative ability, and common action. The home and its environment are the most potent ecological factors in individual and family life; they are the breeding ground for many manifestations in the social life of the people which may be reasonably well oriented and controlled through housing and neighborhood design. It is this kind of understanding of what people are, what their reactions might be, and how they are affected by their home environment, that comes under the study of people. The superficial yielding to fashions, the whim of the reformer, or the requirements of some special class, have brought housing within the pale of reform theories and removed it to a large extent from the more normal field of creative social endeavor. *Housing is not a corrective alone; it is a dynamic force for progressive living, or it can be made so by design.*

Place. In speaking of place, I do not mean the site of the house or agglomeration of houses. I mean its entire relation to the community, its place in the pattern of industrial and commercial distribution, its relation to the open country, its character as a place where homes could be built and maintained in an environment subject to the least deterioration and having possibilities of that neighborhood unity which is so rare in even our best housing developments.

It is not enough to know how to build or even how to design a great mass of homes in proper relation to each other. One must know that there is a clearly definable strategic location of housing which has to do with drifts of population, with the ebb and flow of industrial development, with the convergence of traffic, with the opening up of hazard-producing streams of travel. One must know that improvements which may be to the benefit of the city as a whole, may mar the effectiveness of the privacy and comfort and peace of the residents of a section which is intended to meet all these needs. The architect, or those whom he employs to furnish him with the necessary data upon which to base his housing objectives, must be sensitized and enlightened regarding these dangers to the future of a proposed housing scheme, so as to avoid the pitfalls which destroy the economic and social values of many a well intended undertaking. The coefficient of land value for housing purposes is not the same as the coefficient of land value for all other purposes, and it is this coefficient that the architect must learn to find.

In a series of articles which I published in 1932 in *Real Estate*, I pointed out the various difficulties which arise from the assumption that the location of either housing or business is no longer a matter of values and business opportunities, but a scientific field of inquiry in which a great variety of factors must be taken into account, and in the determination of which the public authorities have a responsibility much greater than the landowner or the building investor. What we need is not momentary fitness, but the kind of foresight that would keep the community from undergoing shifts and changes which jeopardize both social and economic values and make community interpretation impossible.[1]

Time. The element of time which we are here considering has to do with the lasting character of the buildings and also with the lasting character of their surroundings.

It has been said that the longer a building lasts, the cheaper it is in the end. That is of course true, so long as the structure remains fit for the use for which it is intended. The fact is that a building is more economical, if it lasts only as long as it is useful and in harmony with the progress of the times. A glance at the map of New York City and particularly Manhattan Island, will show that the vast majority of dwellings have survived more than a generation. It is well known that many of these dwellings are survivals of the dark ages of the railroad and dumbbell tenement. The first attempt to improve housing conditions by legislation was made in New York City about a century ago. My familiarity with housing conditions in some eighty cities in the United States justifies the assertion that the greatest source of our housing evils is the lasting quality of the buildings which make up our residential areas. Business buildings, hotels, factories have passed in rapid succession from one form to another, and in many cases a business building which has lasted over two decades is looked upon as a relic. In housing, the process of obsolescence is recognized as a means of reducing rents only when there is an ample supply of housing, but the buildings are preserved with

[1] Aronovici, Carol, *Real Estate*, Chicago, January 9 and 23, 1932.

all the tenacity which property rights and the lack of responsibility of the owner for the welfare of his tenants warrant.

While every epoch in industry and business requires a new type of building, and economy and efficiency demand that such a building be provided, generation leaves to generation the pestilential and obsolete homes of the past. The architect has, of course, to conform to certain essential requirements of safety and endurance in buildings, but this does not justify the projecting of expensive structures which would outlast the service they are intended to render. This may sound like a plea for flimsy construction, but it is in fact a plea for a careful revaluation of the methods of construction with its heavy investment burden, which in the end results in a social liability due to this very lasting and substantial construction.

A generation of progress that does not reflect itself in improvements in the home is a generation partly wasted. Let each generation have its own way of living, expressed in its own way of building. It is only when we have learned to junk houses as we have learned to junk factories and office buildings, that we shall have attained full realization of the relationship between the ways of technical progress and ways of home life.

While we consider the necessity for shortening the life of buildings in some relation to their time of usefulness, it is important to see to it that this time element is guarded with the utmost care and forethought in relation to the neighborhood and the community. In other words, the architect who undertakes to formulate the objectives of a housing enterprise must examine every phase of the community and its dynamic forces for change, so as to synchronize the life of the structures with the pattern of the community, insofar as its lasting qualities are concerned.

Housing is therefore not only a problem in building design, but also is a problem in urbanism: a problem which may require not only knowledge and understanding of the facts but skill in providing safeguards and community implements to render the housing safe from the accidents and incidents of sporadic changes caused by lack of forethought. Dr. Walter Curt Behrendt, in his book *Modern Building*, says: "Building, as a function of the community, is a social art. It is from society that the architect gets his task, it is society that gives him the stuff that has to be molded into form."[2]

"But," the architect would say, "we are not sociologists or economists or experts in human culture. We are designers and builders. Let the sociologist, the economist, the social ecologist and all the other students

[2] Behrendt, Walter Curt, *Modern Building*, New York. Harcourt, Brace and Company, 1937, p. 22.

of the social order tell us what they want and we shall know how to build."

This is hardly the answer. There are no longer lines of demarcation between the social sciences and the professions, except as the scientist furnishes the basic principles upon which the accumulation of social facts must be based in order to make a professional service of value. This is true of law and medicine, engineering, and all the other professions which have to do with service. Indeed, business is slowly coming to the realization that good business is good social service, and that industry which neglects the social implications and obligations toward both employee and consumer has no place in a civilized commonwealth.

What is expected, therefore, of the architect is a new outlook, a new realism, a new form of creative design which would become the syntax of home building. When the architect has reached the point where he can use the elements of people, space, time, and economic reality as the material out of which to develop housing design, he will have interpreted life, and, by interpreting, will have served it. There is no greater art than this.

Housing Education

CHAPTER IX

HOUSING EDUCATION

With the growing popularity of housing as a subject of study, and with the expanding possibilities of professional service in this field, schools, colleges, and universities have undertaken the organization of departments, or sections of departments, devoted to the study of housing and training in housing service. The federal government has recently opened up many opportunities for this type of public service; states and municipalities are making new and substantial provisions for housing study and for the planning and development of housing projects. Thus it is evident that a new line of technical service is making new demands upon our educational resources.

Education, however, is not concerned with the technical skills and knowledge required in the carrying out of a task. Its purpose must go beyond the established theories, principles, and practices of the past. It must pave the way toward a dynamic and progressive checking of these theories, principles, and practices, so that they may be verified and revised or discarded and replaced by new ways of thinking and serving. Within less than a decade, our whole outlook with regard to the place of housing in the social structure has changed. Our whole social and legal point of view has found expression in a new philosophy, a new methodology, and a new economy. These are neither final nor even fully in accord with the realities of the present day.

If we are to undertake housing education on any large scale, it is therefore essential not only to train students in the established practices, but to make sure that the practices which they are led to believe are the best for the moment, may not become obsolete by the time they are free to become leaders and practitioners in their professions.

Unlike medicine, law, engineering, or even the usual practice of architecture, housing implies not alone the method of building, but the vast array of factors which make building possible under conditions insuring the best results. The man or woman engaged in housing must, therefore, realize not only the relation of technical skill to the job in hand, but the relation of this skill to the possibilities for making it count in the interest of those who are to be benefited.

If housing work is to assume this broad aspect, it is essential that the trainee be familiar with all of the social, economic, legal, political, and psychological factors which may affect his work and which, in turn, he may help to clarify and amplify in order to make his work effective. Housing, as has been repeatedly said in this book, is not a machine for carrying on the process of physical living. It is the physical mold into which must be fitted the whole complex set of activities and relationships which insure physical and spiritual well-being. It is not confined within the walls of a house or an apartment, but includes all of those essential amenities of human relations which extend to the neighborhood and the community. Looked upon from this point of view, housing education transcends the practices commonly assigned to the training of architects, and includes the whole science of living within the home and the community.

How to make this philosophy effective, we do not yet know. But considerable experience is being accumulated by educational institutions and by those called upon to express, in terms of site and building plans, their philosophies of home and neighborhood ways of living. There is still much to be learned about the process of giving to living quarters the esthetic form in which social values would reach their fullest realization.

Hilaire Belloc, in his characteristically whimsical book on Paris, gives an interesting and sensitive characterization of his approach to the study of the City of Paris:

> For what shall a history of Paris do? It should, to have any value, show the changing but united life of a city that is sacred to Europe; it should give a constant but moving picture of that "come and go" of the living people in whose anxieties and in whose certitudes, in whose enthusiasms, and in whose vagaries are reflected and intensified the fortunes of our civilization.

It is not the city plan, or the monuments, or the shops, but the life of the people and their ways of using and changing and expressing their lives through the city, that counts. Fragmentary housing reform that produces a few more dwellings, or provides subsidies for a few thousand families incapable of attaining a minimum standard of housing, may alleviate the lot of a few, but it will not lay the foundation for a civic culture the history of which will be worth recording.

Assuming that the point of view which I have endeavored to outline can be made the basis for housing education, let us see whom we need to educate. If we could bring ourselves to look upon the need for housing as the Middle Ages looked upon the construction of a cathedral, and if we applied to the purpose the same communal cooperative devotion and purposefulness of design, we shall gain some conception of the wide sphere of influence which would have to be embodied in a housing program.

We have at first the occupant, the tenant, the owner of the home. He must be educated in the ways of living and using his home. His conception of the right to live decently, and his articulate demand for the kind of home that will bear ample relation to his needs, is of prime importance. This task can not be accomplished without reaching down into our educational system, as represented by the public schools, and moving upwards into the press, the public platform, the church, the club, the radio, the theatre, and the moving picture. One can not hope to approach the ideal without making the realization of this ideal conceivable and attainable. The teaching about slums and blighted districts, and the benevolent efforts of the rich and powerful, are just so many phases of a negative social economy, which removes the individual most concerned from the field of dynamic cooperative effort to attain an adequate standard. We have had too much of the superimposed philanthropic effort, appeal to sentiment, and division between those who have, and those who can not have, what civilization through systematic organized effort could attain.

If an educational program regarding housing is to be evolved that will last and be fruitful, we must begin with the men and women from the time they become conscious of the need for shelter, and set their course in the direction of the type of house they should have, the way a home can and should be used, its place in the pattern of community life, its relation to the masses and spaces which make up the community, and the interplay between living, working, and the use of leisure time, as they are implemented by city, town, or village, or even in the open country.

We must, of course, be concerned with the slum, but this should not be the basis of housing education, any more than crime is the basis of our social organization.

The development of a housing philosophy in the consciousness of the masses is, however, not a simple problem of adding courses to our overburdened school curricula, or the setting up of propaganda machinery. The present need is for an enlightened leadership free from dilettantism or hobbyism. Already we have too many leaders who do not know where they are going, and many others whose leadership has for its goal a mild meliorism, which will bring about just enough improvement so that we would not move too rapidly in bringing about necessary fundamental changes.

Before we undertake housing education, therefore, it is important that we take stock of the kind of leadership we should develop, the agencies which have a contribution to make toward the setting up of practical and attainable objectives, and the eventual equipment that leaders should possess.

Colleges and universities, schools for social workers, technical and specialized schools of engineering, architecture, business administration, government, law, public health, can play a part in the development of housing leadership. Even teachers' colleges may find a vast opportunity for bringing, within the range of the new pedagogy, the study of housing as a pivotal point around which a great system of coordinated knowledge may be built to the advantage of useful learning and of civic and social vision.

It is well known that the techniques of housing construction, such as those practiced by the engineer and architect or the ordinary builder, have long been divorced from the more inclusive considerations of human needs and community structure. The educational imperative of the new training should tend to restate the economy of the home as a dynamic force in creating and conserving human values. The technician would be powerless, however, to achieve these ends without the aid of leadership in law, government, finance, and a social outlook which would lend vision to honest purpose.

Many educational institutions, either because of a realization of the importance of housing, or because of the newer consciousness of the need for housing reform, are actually carrying on educational work intended to develop housing leadership and technical skills. Whatever the motive of this new development in educational specialization, the important consideration must be the principles which underlie the professional or educational objective.

Perhaps we could best clarify this point by raising a number of questions, the answers to which will depend upon the type of education contemplated, and the kind of leadership that may be expected to shape the future of American housing.

1. Is housing education to deal with the immediate opportunities for service in improving and modifying the lot of the underprivileged, or is this education to be directed toward a new outlook upon home life, home standards, and the relation of the home to the entire community?

2. Are the present social, economic, and legal limitations to be accepted as the framework under which housing improvements are to be achieved, or is housing to be taken as a basis for such fundamental changes in our social structure as will make the reorientation of our

entire community economy the basis for a new and better way of living?

3. Is housing education to be departmentalized as a profession, or is it to be made the means of synthesizing the vast ramifications of this subject in the remoter fields ranging from finance to social psychology?

4. Is technical training to be limited to the development of skills, or is it to be made a part of the newer outlook, which is concerned not alone with the laws of construction, but with the principles which harmonize skill with social purpose?

5. Is housing to be looked upon as a new field of professional reform, or is the study of housing to be brought within the scope of all professional and business training, which may have some part in shaping broad housing policies.

Whether an educational institution approaches housing as a task intended to develop professional services, civic leadership, or business methods, the answers to the above questions will determine our way of living in the future.

It should not be assumed that the broad knowledge, skills, and experience required in housing may be centered in the training of a single individual. Specialization will be necessary, both for the purpose of developing the peculiar qualifications of individuals, and in the interest of high standards of service. In view of these considerations, the following lines of specialized training might be undertaken:

1. *Clinicians*. It would be the business of the clinician to gather, classify, analyze, and evaluate the social and economic facts of a given community, neighborhood, city, or individual project. He must be able to formulate a program consistent with the realities of all the factors that may lead to practical results. This would mean a knowledge of the economics of land, the financial resources and problems involved in securing funds and assuring their safety, a knowledge and understanding of the promotive and restrictive legislation that may be called into play in improving conditions, a general knowledge of the economic status of the tenants or future home owners, and their rent-paying resources. He must be aware of the movements of population and their effect upon the stability of housing investment. He should have a knowledge of city planning and zoning insofar as they affect the character and location of housing enterprises, and a knowledge of many other aspects of our social and economic life as they affect the home. This group of clinicians should find a field of great usefulness both in public and in private enterprise. The day of slumming is over, and legislating the slums out of existence has proved a tedious and almost

fruitless task. The training of the clinician in the wider implications of housing as a socio-economic problem may refocus our housing economy in a manner that will produce beneficial results for both those to be housed and those whose business it is to derive a profit from housing others.

2. *Leadership*. The most casual examination of our present business methods, our ways of legislative control, our planning technique, and the general manner in which the providing of housing has been carried out by both private agencies and public enterprise, suggests the need for leadership, not alone in what should be done but in altering the mechanics of doing it. Our laws, our taxation system, our methods of safeguarding investment, our ways of fostering public participation in housing finance, can not—judging by past results—be assumed to be adequate. A large number of changes in these methods must be effected before we shall have built up public policies and private practices which would make better housing possible. To achieve this end, leadership of an enlightened kind is essential.

3. *Technicians*. It is the task of the technician to give physical form to the synthesis of all the forces which, when combined in their proper relation, will produce housing. It is therefore important that the technician be not only a designer of sites and buildings, but that he make that design the expression of all of the possibilities afforded by a given condition.

Architecture is, of course, an art. Its main function has heretofore been the lending of a sense of fitness to utilitarian purposes. To this form of professional skill must be added the element of function in terms of specific conditions—social, economic, personal, and communal. Thus design must not be functional, merely as a dwelling in a social vacuum. It must express relationships, the radius of which should extend to the physical pattern of the community and the pattern of society.

To achieve this the technician must speak the same language as the clinical student of housing. He must be able to incorporate, in the conception of his plan, his conception of human life in human relations. He must keep in mind not only the present, but a changing, community and advancing standards. He must be aware of the limitations of investment and management economy. In short, he must transform the art of building into a social synthesis which transcends the narrow limits of mass and space.

4. *Management*. While housing management has long been a field of employment demanding special ability and knowledge, it is only within the last few years that it has gained standing which may lead to

the development of a new profession. Government housing has given a certain zest to the training for this profession, and much of the information and experience of the past is being assembled into a coherent set of principles which, at least in the past, have governed management practice.

In view of the fact that management plays an important part in the social as well as financial success of housing enterprise, the training of housing managers should find a place in the field of housing education.

Heretofore management has been a service called for after the building was constructed and ready for occupancy. As the problems of design are solved more and more in human and economic terms, the problems of management, at least insofar as they may depend upon the physical plant and equipment, must be met before and not after the design of the building is completed. In fact, this is the present practice in the design of some of the government housing projects.

It is difficult to outline all the functions which housing management may include. Past experience has shown that it is not merely a matter of rent collection, building care, and the incidental services connected with tenant-owner relationships. In its broadest implications, particularly in subsidized or government housing, where service is at least as important as revenue, management must deal with many human relations, including the relations of the families to each other, the incidents and accidents of sickness, unemployment, leisure-time use, and many similar aspects of life. The management under these conditions becomes a human-relations service, in which the manager may be called upon to exercise many functions. He must be ready to advise and assist in matters of relief, employment, hospitalization, child discipline, domestic relations. The training of managers must, therefore, take on a new social aspect which borders on a great variety of social services, or he should at least be familiar with every service available in the community that may be called upon to assist in solving the problems of the tenants.

Efficient housing management implies not only knowledge, but experience and tact in handling human problems. The manager is in most cases the determining factor between failure and success of housing enterprises. He must have peculiar talents for this work, but must be trained so that his talents may be used to the best advantage.

SUMMARY

We have seen that the creation of conditions conducive to high housing standards is dependent upon knowledge and experience reaching into nearly every social and technical science. Economics, political science, sociology, law, engineering, medicine, city planning, education, business management, social service—all make their contribution toward the setting up of standards and their practical realization. Indeed, the field of research and the fields of practical service afford opportunities for employment so vast that almost every professional school could with profit set up courses in housing, insofar as these professions may be able to make a contribution toward housing. The schools of architecture and the schools for social work have so far had a monopoly in this type of educational effort.

I believe that universities and colleges would render a valuable service to society if they were to set up housing institutes in which the educational and research resources of the entire institutions were to be coordinated. This would afford the students of housing access to every authoritative source of information which touches upon housing. At the same time, the teaching staff would find a field for contributing their share of knowledge and experience to the solution of the most pressing problem of the day.

Photograph by Federal Housing Administration.

COUNTRY CLUB APARTMENTS, GREENSBORO, NORTH CAROLINA. FINANCED BY NEW YORK LIFE INSURANCE COMPANY. FEDERAL HOUSING ADMINISTRATION INSURANCE.

RADBURN, NEW JERSEY. A COMMUNITY FOR THE MOTOR AGE. PEDESTRIAN WAY. CLARENCE S. STEIN, ARCHITECT.

The Housing Survey
and
Housing Research

CHAPTER X

THE HOUSING SURVEY
AND
HOUSING RESEARCH

It may seem presumptuous to include in this book a chapter on survey and research in housing. However, after a careful study of some hundreds of housing surveys ranging in scope from a few families to the Real Property Inventory, which covers real properties in 64 cities throughout the United States, I am persuaded that some clarification is necessary of the relation between housing surveys and research in the same field.

NATURE AND DEVELOPMENT OF THE SURVEY

Professors Odum and Jocher, in their otherwise fine work *An Introduction to Social Research*,[1] state that the survey "is an inductive method—that it is built up from the particular to the general." It is this misconception of the survey that has led to so many assumptions as to the value of the survey and has often resulted in mistaking surveys for scientific inquiry. The fact is that no survey which is intended to be used for the devising of a particular set of reforms or improvements proceeds from the particular to the general. Rather is the process reversed, so that, assuming certain generalizations, a measuring of social facts is undertaken in order to ascertain the extent to which these facts measure up to the preconceived and presumably accepted generalizations.

Taking the field of housing as our immediate concern, it is obvious that a housing survey like any other survey must approach its task with a well-assorted set of generalizations. It is only by this method that we can discover to what extent these generalizations can be fortified in devising measures for the improvement of existing conditions. We believe, for example, that substandard housing is bad for the health, and we proceed to find out to what extent bad health is more common where housing is substandard. We are convinced that delinquency is a result of a bad home environment, and accordingly we attempt to demonstrate that families in the slum areas are more particularly prone to fur-

[1] Odum, William W., and Jocher, Katherine, *An Introduction to Social Research*, Henry Holt and Company, New York, 1923, p. 249.

nish a high quota of juvenile and other forms of delinquency than the better-housed families.

One of the more recent developments in the housing survey field is the generalization that bad housing places a greater burden upon municipal budgets than does good housing. In New York City and in Cincinnati surveys of slum areas proved beyond the shadow of a doubt that the taxpayer's burden in the slum areas is greater than in the better-housed sections of these cities. Home ownership is another of those superstitions which pass for sociological generalization and which have so often misguided "practical" housing specialists into survey enterprises, in order to demonstrate that the social conditions in areas where ownership is relatively light are less desirable.

The main difficulty with the housing survey, as with surveys in other fields, is the fact that a survey requires a stock of generalizations from which to proceed and that often these generalizations have been arrived at, not through careful scientific research, but through devious ways representing a combination of traditional beliefs, prejudices, habits of thinking, sentiment, social superstitions, and ignorance or deliberate misrepresentation of the fundamental principles, forces, and processes which determine a particular condition or set of conditions. *A survey is often merely evidence that, under a given set of wrong assumptions or generalizations, one can build up a set of facts which would justify action in harmony with these assumptions.* If the assumptions are wrong, the action is bound to be wrong, regardless of the mass of facts accumulated, their accuracy, or apparent close relation to the objectives desired.

The colossal failure of this country to evolve a well-rounded program of housing reform is clear evidence that the survey in this field has failed to supply the necessary evidence and the scientific background for a far-reaching and effective program. We have had agitation, propaganda and honest effort in many directions, but when, in 1932, we were faced with the task of utilizing an economic crisis as a springboard for a housing program, we were as much in the dark as if we had never had any surveys.

It should not be assumed that the surveys have been entirely without scientific value, but where such value has been derived, it was the result of a careful coordination between scientific generalizations and social diagnosis. I shall go even further and grant that, in many cases, surveys have helped to correct and thoroughly reorient scientific thinking, as the result of an accumulation of facts not otherwise available. The fundamental error in the survey is not its accumulation of facts, but its assumption that these facts are intended to promote social action rather than add to the mass evidence essential to the formulation of new principles and generalizations.

Another fallacy of the survey is the assumption that the measurement of separate social entities is possible without considering the close relationship of social institutions. The danger that arises from assuming that an immediate relationship between conditions existing within a circumscribed field of social life represents the cause of this condition has not often been obviated by our surveys. That there is a close correlation between bad health and housing can easily be proved statistically, but that this ill-health is caused by bad housing is still a question that has not been fully answered. Again, it is obvious that delinquency is prevalent in the slums, but that delinquency has any relation to the condition of stairs or the existence of an adequate water supply is not so certain. The survey is therefore faulty insofar as it fails to test its assumptions in the light of the social and allied sciences before following a line of reasoning which correlates cause with effect. The facts may be accurate, the measuring standard may be beyond reproach, the terminology may be borrowed from the latest and best scientific vernacular; and, yet, the conclusions may come dangerously near destroying the real objective sought in improving existing conditions.

I may seem to insist too vehemently upon the necessity for testing the relation between cause and effect, but I have seen from long experience too many reforms which have defeated the very purpose for which they were intended because those who presumed to gather the evidence on which to base such reforms were novices in the field in which they were engaged and mistook facts for evidence. Often facts of unquestionable value to science may, at the same time, be a positive menace to constructive social action. It is therefore important to discriminate between a survey which is intended to contribute to the sum total of factual knowledge and enriched scientific experience, and the survey which contemplates social action.

The latter type of survey is justified only when, in the gathering, classification, and analysis of the facts, it extends its field of investigation over a sufficiently long radius of social causation to avoid the incidence of a too-narrow interpretation of cause and effect. Only thus can a program of social improvement be harmonized with the social processes and scientific outlook.

The survey is not the invention of American social workers. The problems that have arisen in civilized society have long ago been subjected to careful and minute study, and the results have been utilized either in enriching the factual material upon which social theory may be based or in propounding social panaceas intended to reduce the social inequality or injustice which every social order affords. The history of the survey may be traced to Plato and his *Republic*, but we shall only attempt briefly to consider the more recent efforts in this direction and the specific manner in which these may be distinguished from our more modern American method. For the earliest examples of surveys we must go to England, where John Stow first attempted a study of the City of London. He published *A Survey of London* in 1598, a most accurate and carefully compiled chronicle of the city, its history, geographic character, and existing conditions. This represented the first effort in the direction of giving a picture of a particular community in which every aspect of the life, labor, and resources of the people was considered. It was also the first time that the word "survey," so far as we know, was used in connection with such a study. This was not an effort to advocate reforms, but merely to state facts. Twenty-seven years later Samuel Purchas published a work of a similar nature, but here we find more than mere statement of fact, as revealed by the title of the work itself, which reads: *Purchas, His Pilgrim; or Microcosmus, or the Historie of Man, with the Methods of His Generation, the Varieties of His Degeneration and the Necessity for His Regeneration.* Here is a title that should make the average surveyor green with envy. As Purchas was chaplain to the Archbishop of Canterbury, his title can be attributed to divine guidance.

The man who, in my estimation, made the largest and richest contribution toward the technique and scientific outlook of the survey is Pierre Guillaume Frédéric Le Play, who, in 1855, published his *Les ouvriers européens* (*The European Workers*). This was a study carried on during leisure periods in his life, when he travelled from village to village in order to ascertain, not some specific facts about a particular problem, but to gather data on the life and labor and physical environment of the working population.

This was no task conceived under the impetus of reform, but rather an exploration into the realm of living carried on by a skilled engineer concerned with people and their ways of living. It was not until nine years later that he attempted, in his work *Réforme sociale en France*, to lay down some principles of reform which, in the light of his comprehensive and first-hand studies, seemed necessary. How great an influence Le Play had upon social investigation is difficult to tell. There is, however, no doubt that his influence upon social thinking has been largely in the direction of clarifying the intimate relationship between the individual, the family, and the geographic environment. Indeed, this form of social thinking affected even the literature of the latter part of the nineteenth century, of which the most outstanding example is Emil Zola's *Les Rougon-Macquart*, a twenty-volume work in which the history of a family is made the vehicle for a minute study of the social, economic, political, and cultural life of a whole people.

So important was Le Play's work considered that a society for its continuation was organized first in France and later in England. Both of these organizations have rendered valuable service in encouraging surveys and in directing public opinion, not alone toward their value, but also toward the type of technique that avoids the pitfalls of dealing with problems in insulated social segments.

While Le Play's work was essentially confined to personal observations, it must be emphasized that few surveys can be carried on by this method. In the first place, the time factor often must be reckoned with, especially when an investigation covers a considerable territory and involves the recording of many facts. Frequently surveys are undertaken under the leadership of a skilled investigator, who must seek help from others less capable and less familiar with the object of the investigation. This means evolving methods of fact finding which can be employed in delegating the task of observing and recording to others. Certain methods of observation and measurement must therefore be found which would make possible the delegation of investigation to a staff who may be depended upon to select and record facts which, in the end, would have a common value, regardless of the personal equation of the investigator's knowledge or skill. Quantative measurement of specific facts commonly definable is therefore the most important consideration in a survey. In this respect, statistical methodology becomes essential but, at the same time, extremely dangerous.

Taking their cue from the development of mathematical science as applied to social phenomena, a galaxy of thinkers have tried to apply mathematics to social phenomena, in the hope of evolving some kind of a science of social mechanics. Although there is no intimate connection between housing and mathematical calculations as applied to human society, it may not be out of place here to review very briefly the efforts in the direction of calculating social phenomena in quantitative terms.

Blaise Pascal (1623-1662), the French philosopher and mathematician who evolved the theory that environment is a factor in determining justice, also developed the theory of probability, which, when applied to social phenomena, makes possible social forecasts. It was Jacques Bernouilli (1654-1705), the Swiss thinker, however, who connected the idea of probability with the idea of regularity in social events. He was perhaps also the most advanced in the matter of relating "civil, moral, and economic" phenomena to the technique of measurement, or mathematics. In England, we find William Petty (1623-1687), in his *Political Arithmetic*, applying statistical data to political events and social phenomena. Around 1662, John Graunt developed the first mortality table ever prepared in any country. Dutch mathematicians of the seventeenth and early eighteenth centuries went a good deal further than Pascal in their efforts to interpret social, or rather historical, facts as having a causal relation to each other and a certain continuity. This was the result of the influence of one of the greatest philosophers of that time, namely, Gottfried Wilhelm Leibnitz (1649-1716), who anticipated this development in social thinking. Buffon (1749-1789), in his *Natural History of Man*, used mortality tables as a basis for his arguments. Depercieux (1703-1768), who wrote an essay entitled, *The Probability of Human Life*, made the first effort toward giving some idea of longevity. J. L. Lagrange (1736-1813) developed his *Essay on Political Arithmetic*, using much of Lavoisier's work in his calculations. Laplace (1749-1821) and Joseph Fourier (1769-1839) developed the idea that statistical measurements are essentially a mathematical tool used in the development of social science.

In Germany, a very interesting development in the study of social phenomena took place when Peter J. Suzmilch (1707-1767) decided that statistical measurements might be used in the development of social laws. The philosopher Kant went further and demonstrated that, no matter what free will may do in the case of individual action, the group acts with certain regularity and precision which can be statistically measured. The French statistician Quételet (1796-1874) advanced still further in the development of the relation between various social phenomena by evolving the concepts of "average," "maximum," and "minimum." Karl Marx took much from Quételet, in particular the idea that there is a close relation between social, moral, and political phenomena and the economic structure of society. Quételet further developed the theory that, while population might advance in geometric progression, as pointed out by Malthus, this increase is retarded by obstacles which eventually tend to bring population to a standstill. Here is a clear deduction, purely mathematical, which we find to be working out in every civilized country.

This brief review of the development of the study of social science through quantitative measurement is intended to show the evolution of social measurement theories, and is important as a basis for both research and survey work. Statistical measurement is essential in determining scientific symmetry in social phenomena.

The survey is intended to give the key to this symmetry and, in its full development, might give rise to a new science or method of "social meteorology" or "sociometry," which would have for its purpose the measurement of the state of civilization and the extent to which this civilization has permeated the masses of the people and has served to bring them within reach of the resources of social progress and civilization. That is all that the survey could aspire to be when it is developed beyond the narrow confines of a given problem to be solved within a limited pattern.

HISTORY OF THE SURVEY

With characteristic minuteness the Germans started to develop an historical school of surveys which dealt with the evolution of certain social manifestations. Bucher in Germany, and his contemporary, Brentano, began certain economic studies of specific problems rather than general economics while Ratzel was at work on his theory that geography is a very potent factor in the development of the social order and of racial traits.

The geographic factor, which was so fully developed in Germany by Ratzel, was not without preparation. The English Ordnance Survey was begun in 1745, when it was discovered that the country was unprepared to meet rebellion. In consequence, the war office of England undertook a geographic survey of the Scottish Highlands. At the end of the eighteenth century, Napoleon frightened the English into extending this work to other parts of the country. After Napoleon was safely lodged at St. Helena, the army officials lost interest. By this time, however, it was found that the maps were of value in making local improvements, for recording titles, mortgages, taxation, and so on. It was not till 1815, the year of Waterloo, that the work was complete. It has been revised and kept up to date ever since.

The relation between geography and the social sciences became more and more obvious, and the survey idea in relation to geography found increasing support. Patrick Geddes, who was perhaps the leader in the survey movement of England, was in the meantime working at his civic tasks. Geddes felt that geography was most important in planning for human welfare, and devised the formula that we must know first the place, next the work, and finally the folk. His influence has been felt on three continents, and there has never been anyone who could focus facts upon civic problems better than he could. It was under his inspiration that the Le Play Society was organized in England, and the Outlook Tower in Edinburgh was his contribution to organized thinking in terms of human geography. The Outlook Tower, which was the first survey laboratory organized under the inspiration of Patrick Geddes, combined the idea of Quételet with the more advanced concepts of mathematics, history, geography and the social sciences as essentials in the development of a survey technique which could be relied upon to give every social inquiry a scientific backing.

Out of this grew the movement for regional study, which implied a new alignment of geographic areas based on organic, geographic and social entities, and represented a certain symmetry between the intent of nature and the possibilities for economic and social progress. This movement has only recently found expression in America through the National Resources Board, which is attempting a scientific breakdown of the elements which make our civilization and their future possibilities.

In the United States, we can do no better than begin with the regional surveys which George Washington undertook personally. Even before peace with the British was finally concluded, General Washington explored the Mohawk route with a view to coordinating the natural resources of that region with a planned economy. He reported on his explorations to Chevalier de Chastellux, in a letter dated October 12, 1783, and later wrote to Thomas Jefferson (March 29, 1784) regarding certain connections which might be developed between the Ohio and Potomac Rivers.[2]

The most important series of surveys in this country is represented by the United States Census, which had its beginnings in 1790 and by 1850 had reached a degree of thoroughness and efficiency which makes it invaluable as a means of studying the history and development of the United States. While at its inception it had merely a political purpose, namely, the determining of political representation, its subsequent development reached into a vast number of phases of our national life which makes its use for social study indispensable. While sometimes important aspects of our social life could easily have been incorporated in the systematic canvassing schedules of the census, thus laying the foundation for accurate knowledge of our social conditions, pressure from various sources and the point of view of the director and the census board stood out against such widening of the scope of the census. However, much has been accomplished and constant extension of its functions promises to bring about broadening views as to the social function of this instrument of national measurement.

Aside from the United States Census, there was little concern with the survey method in this country. The earliest record that can be

[2] See Hegemann, *City Planning–Housing*, Vol. I, pp. 10-11.

found of any specific investigation of social conditions in survey form is, strangely enough, an investigation of housing in New York City. While traces of housing regulations are found as far back as 1647, the first investigation was made under an order bearing the date of September 30, 1793, of the Common Council of New York.

The annual report of the inspector of health, made by Garrett Forbes, contains information regarding housing conditions in New York and calls attention to the high death rate which is alleged to be caused by the filthy conditions of the dwellings. The report declared that it is to be "regretted" that there were so many mercenary landlords who permitted their tenants to live in surroundings unfit for habitation. The population of the city at that time was 270,000.

A more thorough survey was made in 1842, when Dr. John H. Griscom, of the Board of Health, revealed that 7,196 people lived in 1,459 cellars and that fire risks prevailed, beside overcrowding and filth. But it was not until the Association for Improving the Conditions of the Poor undertook its study of the housing problem in New York that we find any record of concern with housing by a private agency. In 1846, the Association undertook a survey which was published in 1853. Attention was called in this report to many old houses unfit for habitation, the smallness of the rooms, the prevalence of boarders and roomers, and the presence of stables in the rear of houses which had been converted into dwellings.

Prompted by the findings of the Association, the New York State Legislature, in 1856, appointed a committee to make a study of the "tenant houses." This report re-emphasized the findings of the previous surveys, but a recommendation for the appointment of a board of home commissioners was not adopted by the State Legislature.

Despite these inquiries and the agitation following the riots of 1863, which brought to public attention the conditions under which human beings had been living, no serious effort was made to bring about fundamental changes in the regulation and control of housing conditions.

In 1864, however, the Citizens Association of New York, prompted by the alarming conditions that were developing in that city, undertook an investigation of the sanitary conditions of the city. The investigation was conducted by the Council of Hygiene and Public Health. It consumed two years and is a document of great value, both because of its broad approach to the whole subject of health and because of its thorough consideration of the housing conditions. Among the members of the investigating committee we find such persons as Hamilton Fish, John Jacob Astor, and Robert B. Roosevelt. The investigation of each district was entrusted to a physician, and a uniform plan was used in securing information and in reporting the results. The maps and drawings are particularly valuable and should be studied, by those making housing surveys at the present time, as samples of graphic ways of driving home a point. This report is particularly interesting for its accurate and specific descriptions of buildings, accompanied by floor plans and other evidence revealing the evils that prevailed and where they were located.

Between 1866 and 1880 we find very few instances of surveys of any importance, either from the point of view of housing or other aspects of social life. In France the followers of Le Play carried on special studies of specific industries and expanded their work of family records, but the main emphasis seems to have been placed upon perfecting statistical methods and promoting the institution of official agencies for the gathering of uniform and reliable statistical data.

However, we find that many of the European countries were becoming aware of the seriousness of the housing situation. From many quarters came evidence of existing evils. Thus we find Villermé, through the publication of his *Tableau de l'Etat physique des Ouvriers*, bringing the matter of housing into sufficient prominence to prompt legislative action in the interest of housing. His revelations took ten years to produce results. A decade later Adolphe Blanqui, a distinguished economist, undertook an independent study of housing conditions, and in 1866 Jules Simon further dramatized the lot of the French worker in his relation to the home.

In England the movement toward improving housing conditions by calling attention to existing evils began with a remarkable report published by Drs. Arnott, Southerland, and Smith, in which attention was called to conditions of overcrowding in London. The subsequent survey made by M. E. Chadwick in 1842 for the Public Relief Commission was so impressive in its revelations that a number of societies for the improvement of housing conditions were formed, and the first movement for housing legislation had its birth. The various surveys had not only the effect of influencing legislation, but they served as an inspiration for literary efforts and various reform writings which helped to bring housing reform into popular favor. An interesting character who undertook to spend his life seeking a solution of the housing problem is Arthur Rafalovitch, who traveled through the length and breadth of Europe in order to secure some knowledge about the way to improve housing conditions. Here is a case of surveying not conditions but the

efforts and experience which society has to offer, and also the evaluation of these efforts and experience.

Up to 1880 certain gains in the interest of improved housing legislation had been achieved in practically every western country in Europe
and in the United States. From that time on the survey shifted from
the housing field or other specific problems to the consideration of general community conditions in relation to the poorer classes. The most
monumental work came from the pen of Charles Booth, who in 1886
began his investigation and published *Life and Labor of the People of
London*, in 1891-1892. *Darkest England and the Way Out*, by William
Booth, was published a year before Charles Booth brought out the results
of his investigations. These two surveys marked a new epoch in this field
of investigation and gave a much broader meaning to the relationship
between the condition of the poor as economic entities and their lot as
inhabitants of a community unsuited for decent living standards. Ten
years later B. Seebohm Rowntree published *Poverty—A Study of Town
Life*, which further developed the idea of the intimate relationships
between various social factors that determine social conditions.

In the United States, aside from a number of local studies of no great
import, we have no outstanding studies of social conditions, except perhaps the report of the Industrial Commission, which carried on extensive investigations of industrial conditions in the United States but did
not extend its field beyond the specific problems that concern labor and
industry. It is rather difficult to draw the line between studies which are
undertaken as a result of a specific interest of a public nature, prompting
the government to seek information, and surveys which either are the
result of public interest in a specific problem or are prompted by the
normal interest in the accumulation of knowledge valuable in the up-
building of the science of society. The studies we have cited so far are
significant either because of the technique employed or because they
marked a point in public policy where information of an impartial nature
was essential in devising ways and means of alleviating the conditions
of certain classes of people.

Jacob Riis, the Danish-American journalist, in his book *How the Other
Half Lives*, laid the foundation for a new effort in the interest of
better housing in New York City. This book, based on first hand information of conditions and prompted by the author's sense of justice, was
the inspiration of a new awakening to the need for further study and
effort in behalf of the tenement dwellers of the great metropolis. The
activities of the Tenement House Committee of the Charity Organiza-

tion Society, the studies and lectures of Dr. Felix Adler of the Ethical Culture Society, and the work of the Association for Improving the Condition of the Poor, finally brought about the appointment of the Tenement House Commission, which under the leadership of Robert W. DeForest and Lawrence Veiller produced the most complete and thorough study of New York housing conditions.

This report was issued in 1900, and in 1901 the Tenement House Department was created as part of the machinery of the City Government, entirely separate from the Health and Building Departments of that city. The report was the most epoch-making document in the history of housing surveys. Nothing so thorough has been done since in any city of the United States. So impressive was the evidence gathered and so sweeping was the legislation enacted, that a veritable avalanche of housing surveys followed in every corner of the country. The results, however, were not so satisfactory as they might have been, as those who made the surveys were often prompted by sentimental impulses without having the knowledge necessary either to make the surveys or to frame legislation which would meet local conditions. Often the New York Tenement House Act was copied almost *in toto* in order to meet conditions that were fundamentally different from those prevailing in New York City. Indeed, there are today on many statute books laws which emulated the original Tenement House Act of New York City, while in New York the law has been changed in many fundamental respects in order to remove original defects and because of changing conditions and new needs.

One can not close the account of investigations up to the first year of the present century without mentioning the studies of Jane Addams at Hull House in Chicago, and Robert A. Wood's *The City Wilderness*, which made upon the conscience of the nation lasting impressions as to the conditions under which people work, live, and have their being.

The most dramatic survey with the most dramatic results in the first decade of this century was Upton Sinclair's *The Jungle*, a study of the packing industry in Chicago and the human elements involved in this great industry. *The Jungle* was published in 1906; it swept the country like a flaming torch and resulted in a great variety of public investigations and legislative enactments. This was not a survey in the ordinary sense of the word; it was a cry out of the wilderness that thrives on the fringes of our civilization. The cry was heard by the President of the United States, as well as by the humblest men and women with a social conscience.

Here perhaps it might not be out of place to comment on the value of the literary presentation of social facts. Many of our surveys have lacked the vital force of literary treatment and have been presented in forms devoid of the quality of readability. They have often become merely documents to be read when we prepare other documents, or to be filed away in the storehouses of sociological facts, from which only experts may derive benefit.

Up to 1907 there was in this country no organization of a private nature which was intended as a clearing house for social investigation and which was not concerned with some specific problem of reform. In that year Mrs. Russell Sage, who had the full freedom to dispose of the Russell Sage fortune, created, under the guidance of Robert W. DeForest and John Glenn, the Russell Sage Foundation, the purpose of which was the improvement of social conditions, and, especially, the ascertaining of social facts.

The first and most outstanding single undertaking of the Russell Sage Foundation was the Pittsburgh Survey, under the leadership of Paul U. Kellogg, at the time editor of *Charities*, a social worker's publication. It was due to Paul U. Kellogg, with his long experience and sensitiveness to social problems, and later to the skill of Shelby M. Harrison, who became associated with the Russell Sage Foundation, that the Pittsburgh Survey assumed the proportion and character of a city-wide study, balanced in its social conception of main issues and without concern as to the interests involved that might be affected by the findings. The Cleveland Survey followed the Pittsburgh Survey, and finally came the Springfield Survey. These three surveys, broad in scope, diversified as to the character of the communities studied, and scientific in their technical approach, are beyond a doubt among the most outstanding achievements of the first quarter of this century in the United States.

There were, of course, many other surveys undertaken during this period, and, insofar as housing surveys are concerned, there are not less than four hundred in the files in the Library of Congress, the New York Public Library, the Library of the Harvard University School for City Planning, and the Russell Sage Foundation Library. Most of the investigations are, however, fragmentary and often too closely focused upon some specific problem limited in outlook and circumscribed in its geographic area. With the exception of such city-wide studies, as George F. Kenngott's *The Record of a City—A Social Survey of Lowell, Massachusetts*, and a few less meritorious efforts, we have no outstanding complete community surveys.

In 1929 *Middletown* was published. This was the most thorough examination into the social life and manifestations of a city that had been produced in this country.[3] Written by Professors Robert Lynd and Helen Merrell Lynd, two outstanding sociologists, it represents a new technique in community study, and is a model of clarity and thorough methods of social investigation. Its sequel, published in 1937, has an added value in the fact that it reconsiders the same social aspects of community life eight years later. It presents a picture of the changes which took place in the community over a given period of time. We have no similar study of any other community in this country.

I should now like to turn to one more survey of national significance which, although first initiated as a private enterprise in the city of Cleveland, eventually was extended by the federal government to sixty-four cities scattered throughout the country. This is the Real Property Inventory. As a record of information it is the most extensive ever undertaken. The Real Property Inventory was carried on under the direction of the Department of Commerce, Bureau of Foreign and Domestic Relations. Although considering only part of each city studied, it revealed facts regarding conditions, financial status of properties, interest rates, rental rates, overcrowding, and similar aspects of the housing problem which, under careful analysis, should be valuable as a guide in the development of housing programs covering a large number of phases of the housing problem. It is to be hoped that, out of the evidence gathered through the Real Property Inventory, will grow the conviction that housing should become a part of the periodic record which the Bureau of the Census gathers in connection with population, industry, mining, and similar subjects. The only way to measure progress in housing is to provide for periodic records of a systematic character, and to continue this measurement at stipulated periods comparable with similar measurements in other fields of our social and economic life.

FEDERAL HOUSING AND THE SURVEY

The federal government has been concerned with housing only as incidental to some other phases of its great variety of social studies, and the Department of Labor has from time to time published reports dealing with specific housing conditions. It was not, however, until 1932 that, under the promptings of a reconstruction program of our economic structure, housing received consideration. Under the promise of assistance in the solution of local housing problems, the communities throughout the United States began to vie with each other in their demonstrations of the need for better housing. The Real Property Inventory was the most outstanding effort in this direction. Later each com-

[3] Middletown is presumed to be the city of Muncie, Indiana.

Photograph by Sekaer.

LAKEVIEW TERRACE, CLEVELAND, OHIO. UNITED STATES HOUSING AUTHORITY
PROJECT.

WESTFIELD ACRES, CAMDEN, NEW JERSEY. PROJECT UNDERTAKEN BY THE UNITED STATES HOUSING AUTHORITY.

munity which was seriously considering Federal Aid for housing made surveys of local slum conditions and assembled evidence of the possibilities for their removal.

One such study was undertaken in New York City under the leadership of the Slum Clearance Committee of New York. The report of this committee is a very able presentation of facts which were generally well known. The form of the report, however, makes these facts easily understood. More intensive studies of similar nature were carried out by the Orientation Study, organized under the auspices of the Columbia University School of Architecture under the direction of the writer. Most of the material assembled was displayed at a housing exhibit held at the Museum of Modern Art of New York under the auspices of a number of social agencies. This exhibit was visited by more than seventeen thousand people in the course of two weeks.

In this account of housing surveys, I have not mentioned one of the most complete and scholarly studies of housing, namely, Dr. James Ford's study of New York slums. This study was financed by E. Phelps Stokes as part of the work of the Stokes Foundation, and should be looked upon as the most thorough investigation available on slum conditions.

APPROACH TO THE SURVEY

Enough has been said of the general character of various surveys to justify an attempt at defining the approach to the subject, insofar as it represents not only a commodity which every person must consider as essential to his personal and family well-being, but also the expenditure of enormous national resources in the production of this commodity. The individual investor, the banks, the consumer, the insurance companies, and the motor revenue of our municipalities, are inextricably related to each other in any consideration of housing.

If surveys are to be undertaken, it is therefore essential that not alone the conditions and the causes and effects of housing be studied, but that these studies be undertaken with a view to ultimate, rather than momentary, solution. I am aware that some studies are needed to meet immediate situations or to emphasize some specific phase of the subject at a crucial moment in legislative enactment, but these are not surveys in the strict sense of the word; they are merely the accumulation of information intended to serve a purpose which is ephemeral in character and seldom likely to have lasting value.

I have often thought that the term "survey" is misleading. It is a phrase which denotes taking a general view rather than making a more minute study of conditions and facts. It is probably too late to advance a new name for this type of study, but its use certainly is not justified in the case of most social studies.

TYPES OF SURVEYS

It is quite difficult to devise a classification of surveys without running the risk of leaving out certain studies which meet the requirements of several classifications. We can, however, formulate a general set of types of surveys, which may depend for their classification upon their purpose rather than their ultimate content. The following classification would seem to me to include most of the studies thus far undertaken as surveys: descriptive surveys, analytical surveys, problem surveys, propaganda surveys, test surveys, and project surveys. We will now take up each type more fully.

The Descriptive Survey. This type of survey is essentially devoted to the accumulation of details and analysis of specific social phenomena, whether they be housing, crime, health, or other social manifestations. They may not necessarily apply to abnormal conditions, but may merely be intended to enrich the stores of social facts. These might be descriptive or statistical, or both.

The Analytical Survey. This survey is more in the nature of sociological analysis of conditions, their causes and effects, carried out in the light of a specific social philosophy or for the purpose of deriving evidence upon which theories or principles may be based. Herbert Spencer hired agents to gather data for his sociological work. Others gather their own facts, or derive them from the store of evidence gathered from available sources of various kinds. Much of the work which was done by the President's Research Commission on Social Trends, while of the highest order, was primarily based upon existing data. The conclusions reached in this report are of great value and present a new field of exploration for both public and private agencies, whose function is to provide and help to secure the adjustments recent social trends suggest.

The Problem Survey. This is a special type of investigation which assumes that a specific problem exists and sets for its purpose not only the measurement of the problem, but the discovery of the factors which must be taken into account in finding a solution. The problem survey is not concerned with the conditions, except insofar as the condition justifies its being classed as a problem. Its main object is a solution which would be in harmony with the facts, and would include all factors which may contribute to the presence of the problem and all factors which might play a part in devising solutions. This survey may or may not endeavor to discover all of the ramifications of the problem insofar as they affect society, but it does take account of all the factors which may help or stand in the way of a solution. Professor James Ford's *The Slums of New York* is an example of such a problem study.

The Propaganda Survey. This type of study is generally made with a specific aim in mind and is perhaps the least valuable of all, except when emergencies arise. Most of the housing surveys we have so far made are propaganda surveys. Their motivation may be beyond reproach, but their regard for relations between facts and social reality is not above reproach. They are likely to be fragmentary, one-sided, and careless of the larger implications of the problem.

The Test Survey. This survey is a form of investigation which deals largely with conditions and results achieved through various efforts toward conscious social change or improvement. We have few of these surveys; or, rather, this form of survey is often made part of other studies. It has seemed to me that, in view of the many reforms which have been inaugurated in this country within the last generation, it would be an extremely valuable service for some students of social action to subject many of these reforms to the test of adequacy in the face of the problems which they expected to solve. We have had many reforms intended to improve housing conditions, home ownership, land control, taxation, and so on. It would be of the greatest benefit to social science and to reformers if these efforts toward improving social conditions were to be subjected to the test of efficiency in the light of the original objectives. These surveys should be made not as general studies but as localized investigations of specific areas and the effect upon these areas of the reforms under scrutiny.

The Project Survey. This is the form of investigation which is used when a general solution of a problem has been settled upon and the question of adjusting the solution to the specific area and conditions must be projected on a basis of fact. In the case of housing, the project survey is particularly important, because after all the factors of general importance have been considered, there is still left the problem as to how to express in structural and site-plan details the general objectives to be attained in relation to the physical site and community conditions into which the project must be fitted. Within the last few years most government housing projects have been conditioned upon such studies. Many of them have been less thorough than conditions justified, but on the whole they have opened the way toward a clearer understanding of the social, economic, psychic, and governmental factors that govern the carrying out of an effective housing scheme. Clarence S. Stein, the New

York architect, who has had a very wide experience with large-scale housing, long ago developed a technique for the carrying on of such studies. The proposal for the reconstruction of a certain section of Astoria, a division of Queen's Borough of New York City, made by a group of architects and housing students, may be cited as an example of the more general phase of such study. More recently most housing projects of any magnitude are planned only after a careful project survey is completed, so as to bring the objective as close to reality as possible.

THE SURVEY AND RESEARCH

It is difficult to draw the line between the survey and research. Often the term "research" is used when "survey" is meant, as it has become fashionable for people to use the former when they are carrying on a minor investigation of some kind.

While it is quite impossible to draw a clear line of distinction between the survey and research, there is no question that, in the case of research, the object is to discover theories, principles, methods, and techniques. In the case of surveys, the main purpose is to gather, classify, and analyze a set of facts which, considered in the light of accepted theories, principles, methods, or techniques would yield certain conclusions and point to certain types of action which would result in changes and improvements consistent with recognized and accepted standards.

While the essential requirements of accuracy, knowledge of the subject to be studied, familiarity with the science or sciences which are to be relied upon for proper interpretation of the facts, are similar in the case of both surveys and research, the methods and objects differ.

Statistics. A survey implies measurement and, therefore the use of statistics as a tool. As already stated, the emphasis has been placed too confidently upon the fact that statistical evidence has been gathered, and the results have been taken for granted as indicative of the conditions which the survey is intended to reveal. It is well-known that often statistical information, no matter how accurate, may be misleading unless the facts are of sufficiently broad scope and bear to other causal facts a close relationship broad enough to give the subject studied a rounded-out aspect. Often the evidence is quite complete, but fails to meet the requirements of comparison with similar conditions in other areas. In other cases, statistical relationships are easily demonstrable when the actual social relationship may be of a doubtful nature. For example, tuberculosis and bad housing can easily be correlated in almost every slum area. The extent of the accuracy of this correlation may not be capable of actual proof, unless we consider the better housing conditions and their tuberculosis rate. Even then it might not be a true basis of comparison, as the people living in better houses are of a higher-income group and can send their patients to private sanatoriums and even out of the community to more favorable climates in order to cure the disease. Another instance to which we have already called attention is the claim, statistically demonstrable, that the social and other public services required by the poorer sections of the city where slum conditions prevail are a heavy burden upon the community budget, and that if housing were improved there would be a very material saving in municipal expenditures. These statistical demonstrations, so dear to the heart of the housing reformer, are sheer propaganda material, as can easily be proved by broader studies of the subject. The poor live in slums, but the slums alone do not make the poor. Low income is caused by other conditions. These same people, moved to palaces or the most expensive elevator apartments in any city, would still remain poor and without the means of caring for their sick, without proper means for educational development, or recreational facilities. They would still have to be supplied with the many services for which they could not pay.

One of the most interesting revelations of the Real Property Inventory is the fact that, in most cases where the rent is lowest, the rent delinquencies are most common. This does not mean that the slums produce rent-paying delinquency, but rather that as the ability to pay rent decreases there is a tendency to move to cheaper and cheaper quarters.

Qualitative Analysis. One of the most serious and, at the same time, the most difficult problems in carrying on a housing survey is the determination of the facts which are to be gathered and the definition of these facts in clear terms, so there will be no chance of misunderstanding the meaning of the findings after they have gone through the process of statistical analysis. In the case of housing this is a particularly difficult problem, as many of the terms used in a survey are open to different interpretations and, from the point of view of the field workers, are subject to personal viewpoints.

I am aware that it is often difficult to define a term, but we should then so circumscribe it as to provide a common definition of each word, thus affording little chance for confusion. The term "unfit for habitation" may mean different things in different communities and under varied conditions. "Room overcrowding" means practically nothing, unless we know how large the rooms are, and what the relationships and ages are of those occupying the rooms. We might even go so far as to say that racial characteristics would have much to do with the conditions of room use, although overcrowding is not desirable under any conditions.

"Rent" may mean the amount paid for a dwelling. But when we consider heat, hot water, refrigeration, and other services which relieve the family budget of extra expenditures, it would constitute a different item in the family budget. We could go on citing other instances, but suffice it to say that before any survey is undertaken the terminology to be used should be as clearly defined as qualitative and quantitative terms can be.

A number of students of housing have from time to time resorted to a scoring system which avoids in some respects the danger of personal variants in both the answers to questions and the method of recording. These score cards, however, are subject to many of the same dangers as the direct question without scoring. In 1919, the Whittier State School, an institution for delinquent boys in California, undertook to devise a guide to the grading of neighborhoods. I do not know to what use this guide was put by this institution, but a reading of the questions and an examination of the method of grading makes it obvious that there was much room left for personal discrimination and points of view. The values attached to specific factors seemed open to a considerable range of differences of opinion. There seemed to be serious confusion between values and attitudes and a stress on the relation of the neighborhood to the delinquent boy, rather than stress on the neighborhood as a place in which normal families might live. The assumption seemed to be that, if a certain condition produced a certain effect upon a boy of a particular mentality, this condition is undesirable from the point of view of the people in the neighborhoods.

A similar study carried out recently in a slum district of New York revealed the fact that in a larger majority of cases the boys coming from homes of better conditions in the same district of New York were more prone to fall into habits which would land them in the hands of the police than boys living under less favorable conditions. I am pointing out these dangers of connecting facts and assuming standards because, in the field of housing, we have accumulated a considerable number of prejudices, superstitions, and habits of thinking which befog the issue and confuse the investigators, so that they accept beforehand meanings of words *and correlations of facts which have no scientific value and which, in the end, are incompatible with the main objects of housing studies and the application of the findings to housing reform.*

Indeed, I am persuaded that qualitative studies, largely descriptive and often unyielding to statistical tabulation, are of greater value than statistical data leading to generalization and having no basis in reality. As Professor Mitchell expresses it,[4]

> Even in the work of the most statistically minded qualitative analysis will keep a place. Always our thinking will cover a field larger than our measurements; the preconceptions that shape our ends, our first glimpses of new problems, our widest generalizations will remain qualitative in form.

Indeed, it may be said that in much of our social investigation we are often confronted in statistical generalization by the facts which had been secured as a short-cut to mass evidence, as a substitute for the more laborious, but often more accurate, qualitative evaluation.

To be sure, qualitative analysis requires as much, if not more, knowledge and skill in evaluating facts and in relating them systematically to the main object of the study. But granted that these qualifications are present in the investigator, a descriptive study of a few families in their relation to housing would be vastly more valuable than a mass of statistical data in which there is lacking a clear definition of the items to be measured and a symmetry of the facts bearing upon the problem.

The Elements of Space and Time. It has been pointed out that a dwelling is part of a larger and more complex set of communal and neighborhood patterns, and that in recent years it has been realized that frequently conditions which are not difficult of improvement structurally are surrounded by such unfavorable communal conditions that no localized effort to improve individual buildings would materially change the general living conditions. It would not be contrary to common experience also to assert the opposite view, namely, that a neighborhood with obsolete and substandard housing, in a general environment of open space and adequate provisions for communal living, would hardly come under the heading of a slum. It is often the relation between the outer conditions and the house itself that gives an accurate conception of the way people are living or can live.

As the location of the house bears a close relation to the community and the neighborhood, it is essential in all housing surveys to ascertain within what physical space the study should be geographically confined. The neighborhood is often taken as a unit of study. But what is a neighborhood? I doubt if a satisfactory definition, upon which agreement could be reached by a number of social students, is available. It is a term which has found much popular use, but even the dictionaries have avoided it as undefinable.[5]

[4] Mitchell, Wesley C., "Quantitative Analysis in Economic Theory," in *American Economic Review*, Vol. XV, 1925; p. 12.
[5] See the *Columbia Encyclopedia*, Columbia University Press, New York, 1936.

Yet there is no doubt that within every community there are certain areas which, because of homogeneity of populational make-up, tight geographic street plan, historical background of facilities, agencies, organizations and institutions, human relations, and ways of living, are closely knit. In many instances there has grown up a consciousness of neighborly community of interests which has found expression in a whole series of economic, cultural, educational, and social organizations. These become potent factors in holding the population together. How to draw the line on a map which would relate the neighborhood as a social entity to the geographic boundaries is a difficult and sometimes impossible task. The fact remains, however, that frequently the proposals for the removal of a slum district and the opportunities for better housing in another district meet with serious resistance because in many cases the individual families are not separate groups of individuals of blood relationship, but that family groups rather than the individual family have become the unit for consideration. One reason why it would be difficult to resettle the Italian or Jewish tenement dwellers on the lower West or East Side of New York in other parts of the city is that they have built up a social structure and human relationships which must be taken into account in all projects contemplating the rehousing of large numbers of families.

In a recent study of a housing project which was to be located on Long Island, New York, the problem of transportation to and from work or shopping centers was a minor consideration compared to the questions of how the families moving into the new housing would be able to reach the neighborhood from where they came, in order to keep up their neighborly relationships in a district in which they were no longer residents.

A few suggestions as to the main considerations which would assist in the creation or in the delineation of a neighborhood are set forth below:

Geographic Isolation. Most of our cities have been made up of smaller communities which have either remained stagnant for a while and then have suddenly become the center of new activity, or have been absorbed into larger cities as these cities extended their political tentacles into the outlying districts in order to expand their tax resources or voting power. At any rate in a large proportion of our cities we find cells of community centers, around which there are other cells with a rather indistinct or uncertain character as to residential, business, or industrial activities or a combination of all of these. Geographically speaking, these little communities have often retained their character, and a large proportion of the buildings have survived from a generation to more than a century. They have thus kept the district from radical transformation. We find these conditions in Chicago in the very shadow of the Loop skyscrapers, in Boston where an aristocratic neighborhood has survived the pressure of business expansion, and in New York where Wall Street and Broadway and all of the great financial institutions of Lower Manhattan have failed to wipe out the remains of old neighborhoods—the quaint, but not altogether desirable, old buildings which present the most fantastic contrast between the bustle of big business and the sordid remains of a dead age.

Greenwich Village, the alleged center of the artistic population of New York City, has remained a reasonably well integrated neighborhood, despite the presence of a great university, hotels, and luxurious apartments near by.

The street plan often the residue of earlier development, the presence of transit lines which keep the community from becoming popular with a different class of residents, the closing in of a district by main arteries of travel which are dangerous, the old boundaries of two adjacent communities which once had their separate political entities and street plans—these factors tend to preserve neighborhoods and may be depended upon as guides in the study of neighborhood character and activities. The configuration of the land is another important factor in creating and perpetuating neighborhood boundary lines.

In the early days of American community building, the church and the village green were the pivotal centers around which the community was built. This was more true in European countries, where the church was the protecting element in human settlements. Nevertheless, we have many illustrations in our own cities in which the church has remained an important center around which neighborhood growth, if not neighborhood activity, has taken place.

Whatever may be said about the rapidly shifting centers of activity in the United States and the vast migrations of population from the center to the periphery of our cities, there is ample evidence to show that neighborhoods persist not alone as aggregates of human beings, but rather as geographic entities which show the same perpetuating trends as our street systems, which even the automobile has failed to affect materially insofar as the old-established lines are concerned. Geographic boundaries alone, however, are not sufficient to determine fully the lines of demarcation of a neighborhood as a social entity.

Economic Levels. While we are living as a democratic people in the political sense, the economic level of the people finds its counterpart in the type of habitations which they occupy. This is particularly true of cities. There are, of course, families of some wealth living in the congested areas, but their presence is largely due either to a lag in their aspirations for better conditions, or to business interests which are located in the poorer sections of the city. On the whole, however, the stratification of our population is not difficult to delineate with reasonable accuracy on the map of any city. There are some fluctuations as to rental ranges and building conditions, but on the whole the incursions of better dwellings suited for a higher income level are few and far between, as the investment in such dwellings would hardly bring the returns which it would bring in other locations. Thus the level of incomes also determines the level of community conditions and the make-up of the neighborhood population.

I venture the assertion that, within certain limits, a study of wages and rents would reveal also the lines along which the neighborhood boundaries might be drawn. There is no doubt that in many instances changes are taking place on the fringes of these neighborhoods, but on the whole the neighborhood lines would correspond roughly to the income and rent levels.

Where the characteristics of the population's country of origin have been preserved, we find that many of the most highly integrated neighborhoods are to be found. To be sure, the income factor has been potent in determining the choice of the neighborhood, but on the whole the national lines, within certain limits, have been more important than income levels. If one undertakes to study the institutions which have persisted in various neighborhoods after being created to meet a need peculiar to a given national group, one finds that they are drawn along the lines of neighborhood boundaries and seldom include outsiders as active participants.

The settlement houses and the various social centers located in these neighborhoods have had to develop their activities to meet the inclinations and group proclivities of these national groups. Hull House in Chicago, Greenwich House and The University Settlement in New York, as well as the many hundreds of other centers of this kind, have had to draw clear lines in their activities to meet neighborhood needs in terms of neighborhood character. Their entire success has been based upon an understanding of the desires and needs of the people and not upon some abstract concept of culture or Americanism, or some other social philosophy alien to the people.

Race is another factor in the development of neighborhoods. Many of the racial groups which have created neighborhood entities have done so not alone because of their economic level or a desire for carrying on their own life in their own way, but because of certain elements of discrimination which prevail as much in the North and West as they do in the South. The Chinese and Japanese in the West have to meet similar conditions, and have created their own centers or neighborhoods in the areas where they could find space to settle, or where through heavy sacrifices in rents they could get a residential foothold from which they expanded as their number increased. To overlook the race and national character of people, and to disregard both the prejudices which have developed against them, or the prejudices which they have acquired against certain American ways of living, is to overlook a most essential condition of housing.

Where these requirements have been overlooked in a housing project, the project has been a failure even under conditions where the shortage of housing is serious and the advantages offered by the new housing are quite out of the ordinary both in rental rates and surroundings.

Cultural Levels. It is strange that cultural levels play a comparatively small part in the determination of neighborhood organization. In each neighborhood there are varieties of categories of cultural levels and cultural activity which in no way interfere with the integrity of the neighborhood. As the cultural level of an individual becomes incompatible with the neighborhood atmosphere, he may leave the neighborhood, but he will not be likely to find another neighborhood in which he could meet those of his cultural needs. On the contrary, as the cultural level rises, the migration is merely away from the original neighborhood and not of necessity into a neighborhood more congenial from the cultural point of view.

I believe that as incomes, culture, and traditional ways of living and thinking and praying either change or become liberalized, the ties of the neighborhood are loosened. While there is a sense of relationship always coming to the fore in neighborhoods which hold the homogeneous lower-income classes, in the better housed sections of our cities an increasing social distance is developed, and this makes of our select residential areas (except perhaps in small suburban towns) merely an incoherent massing of people whose interests, social relationships, and cultural contacts are scattered over large areas with complete disregard of the next-door neighbor. Professor Robert E. Park, who first introduced the term "social distance," and Professor Emery S. Bogardus and Professor Pitirim Sorokin, who have elaborated the significance of the term, present peculiarly interesting opportunities for study in connection with the change that takes place in this social distance when people are moving from an established neighborhood to a new and more prosperous one. This aspect of increased social distance in neighborhood disintegration presents an extremely important problem in the planning of large-scale housing projects.

In connection with the often-mentioned slum clearance efforts, there is always a serious difficulty that must be met if the rehabilitation is to be social as well as physical. As far as physical rehabilitation is concerned, there is little advantage to be gained by merely bringing new investments into a dilapidated residential area. The advantage contemplated is usually assumed to be an advantage to the residents of the district, the so-called neighborhood. My friend, Clarence A. Perry, author of the splendid report *The Rebuilding of Blighted Areas*, gave the study a significant subtitle, *A Study of the Neighborhood Unit in Replanning and Plot Assembly*. It is not quite clear from the report whether the replotting and replanning is for the physical rehabilitation of an area or the rehabilitation through physical replanning of a neighborhood in which people previously in the slums are to be given, through planning, an opportunity for better neighborhood conditions and a more suitable home environment.

It seems to me that the whole movement for slum and blighted area rehabilitation has overlooked the people living in these areas prior to rehabilitation. In this respect I should like to suggest that, before any slum rehabilitation is undertaken, it be made an essential condition for the undertaking that all the manifestations having to do with the human relations be examined and evaluated, and that values worth being preserved should be provided for in the new plotting and planning. Physical rehabilitation of a district resulting in a new standard of tenant selection which completely disregards the original occupants and sets up conditions of occupancy which destroy the original social relations between the people, fails to restore to the people the social value that the slum might contain.

There are few adequate studies of neighborhoods. Many attempts have been made to divide cities into neighborhood units, but in most instances this division was artificial or intended to deal with certain specific problems rather than the more important and more constructive values of normal human relations. If slum rehabilitation is to be made a part of our housing program, it must be backed by certain efforts toward conserving the neighborhood and the pattern of the neighborhood life, which is much more valuable to the lower-income groups than to the higher.

This means that before the process of slum destruction begins, there should be an inventory made of all the assets inherent in the human relationships already established in the district.

A recent statement issued by a member of the New York City Planning Commission contended that slum clearance was of the first moment in housing in this metropolis and that it should, for the time being, take precedence over housing enterprise in outlying districts. I have been unable to find any evidence that this is the best course. In slum clearance the assumption is, either that the people now living in slums would be rehoused in the same neighborhood, or that it would merely mean the clearing up of the slum areas with the purpose of devoting the space to other uses. As slum clearance is carried on by the various public authorities, it is quite obvious that the clearance would have to be fragmentary unless huge sums of money are to be made available for this purpose. Otherwise, individual projects would tend to break into the natural neighborhoods and, owing to the higher rents in the new dwellings, exclude from these neighborhoods families which have a close relation to its life and who could not afford to be rehoused in the new dwellings, unless the subsidies were sufficient to make up the difference between their original rent in the slum and the rent of the new project. What these families could do to secure housing during the interim of reconstruction has not been indicated by this statement. The new occupants of the cleared slum areas are generally alien to the neighborhood and must begin to build up their own neighborhood structure. The facilitating of this process is of the utmost importance.

In the following outline, I have endeavored to give only general suggestion of the lines of inquiry to be considered in the examination of neighborhood manifestations and values. These studies might be extended to include certain psychic factors, as racial conflicts, the stability of the family, the conflicts between various cultural group levels, religious prejudices, public opinion in matters of changing trends in the composition of the population, labor unrest and economic solidarity, and a host of other aspects of the life of the people. What follows should, however, be suggestive of two aspects of the problem of determining the character of neighborhood life and the elements which should be incorporated in any plan which would lay the foundations for housing enterprise as integrated neighborhood centers, rather than as isolated entities having for their function mainly shelter and the usual housing amenities. There is still much to be done by way of study and research before a new concept of neighborhood life could be evolved in harmony with our changing ways of living.

GENERAL OUTLINE OF NEIGHBORHOOD STUDY

GEOGRAPHIC LOCATION

1. Specific character of the land and its configuration.
2. The incidence of access from the rest of the community.
3. Advantages and disadvantages from the point of view of exposure to the elements, vegetation, drainage, water supply, suitability of the land for building purposes, priority of settlement due to access to certain basic occupations or sources of population, and so on.

POPULATION—RACIAL DISTRIBUTION

1. Distribution of nationalities.
2. Families and family sizes.
3. Distribution of ages, birth rates, mortality rates.
4. Susceptibility to certain diseases.
5. Density of population in relation to rooms, floor space, and land area.
6. Drifts of population within the neighborhood, and interneighborhood trends.
7. Length of stay in neighborhood.

ECONOMIC LEVELS—TRADES AND OCCUPATIONS

1. Prevalence of work among married and unmarried women.
2. Period of industrial efficiency and self-support.
3. Child labor.
4. Prevailing wages.
5. Trade unionism.
6. Relation between services, trade, and industrial occupations.
7. Property ownership and home ownership.

ECONOMIC ORGANIZATION—LOCAL AND COMMUNITY BANKS

1. Savings institutions and the per-capita savings in given periods of time.
2. Cooperative organizations for business and for mutual aid.
3. Building and Loan Associations.
4. Mutual insurance organizations.
5. Local relief organizations.
6. Burial organizations.
7. Fraternal orders with an economic purpose.

In connection with the above phase of the inquiry, emphasis will be placed upon the race and nationality, affiliations, and such cultural differences as might play a part in selecting memberships and participants.

FINANCIAL CONTROL

This study will deal with the extent of economic control emanating from within the neighborhood and the control which is in the hands of people and agencies living outside of the neighborhood. The investment in various neighborhood enterprises, and the sources from which the money in these enterprises has been derived, should give some idea of the amount of economic independence which the neighborhood enjoys. Property ownerships, mortgages, control of financial institutions, and investments in business, industrial, recreational, and educational enterprises, should furnish some conception of the economic independence of the neighborhood.

POLITICAL COMPLEXION

This study should give some inkling of the relation between political affiliations and the character of the population. Occupational, national, racial and religious groupings, education, connection with some labor or political organization, earning capacity, property ownership, economic level, and the employer factor in politics should be considered.

INDEPENDENT POLITICAL ORGANIZATIONS

This would include every expression of political organization within the limits of the neighborhood which functions, either in local organizations forming part of a city or nationwide political party of the recognized order, or as subversive organizations having for their purpose a new order of things. The sizes of memberships, the political philosophy underlying these organizations, and the manner in which they are organized and function would be essential subjects of the study. The various activities of those organizations as economic, educational, cultural, political, and propaganda agencies would reveal their value as factors in neighborhood solidarity and cooperation.

STANDARDS OF LIVING

These studies would include not only a sampling of typical family budgets, but also a study of the relation between incomes, rents, room occupancy, education afforded to children, education-continuation activities among the adults, special training for children, forms of and expenditures for recreation, travel, books, phonographs, telephones, automobiles, radios, and so forth. It would also include memberships in various organizations having as their objectives educational, recreational, and cultural activities of various kinds. Some differentiation might be made between the various types of the population.

EMPLOYMENT

1. Segregation and distribution of centers of employment.
2. Radii of travel between homes and employment centers.
3. Business classification in relation to population and employment load.
4. Comparative studies of employment data for city and neighborhood.
5. Wage scales and standard union or legal wages.
6. Unemployment, ages, sexes, occupations, and organized and unorganized trades.
7. Subsistence margin of the unemployed.
8. Unemployed, and stability of population.

BUSINESS CAPACITY

1. Volume of various types of business, as to money and quantity.
2. Relation between population and business.
3. Zoning:
   a. Maximum capacity uses in relation to business, industrial zones.
   b. Actual and legal zones.
   c. Standards of living and local market prices as a basis for business security.

4. Ephemeral business development.
5. Forms of business exploitation.
   a. Rackets.
6. Bankruptcies.
7. Credit methods for wholesale and retail consumers.

HOUSING

1. Rents.
2. Space available.
3. Space occupied per person and per family—congestion.
4. Home ownerships.
5. Condition of buildings.
6. Types of buildings and types of construction.
7. Floating population in its relation to family, commercial, charity, or municipal accommodation.
8. History of the housing development of the district.
9. Legal factors.
10. Planning factors.
11. Business and industrial factors.
12. Obsolescence of buildings and appurtenances.
13. Transitions in occupancy and their consequences.
14. Rental history.
15. Steps in assessing methods and valuations.
16. Tax delinquencies.
17. Foreclosures and mortgages.
18. Present distribution and character of ownerships.
19. Relation of ownerships to maintenance.
20. Relation of ownerships to rent.
21. Rents and incomes, accommodations, and family sizes.
22. Levels of rent in relation to specific floor occupancies.
23. Cellar habitations.
24. Methods and extent of remodeling in relation to cost and rents.
25. Housing shortages as a whole and according to sizes and types of habitations.
26. Available open spaces within building blocks.
    a. Possibilities of using these spaces for light, ventilation, and recreational activities.
27. Fire protection in buildings.
    a. Fire-resisting construction.
    b. Fire-protecting devices.
    c. Fire-protection service.

OPEN SPACES

1. Street—amount of space, width, and uses.
2. Uses for transit.
3. Uses for business—pushcarts, sidewalk trade.
4. Play types—number of persons, ages, sexes, and so forth.
5. Local traffic classified.

APARTMENT HOUSE, GREENBELT, MARYLAND. A FARM SECURITY ADMINISTRA-
TION DEVELOPMENT.

Photograph by Farm Security Administration.

APARTMENT HOUSE IN GREENBELT, MARYLAND. A FARM SECURITY
ADMINISTRATION DEVELOPMENT.

6. Through traffic classified.
7. Streetcars.
8. Cleaning.
9. Washing; snow removal.
10. Repairs.
11. Lighting.
12. Policing.
13. Planning.
    a. Changes in character of street.
    b. Street orientation in relation to city.
    c. Possible changes in traffic trends.

MARKETS

1. Extent and character.
2. Types of food.
3. Patronage.
4. Method of renting spaces.
5. Places of residence of tradespeople.
6. Radius of patronage.
7. Ownership and arrangement.
8. Public control.
9. Cleanliness.
10. Rents and volume of business.

PLAY SPACES

1. Parks.
   a. Sizes, types, and relation to distribution of population uses.
2. Playgrounds.
   a. Municipal.
   b. School playgrounds and roof spaces, with studies of amount and type of use similar to play-area studies.
   c. Social service organizations.
   d. Churches.
   e. Private organizations (clubs, fraternal orders, and lodges).
      Note: Studies of playgrounds should include: (1) forms of activity; (2) supervision; (3) clientele; (4) relation to population, children, adolescents, adults; (5) special neighborhood outdoor activities—traditional, racial, national; (6) unused open areas capable of development for playgrounds: public lands, private unoccupied areas, backyards, abandoned waterfront structures, and so on.

OTHER PLAY SPACES

1. Range of use of play and recreation spaces in adjoining areas.
2. Cooperation and antagonisms.

COMMERCIAL AMUSEMENTS

1. Local neighborhood.
2. Adjoining areas.
3. Types of clientele.

4. Competitive elements.
5. Effects upon the neighborhood.
6. Police control.
7. Relation between delinquency and commercial amusement.
8. Changes in character of amusements.
9. Business volume.
10. Relation of population to attendance.
11. Competition between non-profit and commercial amusements.
12. The development of commercial recreation over a period of a year.
13. The investment represented by commercial recreation.
14. Profits derived from commercial recreation.
15. Contributions in various forms of taxation.
16. Cost of public supervision in relation to special recreation taxes.

EDUCATION
1. Public institutions.
   a. Various types of children's schools.
   b. Capacity and minimum requirements.
   c. Access to places of residence.
   d. Traffic in relation to safety, noise, discipline.
   e. Traffic arteries as factors in school location.
   f. Age of schools and adequacy of building standards.
   g. Obsolescence in school construction.
   h. Mobility of school population.
2. Human elements in schools.
   a. Distribution of grades by ages, sex, race, nationality, with comparative data for city and other neighborhoods.
   b. Range of ages and grades when school period ceases.
   c. Truancy.
   d. Problems of school and extramural discipline.
   e. Selection of teachers, length of service, preparation, and grading.
   f. Management, administration, and discipline personnel.
3. Accessory educational facilities.
   a. Public and private libraries.
   b. Art schools.
   c. Music schools.
   d. Adult education facilities.
   e. Crafts.
   f. Business schools.

These would represent public-school activities, settlements, churches, special cultural organizations, university extension, private institutions commercially managed, and so on.

In connection with this aspect of the study, it may be possible to approximate the cultural needs of the neighborhood and the relation between neighborhood agencies and city-wide organizations.

PUBLIC OPINION
1. Local daily or weekly press.
2. Circulation of papers and literature bearing on matters of public interest.

3. Special organizations devoted to social and economic opinion or specific philosophies.
4. Character and discussion subjects at public gatherings.
5. Protests.
6. Parades.
7. Participation in strikes, and so forth.

This study might develop data upon which to base some conception of the character of leadership and social and economic thinking characteristic of the neighborhood.

DELINQUENCY

A study of delinquency with correlations as to age, sex, race, nationality, type of crime, length of sentence, repeaters, parole, and so on, would of necessity be part of this investigation.

POVERTY AND DEPENDENCY

This aspect of the study would deal with various forms of relief—public, philanthropic, mutual aid, alms. Special emphasis might be placed upon the changes in relief according to types of cases over a period of a decade or more. By including the periods of depressions since 1921, some idea of the margins of subsistence of various groups might be derived.

HEALTH

1. Morbidity and mortality rates by age, sex, race, nationality, occupation, and so on.
2. Prenatal care.
3. Baby clinics.
4. Private hospitals.
5. Private clinics.
6. Dental clinics.
7. Health education in schools, factories, shops, homes, churches, settlements, and so on.
8. Private physicians.
9. Dentists.
10. Medical care of specialized types.
11. Electrical treatment.
12. Baths.
13. Quacks.

This study would involve an examination of standards and relations between needs and service resources, costs to patients, and community or other welfare agencies. Ethical standards, legal control, beliefs, prejudices, fears, and so on, of patients, and the effectiveness of various services, would also be studied.

Inquiries of this kind may give the planner and the architect a new vision of the type of dwelling that would best meet the purpose of bringing people together and making their lives part of a community in which they could function and express themselves as normal citizens and good neighbors.

The neighborhood, if capable of being determined, presents special aspects of the housing problem. In projecting any large-scale housing scheme, it is essential to consider the neighborhood as it may be related to the future of the project, as well as its relation to the community. Thus the concept of housing becomes not alone a matter of considering where land can be secured cheaply and in what quantities, but also one of determining the relation between the choice of a site to the broader factors of the community plan.

In view of the fact that housing is being dealt with as a community responsibility and its solution is dependent upon local authorities, it is not out of place here to point out the fact that many of the sites within those communities may not be as desirable as others outside their political boundaries.

Political Space. This is the study of the site in its relation to the political entity of which it is a part. Much of modern housing is located within the community in which a substandard condition exists. Housing, particularly for the lower-income families, must be placed where it would have all of the advantages of proximity to places of employment, education, amusement, and the cultural requirements of their class and social level. It must not be burdened with land costs in excess of the proportion which buildings normally bear to land cost and should be endowed with all of the free space which the cramped quarters of the average families make necessary for outdoor life. These conditions are not always available in our cities, particularly cities where congestion is prevalent.

There is also frequently a question as to whether adequate parcels of land could be secured in one locality to make large-scale housing possible without heavy costs for land. Some communities in Europe, particularly in England and Germany, have resorted to removal of population from the political areas in need of housing to outlying districts where land is cheap and space plentiful. The London County Council has actually built a large settlement outside the County of London. Such lack of local patriotism in United States cities would be assailed by every real-estate board in the country.

Economic Space. The lower-income groups must meet the cost of transit from home to work and from home to school or other cultural centers. The question as to how housing projects could best be placed, where transportation would be not only sufficient and planned to meet the needs of the workers, but where it would be made unessential to most members of the family because of proximity to both work and other centers, must be met by a careful study of the space to be selected for housing. Rent and transportation must be calculated together. Two or three members of a family may expend in transportation to and from work the equivalent of the rent for an additional room which the family might need.

What is true of the political and economic considerations of space should be applied with equal care to considerations of social and cultural requirements, so that the particular housing undertaking may not only develop its own individuality as a neighborhood, but may find it possible to fit into the pattern of every aspect of the lives of the people and their relations to all the advantages the community affords.

This may imply a different outlook upon housing: namely, the inclusion, in the consideration of site, of all factors which a specific area may require in order to become self-sufficient in respect to all essentials of normal human activities.

The time element may not seem very important, but as cities and regions grow and develop, there are constant shifts in the pattern of population distributions, new and unavoidable encroachments upon established land uses and readjustments due to changes in methods of production, distribution, and working standards. These affect the future of the city or the region, or both, in a manner that leaves much to be desired in matters of stability of investment and continuity of neighborhood development and neighborhood integration. A survey which prepares the ground for a housing project should therefore not only be concerned with the important facts as to conditions and possibilities for meeting all of the needs of the present, but should also take into consideration the permanency of such a project in its relation to shifting communal conditions and trends extending over a considerable period. Most housing projects are designed to meet present-day needs, and yet the life of the investment is calculated to continue a generation or longer. It is therefore not out of order to require of the project survey a consideration of the plans, laws, trends, controls, and advantages which the site of a housing project may afford in the course of a generation. It is only in this manner that controls could be set up to insure permanance of the project.

The Human Element. Housing which disregards the essential human element and the large range of variants in the requirements of its occupants can not be said to be successful. The most up-to-date plumbing equipment, the most careful selection of materials, the greatest protection against fire, and the best sanitary provisions for ventilation, may still fail to meet the human requirements which make housing a device for the carrying on of normal family relations and social well-being. Indeed, the elements which make up family membership are so diversified that their consideration is as important as the structural requirements for safety and convenience.

Age Groups. It is, of course, difficult to develop plans for a specific distribution of age groups, but there is no justification for failure to recognize these groups in planning housing projects. As age groups are constantly changing and their requirements are changing with them, it is impossible to develop individual projects within a given age-distribution standard. It is conceivable that when the same careful consideration is given to private as to public enterprises, the variety of types of dwellings will meet every need and families will select their dwelling places in accordance with their particular needs.

Each age presents its own requirements. A rough classification from the point of view of these requirements might be as follows:

> Children under 2 years of age.
> Children between 2 and 4 years of age.
> Children between 4 and 6 years of age.
> Children between 6 and 10 years of age.
> Children between 10 and 14 years of age.
> Children between 14 and 18 years of age.
> Adults under 21 living with their families.
> Parents under 50 years of age.
> Those over 50.

Each of these groups requires certain facilities peculiar to its age, and these extend to both the inside and the outside of the dwelling. It is obvious that, where little babies are to be cared for, it is essential to make provision for balconies or places where they can be given a certain amount of fresh air. It is also obvious that as soon as they are able to move about, they need certain spaces where, under the supervision of a parent or older person, they can be safe. When the supervision of the parent can no longer be depended upon, playgrounds with proper supervision and the maximum of safety must be provided. The variety of these play spaces can not be dependent upon the number of families housed, but rather must be determined by the requirements of the ages of children living in these buildings and the kind of equipment they need for play.

The adults may also require certain facilities for relaxation and social intercourse. These provisions might consist of a common hall, park areas, a little theatre, shops for carrying on manual activities, cooperative organization facilities, or similar provisions.

A housing project must of necessity assume a certain distribution of ages in order to meet the needs of this age distribution. Whether the age distribution is based upon some hypothetical assumption, or whether it is based upon actual facts as we find them in districts where families are living for whom provisions are to be made, must be determined beforehand. It is true that many projects are developed first, and the selection of the families is made after the buildings are ready for occupancy. It is also true, however, that where the project is developed without a realistic consideration of age distributions, there is difficulty in coordinating tenant needs with available dwelling units.

Insofar as sex distribution is concerned, there is also to be taken into account the fact that after a certain age the separation of sexes among children is quite as essential as provisions for play.

The aged, who have received so little consideration in our housing projects, are also entitled to a place in the scheme. Long flights of stairs, lack of adequate open space away from the noises of the playground, and rooms not sufficiently isolated from the daily hubbub of family life are hard on the aged. We have often resorted to institutional care, a costly and inhuman treatment of normal human beings desiring to remain in the family fold. Is there any reason why in planning housing projects the aged should not receive the consideration that is due them?

All housing enterprise, private or public, must take into account the human factors. The pamphlet prepared by Miss Catharine F. Lansing, entitled *Studies of Community Planning in Terms of the Life Span* and published by the New York City Housing Authority in 1937, should prove of great value to those who prepare the social material upon which the physical site and building plan is to be based.

The Economic Basis. Enough has been said in our discussion of rents and incomes to give a general idea of the limits within which housing built for various groups could be expected to pay. Any community concerned with the solution of its housing problem should, before undertaking any building, determine upon the groups which, in view of their rent-paying capacity, most need accommodations. It is not enough to increase the available number of dwellings and hope that those who most need them would live in them. The community must face the problem and determine beforehand what income group needs to be provided for, and must calculate rents not in terms of costs but in terms of family income. The difference between what they can pay and what they need would have to be made up by the community, state, or federal government. I am not entirely opposed to providing for families which are by no means of the lowest level of income, but I am convinced that the more accurate the calculations are as to the rentals required in the end and the types of families to be accommodated, the sooner we shall gain an accurate picture of the task to be accomplished. In other words, it is conceivable that tenant selection could be carried on before, rather than after, the project is planned. By this I do not mean an advance allocation of families to the particular apartments, but a closer correlation between specific family types and plans.

The Legal Aspect. In the chapter on legislation, I outlined not only the various forms of existing legislation but also the various legal provisions that would help in the improvement of housing conditions. A survey of existing legislation in the light of what is needed and could be attempted under the most favorable conditions would be of very great value. Often lawmakers are ready to provide the kind of laws that are needed, if the advantages of such legislation are clearly pointed out. In March 1937, the National Emergency Council published a *Comprehensive Housing Legislation Chart*, prepared by the Central Housing Committee, which gives in outline the condition of the law in every state of the Union. This chart, while of great value as a guide for local studies, is by no means to be taken as final, since conditions are constantly changing and much housing legislation either applies specifically to particular communities or is actually enacted by these communities under enabling acts of the state legislature. Many building codes and housing regulations are of local character, and many of the methods of enforcement vary with individual localities.

Most of our legislative enactments fail to take into account the lower-income groups and the requirements for economy and simplicity. We can not assume that existing laws are fixed when we consider housing projects. With the growth of large-scale housing as a general practice must come a revision of housing legislation based on the experience of the past and on demands of the new enterprises. A critical analysis of existing legislation is therefore an important part of the housing survey.

The Role of Public Agencies. The development of a large-scale housing scheme can not be conceived of without giving consideration to the services which the community should, could, or might render in order to insure the success of the undertaking. The supply of school facilities, playgrounds, the care of the sick, the building and maintenance of the roads, the fixing of tax rates, the many types of cultural and recreation enterprises—all are essential requirements of housing. It is obvious that, unless these services are available, the mere improvement of the physical character of the building would in no way insure the necessary advantage to be derived from better housing. This consideration implies not alone the legal ability of the various local authorities to render a particular service, but the disposition on the part of local officials to do so. If a school is needed, would it be provided by the local school board? If a playground is required, would the cost of the land and the upkeep, as well as the supervision, be provided by the community without charging the expense against the new development? These are not mere questions of better living conditions, but questions of finance which may so affect rents that the main object of the housing project would have to be modified to meet a new set of conditions and a different range of rental rates.

If a street readjustment is required in order to secure privacy and safety, would the city fathers be willing to abandon streets which are no longer an advantage to the particular housing plan? If grade crossings present a menace to children traveling to and from school, would the municipality or some other agency assume the responsibility and the expense entailed by the required change?

If hospital facilities are inadequate in the district and if clinics are needed, can it be expected that provisions would be made for medical services without additional costs to the project?

In other words, a housing enterprise requires a whole set of new and improved services in order to make it most effective. What is the city, town, or state ready to do in order to make this possible without heavy expense to the owners, whether they are official bodies like the local housing authority or private individuals prompted by philanthropic or purely profit-making interests?

The carrying out of a housing scheme of any magnitude is not a mere problem of planning the right kind of buildings for the right kind of people, but a "team haul" in which every agency which has any social, economic, governmental, or financial interest must participate to the extent to which its service would aid in establishing and keeping up standards.

The Role of the Surveyor. The architect and the site planner are the ultimate authority to whom are entrusted the facts of the survey, so that they may translate them into an economical and socially coherent structure. The nature of the investigation itself is, however, not architectural or of a site planning nature. The facts are social, economic, legal, financial, administrative; in short, they are the key to the human relations that exist between individuals as members of a family, as citizens, as producers, as members of certain cultural, economic, and social strata of society. The question is, do the professional skills of the architect or site planner measure up to the task involved in taking social data and translating them into suitable living quarters? A store, a shop, a factory have clearly defined objectives to take into account; in housing, a whole system of social relationships must be synthesized and given expression.

In this respect, we must say that only a few of our professional men skilled in the art of design and construction are capable of wise social interpretation in relation to housing. This is the reason why so many well conceived housing enterprises have failed to meet their original objectives.

I have outlined in the chapter on education the requirements of housing education, but I must reiterate that unless we combine social knowledge with technical skill we shall never achieve good housing. It is not enough to have accumulated vast quantities of housing facts, no matter how accurate and well conceived they are. The final test is the ability of the architect and site planner to translate the facts into coherent and functioning living entities.

The Role of the Architect. Once the social requirements have been settled, there still remain many problems which the plan must solve. One of these is the matter of the inner use of the building as what Le Corbusier calls a "living machine." This means adjusting function not only to use, but to convenient use and labor-saving use. Alexander Klein, the Russian architect, who has done such careful work in developing these very aspects of housing, has recently published *Das Einfamilienhaus* (*The One-Family Dwelling*), in which he gives careful and, to me, rational plans for the arrangement of rooms, their size, their relation to each other, their connections, and all other provisions which make use easy, safe, attractive, and economical. We have no such studies in the United States. A careful study of the ways of living of various types of families, and the application of the knowledge derived from such a study to the technique of home planning for use, would be of great value to modern architecture.

In this connection it should be kept in mind that the most intelligent floor plan can be made useless by furniture which fails to harmonize with the interior of the dwelling as to either use or esthetic character. There is no reason, therefore, why the architect while designing the floor plan could not also endeavor to plan the furniture arrangements, at least insofar as the wall space and floor use demand. People moving into new dwellings often make radical changes in their furniture. By suggesting rational furniture arrangements, the tenants would be able to evaluate their ability to use the apartment and, incidentally, to have some guiding information when new furnishings are to be purchased. While I make this suggestion as to furniture, I feel that there is danger of architectural enterprise being projected into the design of furniture that would fit the apartment rather than the needs and resources of the family and its habit of life. This would mean a certain amount of investigation into the ways in which families to be housed acquire and use furniture and the ways in which improvements could be made by providing storage space, convertible tables, beds, and so on. Many proposals have been advanced regarding the possible reductions in floor space per apartment. It would seem that such economies of space could be attained only by taking into account the most minute details concerning the ways and requirements of efficient and effective home life.

While the home may be looked upon as a living machine, the fact is that this mechanism must be operated within specifically limited resources and in accordance with a great variety of mental habits and traditional ways of doing things. If his work is to be successful, the architect must approximate a synthesis of many factors. His work of planning must be based as much on providing for smooth functioning of the family as for adequate provisions for the practical use of space.

I recall an instance when one of my friends wanted a prominent architect to design and supervise the construction of a new home. He hesitated to accept the commission. As he was also my friend, I was asked to intervene. The architect finally suggested that his willingness to undertake the work would depend upon the willingness of the client to permit the architect to live in his home for two weeks. "This man is a personality and his house must not only express this personality, but must be suitable to his peculiar needs," said the architect. The commission was finally accepted on these terms. I mention this incident as suggesting that perhaps if the architects would live in some of the old tenements or even in a slum tenement for a time they would learn more about low-cost housing design than is conveyed in the schools of architecture.

SUMMARY

The treatment of the survey from the point of view of its application to housing, which I have ventured upon in this chapter, is by no means to be looked upon as a guide to such surveys. All that I have endeavored to do is to bring before the reader the vast implications which the planning of housing projects entails, to suggest how scientific information and skills must be translated into the fiscal and social plan. It has seemed to me for a long time that the architect, instead of bringing his profession within the range of the newer outlook on housing and the community, has capitulated to the engineer, who has himself been unable to bring modern social science into harmony with structural design.

The architect and the site planner are faced with the task of evolving an integrated philosophy of planning and building. This can be achieved only after they have evolved a social philosophy of living compatible with the realities and possibilities of modern society and its resources. At no time in the history of modern society has the opportunity been greater. The reconstruction of our cities is going on, and large-scale housing is giving the architect and site planner his first opportunity to utilize masses and space in a manner that may give a new expression to efficient and effective living. This is a new mission entrusted to these technicians. Their success will depend not alone upon their skill, but upon their ability to bring within their professional practices a social philosophy that is vital and dynamic.

Conclusions

Chapter XI

CONCLUSIONS

For over three generations housing reform has played an important part in every welfare program in this country. During the last half decade new hopes have come to those who had despaired of any widespread improvements or of any serious financial participation on the part of the government in bringing housing within the sphere of national concern. Splendid examples of comparatively low-rental housing have sprung up in more than fifty cities. The financial structure of the real-estate field has been benefited by the activities of the federal government through the Home Owners Loan Corporation, The Home Loan Bank, The Federal Housing Administration, and in the earlier days of this encouraging era by the Reconstruction Finance Corporation.

It may therefore seem rather gratuitous and ungracious to assume a critical and pessimistic attitude at a time when there is so much promise and action in line with what housing reformers have been striving to attain for so many years. It is hoped that the reader will not be led to the conclusion that we are dissatisfied with the tempo of action or with the various forms of housing activity which have been launched. The fundamental difficulty is not with what is being accomplished, but rather with the failure to realize that these accomplishments are not intended to solve the housing problem for the people who are most in need of better housing. The latter cannot be benefited without more fundamental changes, not alone in government policies and methods of procedure, but also in the basic business methods and public controls of building. Implications as to methods of finance, taxation, land values, market controls, interest rates, location and distribution of land uses, and the relation of habitation to the purposes and functions of communities—all these are involved.

There is no community that is free from slums. Indeed, even in areas which are free from slums and where the general housing standards are reasonably acceptable, the failure in the past to take account of changing conditions and to consider neighborhood and community relationships in building enterprise will eventually result in the type of obsolescence that is mainly responsible for our slums and blighted areas. No one can deny the value of the fragmentary achievements of the past and the bolder achievements of the present. But the fact remains that with seven million families living in slums or near-slum areas, both in large and small cities, it is idle to expect that within a reasonable time government action will wipe out slums and create in their place modern living conditions.

There was a time when we placed our faith in legislation. After thirty-five years of legislative effort, however, the slums have become worse and, furthermore, enlarged by once decent residential areas that have degenerated through neglect, shifts in population, or for other reasons. Even if government funds to the extent of a billion dollars a year were to be made available, it would still take at least a generation before the slums could be cleared of their present substandard housing.

Where government has taken a part in promoting private enterprise, as in the case of the Federal Housing Administration, which only insures and does not contribute to the investment, the standard of housing that can be developed is entirely too high to take care of the vast majority of families with low incomes. Indeed, the standard has in many instances been too high even for the normal earning capacity of skilled workers when their families are of normal size. This is not by any means the fault of the setup of the Federal Housing Administration, but is inherent in the economic factors which control the business of housing and building practice. Although we all have a high respect for the methods of procedure set up by the Federal Housing Administration, we are forced to admit that its effectiveness as a controlling factor, not alone in the promotion of housing but also in dealing with housing according to need rather than according to available investment capital, is practically nil.

The various suggestions for legislation and methods of control which have been made in the course of the present discussion are predicated not upon slum clearance, but upon the clearing away of the obstacles which stand in the way of building enterprise, along lines consistent with the market needs and the purchasing power of the tenants or owners. We need more than a mere housing meliorism which will help a minor portion of the population to live in better houses; we need to create favorable conditions which will raise the standard of all housing without adding to the economic burdens of the occupants. It is not just the slum dweller who is in need of improved conditions, badly though he may need them, but the millions of other families which live in respectable but cramped and unsatisfactory quarters, which although provided with the essentials of sanitation and with the outward trappings of respectability, are nevertheless badly planned for normal family life and are lacking in the individuality and the fitness which help to make home life a spiritual force.

That housing is not an isolated building or set of buildings, but only a component part of a larger neighborhood and community pattern, should be evident to everyone. This means not only the revamping of the economy and technique of planning and building, but also a readjustment of housing to the functions of the community, and the reorganization of the pattern of the neighborhood and the community to the needs of housing. In this connection, it must be admitted that partial slum clearance, which leaves the old confusion with all its evils and obsolete services, can hardly be accepted as a thoroughgoing improvement of living conditions. Slum clearance, therefore, means not alone the clearing away of obsolete buildings, but also the discarding of everything that may render improved housing ineffectual in promoting normal community life.

After nearly thirty years of study and experience in housing I have come to regard this subject not as a special reform, but as an important civic imperative which affects or should affect all of us. A new spiritual vision and a new economic outlook must be developed. Rigid legal forms must be tested in the light of their effectiveness in making the economy of life harmonize with the grace of living. New patterns of community functioning must be evolved, and ways of bringing them to realization must be devised. In fact, a whole new set of fundamental social, economic, legal, and technological principles must be woven into a philosophy of living which will find final expression in a program of housing the masses under community conditions intended to conserve not alone health, but every effort and aspiration which has individual and social value.

Housing Literature

HOUSING LITERATURE

The torrent of housing literature which has kept both government and private printing presses busy during the last half decade has become so overwhelming that we have lost the sense of balance as to what is essential and what is merely ephemeral in the discussion that is raging. Bibliographers have been vying with one another in the length of the lists of books, pamphlets, and public documents which they can record by rummaging through newspapers, other people's bibliographies, library card catalogues, and periodicals. Much of this material is listed again and again, not because of its intrinsic value, but by force of the number of times it has found its way into bibliographical listings. Indeed, a whole book has recently been written as a doctor's dissertation which has for its object the derivation of fundamental principles on housing out of the weight of reiteration of housing commonplaces.

The type of housing bookworm who never ventures beyond the title page and offers a form of literary accountancy which merely lists the goods but gives no intimation as to their value, performs a questionable service. The literary pottage which such books afford confuses and misleads the uninitiated and is of no particular value to the serious and informed student.

The vaster the listing of books, the less likely is it that the record represents actual familiarity with their contents. Even in some of the best of books, we find a mélange of references indicating either ignorance of content or an utter lack of any epicurean discrimination. I should say that a large amount of the writing that has found its way into print in the last half decade is neither palatable nor nourishing. Since it has become fashionable to discuss the subject of housing and to write about it, there has been a lowering of the standards of originality, clarity, and vision so essential to lasting literary value. Much of this writing has served to intensify the emotions, but it has failed to nourish the reason.

So far as emotional values are concerned, the student of housing would do better to read Dostoevski, Dickens, Zola, Arnold Bennett, or any one of a dozen writers who have taken soundings of the depths of our city life and have exposed the mildew which accumulates on the edges of urban civilization and engulfs the lives of the less privileged. Indeed, those who attempt to focus our attention on housing merely as the deterioration of certain of our habitations, rather than on the larger implication for which the whole of our civilization must be held responsible, are like those who, either by design or through ignorance, "bawle for freedom in their senseless mood, and still revolt when truth would set them free."

GENERAL WORKS ON HOUSING

Assuming that to read all the literature on housing is a task impossible and perhaps undesirable, even for the most gullible and those having the most leisure, it is important to give the reader only such bibliographical hints as will fit the framework of the book to which it is appended and be free from those accumulations of commonplace writings which are a hindrance to creative thinking.

As already stated, housing is merely a symptom, an incident in the general accumulation of problems of human welfare and human relations. The presentation of vast statistical evidence of the prevalence of unsanitary conditions, lack of light and ventilation, congestion, lack of privacy, or fire hazards is, of course, important. It is more important, however, to realize and understand what these conditions are doing, not alone to the bodies of people, but to their souls, to their usefulness as members of society, and to society itself. To achieve this end, it is not enough to read a book about housing. I know of no such book which is written with the literary technique, the persuasive magic, and the penetration necessary to vitalize and lend originality and vision to the interpretation of the slum as a moulder of human life and as the tragic expression of our civic failure. For such a work we must resort to the literature of both past and present. The tools of reform must be forged by scientific knowledge. The dynamic force behind these tools must be sampled in the emotional and inspirational realm which belongs to literature and the arts.

In the teaching of housing, we are too prone to circumscribe the subject and endeavor to draw as sharp a line between slums and the rest of the community as our clumsy methods of social measurement will permit. Out of this tendency has grown a sense of special concern that housing be brought to the minimum of decency consistent with an undisturbed social order. The criteria are always limited within the confines of practical politics, practical finance, and practical philanthropy. No suggestions are made for ideal conditions, no dreams expressed of a utopian communal development in which housing would reach the highest, rather than the lowest, level consistent with human capacity to enjoy a better way of living. It seems to me that the time has come for bringing into the study of housing and the building up of its objectives new and wider horizons, and less recognition of the lag which an economic system imposes upon the pace of social progress. Indeed, I should want to see housing taught with a utopian outlook, an outlook that would bring into focus new criteria of ways of living, free from the meliorism of modern philanthropy. Toward this end we should examine not only the theories of the social scientist, but also the dreams of those utopians who see in the city of the future a synthesis of all that human aspiration is capable of formulating and who are working toward its realization. I would feed the imagination of students with the thought-provoking philosophy of Plato's *Republic*, Sir Thomas More's *Utopia*, Campanella's *City of the Sun*, Francis Bacon's *The New Atlantis*, and the scores of other creative works that have moulded prophecies for the future of mankind out of the miseries and discontent of their times. I would not overlook the planning efforts of the more practical idealists of the Renaissance, who, aware of the shortcomings of cities of the Middle Ages, labored to bring about a new form of city life that would meet the aspirations of a new age with a new way of living. Such technicians as Antonio Averlino Filareti, Leon Batista Alberti, Francesco Colonnas, or Francesco di Giorgio Martini—to mention only a few—have made important contributions to the efforts which characterized the Renaissance as a reinterpreter of the meaning of life and its physical implementation. Even the immortal Leonardo da Vinci conceived a new type of city which represented, however, his contempt, rather than his sympathy, for the lower classes.

In so-called "modern" times many ideal city schemes have been presented. These range from the socialistic communities suggested by Fourier and St. Simon and the international proposal of a world center by Hendrik Christian Andersen, to the motor-age town of Radburn. To understand housing, one can not progress in a civic vacuum or only in an atmosphere of benevolence prompted by the misery of a special class. One must brace the concept of housing against a new concept of modern living. This can be brought about only by creating an awareness of factual evidence as to the need for better housing, reinforced by an outlook which has historical perspective and vision transcending the difficulties of the present in laying a foundation for the future.

I have digressed from the main subject of housing literature because I believe that the foundation of all fundamental social advance must be prompted, first, by an understanding of the basic relations involved in bringing about this advance, and second, by the light which a well trained imaginative mind can throw upon the path that must be followed in order to realize social change.[1]

STANDARD WORKS ON HOUSING

Despite the great effort that has characterized the work of housing reform in Germany, the most important single work on housing which embraces the essential phases of the subject as we think of it today is still Dr. Rudolph Eberstadt's *Handbuch des Wohnungswesens und der Wohnungsfrage*. This, although published nearly thirty years ago, is the one work which deals with housing as a broad national problem. No social or economic institution or agency bearing a relation to the subject has been neglected. Aside from the standards of construction, which have become somewhat outmoded, the fundamental principles are as sound today as they were the year the book was first published. It is to be regretted that it has never been translated. Even though its main sources of information are German, its outlook is definitely international. This work was preceded by a two-volume work, also in German, from the pen of Dr. L. Pohle, of Frankfurt, *Die Wohnungsfrage* (Leipzig, 1910). For clarity of statement and general development of the pattern of community planning as the leading factor in a permanent housing program, it has never been excelled.

For a general discussion of housing from the point of view of French urban communities, in particular of the City of Paris, one must look to a small volume published in 1913 under the title *Le logement dans les villes*, by George-Cahen. It is a compact work dealing with the development of the housing movement in French urban communities and with the activities, agencies, and legislative efforts intended to promote better living conditions. Henri Sellier's *La crise du logement et l'intervention publique*, a monumental work in four volumes, published in 1921, gives a thorough picture of the conditions, needs, and measures taken to insure better housing. While this represents a monumental task, it lacks a rounded outlook and is more a survey than a carefully developed discussion of the broader implications of the subject.

For a comparative study of housing reform in various European countries up to 1913, one should consult the book by Henri Biget entitled *Le logement de l'ouvrier*. It is a carefully compiled document of considerable historical value, giving a clear idea of the rate of development of the various types of housing activity up to

[1] For a list of general housing literature, see Aronovici, Carol, "The Planner's Five-Foot Shelf," in *Survey Graphic*, September, 1936.

the time of its publication. It is particularly valuable because it gives the full text of many of the various laws having to do with the promotion of housing enterprise under government influence and with government help.

The literature on American housing is particularly rich in textbooks of a general nature. To this literature no one has contributed more than Dr. Edith Elmer Wood, who has covered the general field in a scholarly manner in three volumes: *Housing the Unskilled Wage Earner* (1919), *Housing Progress in Western Europe* (1923), and *Recent Trends in American Housing* (1931). The last volume does not, of course, contain any data regarding the recent housing movement under the New Deal initiated by President Franklin D. Roosevelt, nor does it deal with legislative enactments which have resulted from the New Deal so far as they affect housing finance and standards. Although one may be inclined to take issue with some of the economic theories advanced by Dr. Wood, her general treatment of the subject is always clear, fair, and based upon a broad social outlook.

Miss Catherine Bauer's *Modern Housing* (1934) will long remain a standard work, both because of its thoroughness and because of the larger implication which she brings into focus regarding the cause of present housing conditions and the necessary remedies. Her knowledge and understanding of the methods and motives of European housing reform make her contribution bearing on this subject particularly valuable.

The newer housing students are prone to forget the vigorous work of Lawrence Veiller, who was largely instrumental in giving housing legislation in this country its first real impetus. While Mr. Veiller was essentially a conservative and has remained so in matters of public financing of housing, his book *Housing Reform* (1910) is still a valuable contribution on the subject, particularly in respect to securing the enactment of favorable legislation. My own little booklet, *Housing and the Housing Problem*, published ten years later, may prove of some use to students who assume that only within the last few years has the discussion of housing reform extended beyond the stage of restrictive legislation.

For an understanding of the background of congestion, slums, blight, and the various land policies which have led to the peculiarities of our city patterns with all their evils, one should read Werner Hegemann's *City Planning—Housing*, a three-volume work of great value. The discussion is rather polemical, but it contains a wealth of significant material which housing students should have at their command. The historical material contained in these volumes has never been explored from the housing point of view and certainly never with a greater sense of perspective.

Two other books should be mentioned in this list of general treatises on housing. One is Charles Harris Whittaker's *The Joke About Housing* (1920), a critical, if rather cynical, analysis of the subject, forecasting the present-day housing movement, and Louis H. Pink's *The New Day in Housing* (1928), a very thorough work based on long social experience and first-hand knowledge of administrative problems related to private investment in housing.

There is a tendency to overlook one public document devoted to a general discussion of all the problems and available facilities and agencies for improving living conditions. This document embodies the reports and discussions of the President's Conference on Home Building and Home Ownership, held in Washington in 1930 at the call of President Hoover. It comprises eleven volumes, edited by John M.

Greis and James Ford, and contains a wealth of information, opinion, and illustrative material of great value to all students of the subject. The material in these documents has never been fully explored.

THE SLUMS AND BLIGHT

Aside from the survey material available for most of the cities of the United States, a very considerable amount of general literature has important bearing on the policies of slum clearance and blight prevention and rehabilitation. One such work of a general nature, which purports to cover all the more important European countries and the United States, is *Slum Clearance*, published by the International Housing Association in 1935. It is a two-volume study in French, German, and English, dealing both with slum conditions and with efforts to improve them. Unfortunately, many errors have crept into the various reports, so that the text can not be used without reservation.

The most outstanding work of this nature in the United States is *Slums and Housing*, by James Ford. This deals with the history, conditions, and policies bearing on slums, and is fully documented. Its main emphasis is upon New York City, but it has great value as a general treatise on the subject. The bibliography is by far the most carefully compiled among those I am familiar with in the field.

For a concise appraisal of "slums and blighted areas in the United States," there is no more valuable work than Dr. Edith Elmer Wood's pamphlet of that title, published by the Housing Division of the Federal Emergency Administration of Public Works. *Urban Blight and Slums*, by Mabel L. Walker, although it contains some confusing definitions and the usual conflicts in point of view that arise when several writers contribute to a specific work, is an important contribution. It is well conceived, clearly written, and fully documented. The discussion of the various efforts directed toward developing remedial methods of prevention and rehabilitation is the best available thus far in book form.

THE LAND PROBLEM

I know of no better short study of land as an economic factor than *Land Economics*, by Professor Richard T. Ely and George S. Wehrwein. Though I am by no means in full accord with all that it contains, I am convinced that students of housing who read this work will gain a clear idea of the relation of land to our community development. Unfortunately, it has never found its way into print, but it is available in mimeographed form in many libraries. *Elements of Land Economics*, by Richard T. Ely and Edward W. Morehouse, published in 1924, is less valuable from the point of view of the housing student.

Students able to read German should not overlook the very excellent work by Professor W. Gemünd entitled *Bodenfrage und Bodenpolitik*. Although this book was published nearly twenty-eight years ago, it has a freshness and close relationship to housing and community planning that no other work has. Its scope embraces every phase of community development having to do with human welfare. Two years later, Professor Gemünd published a second volume entitled *Die Grundlagen zur Besserung der städtischen Wohnverhältnisse*, in which he carries his land studies more closely into the field of housing and community planning. By itself it stands as a singularly well rounded treatise on housing thrown into clear perspective as part of a comprehensive planning policy.

Land Planning in the United States for City, State and Nation, by Harlean James (1926), although having as its main theme the development of general principles of community development as affected by land use, bears upon housing in a manner uncommon to writers on this subject. For a clear and practical treatment of the land problem as it relates to housing, no better statement is available than the discussion contained in a transcript of a series of lectures by Sir Raymond Unwin, made public by the Subcommittee on Research and Statistics of the General Housing Committee in Washington, D. C. I should also like to mention Sir Raymond Unwin's little pamphlet, published in 1912, which bears the incisive title *Nothing Gained by Overcrowding*. It is a short but illuminating discussion of the value of intelligent land planning for group housing. No one intending to subdivide land should overlook this simple and logical treatment.

It would be futile to give a long list of publications on the land problem as related to housing because of the fact that most writers deal with land from a general point of view and without serious consideration of the housing problem. There are some, however, who emphasize some special panacea intended to solve the housing problem through a solution of the land problem. One such book which I have found challenging is Sir Thomas P. Whittaker's scholarly work *The Ownership, Tenure and Taxation of Land*, which deals with a whole series of theories of land and land reform. A more recent book on the subject is that of George Raymond Geiger entitled *The Theory of the Land Question*. This book deals with the Henry George theory that "land is part of the human environment, which is not the sole product of human labor," and draws the conclusion that "rent socialization through taxation seeks to adjust the distributive process by channelizing the flow of social income into social repositories, and by leaving inviolate private and earned income."

Land and taxation of land are inseparable subjects so far as housing is concerned. The device of the single tax on land has often been advanced as the most expedient means of obtaining cheap land for housing purposes, or of obtaining land at a cost merely commensurate with its tax-producing power. Any recent book on taxation will give the reader the essential background for the study of taxation as it affects housing. However, I should like to mention two studies as being both interesting and valuable in orienting the student in those phases of the tax problem which need concern us and which bear on the whole problem of urban land use. The first of these is *Tax Racket and Tax Reform in Chicago*, by Professor Herbert D. Simpson, published in 1930 by the Institute for Economic Research, at Northwestern University, Evanston, Illinois. The other is a test study of the workings of a partial and modified form of the land tax which is in practice in Pittsburgh, Pennsylvania, prepared for the Bureau of Business Research of the University of Pittsburgh by J. P. Watson and published in 1934 under the title *The City Real Estate Tax in Pittsburgh*.

For a systematic study of taxation, one should consult the following: Jens Peter Jensen's *Property Taxation in the United States* (1931), published by the Chicago University Press, and Herbert D. Simpson's article "The Incidence of Real Estate Taxes," in *The American Economic Review* for June, 1932. It might also be of interest to examine the very interesting work by Homer Hoyt, entitled *One Hundred Years of Land Values in Chicago—1830-1933*, on the history of land values in Chicago, published by the University of Chicago Press. This study is an extremely valuable examination of land-value enhancement. It is to be hoped that similar studies will be made in other cities. I can think of no better subject for a carefully planned doctoral thesis than a study of this kind in any community.

HOUSING PROGRAMS AND REHABILITATION PLANS

One of the most interesting documents dealing with housing programs is that issued in 1934 by the National Housing Committee of the British Empire, entitled *A National Housing Policy*, which reviews the various proposals for housing reform that have found expression either in law or in some economic planning set-up.

The United States has, of course, produced many proposals and many programs for housing reform. Sir Raymond Unwin, who has made so many valuable contributions to housing literature, has, with the aid of others, compiled such a program. This was published in 1935 under the auspices of the National Association of Housing Officials and bears the imprint of the Chicago Public Administration Service.

In view of the fact that the Netherlands has achieved a great deal by way of organizing the building industry and producing reasonably low-cost housing, it is suggested that the student become familiar with H. Van Der Kaa's *The Housing Policy of the Netherlands*, published in October, 1935, by the League of Nations, in a bulletin issued by the Health Organization Division. In 1931, the same office of the League of Nations issued an excellent report on the activities of various nations in matters of housing. This report deals with practically every civilized country of the world. A similar report, edited by Bruno Schwan, was published by the International Housing Association under the title *Town Planning and Housing Throughout the World*. It was printed in French, German, and English, and was issued in 1935 by the Wasmuth Publishing House of Berlin.

From the above literature, one can without difficulty glean the various programs followed by different nations and partly evaluate their achievements.

POPULATION

The development of a housing program must, of course, depend upon an understanding of population trends. This subject has received a great deal of attention in recent years. The latest and one of the most valuable contributions to literature on population is *The Problems of a Changing Population* issued in May, 1938, by the National Resources Committee. No student of housing can afford to overlook its wealth of information. Another valuable work is the study of population redistribution published in 1936 by the University of Pennsylvania Press under the directorship of Carter Goodrich entitled *Population and Population Migrations*, with the subtitle "Migrations and Economic Opportunity." I should also like to call the attention of the reader to *Dynamics of Population—Social and Biological Significance of Changing Birth Rates in the United States* (1934), by Frank Lorimer and Frederick Osborn.

Among the more specific studies, we find Professor R. D. McKenzie's *The Metropolitan Community* (1933), a scholarly analysis of the relation of population distribution to metropolitan districts. Its fundamental bearing upon the allocation of housing projects in metropolitan districts is made very clear. *Migrations and Business Cycles*, by Harry Jerome, which was published in 1926 by the National Bureau of Economic Research, Inc., is also important as a general discussion of the relation between housing and business as it affects and is affected by migrations of population.

In *Recent Social Trends in the United States*, a two-volume report of the President's Research Committee on Social Trends, published in 1933, the housing student will find a wealth of important material bearing on the population aspects of housing, incomes, migrations, and other subjects related to the ways of living and the changes that are taking place in the United States. From these studies, individual members of the Committee's staff have constructed several monographs, the most important of which are Professor McKenzie's *The Metropolitan Community*, already mentioned, Warren Thamson's and P. K. Whippleton's *Population Trends in the United States*, and T. J. Whoofter, Jr.'s, *Races and Ethnic Groups in American Life.*

INCOMES AND HOME OWNERSHIP

The United States Census Bureau has gathered statistical data regarding incomes which should be studied with great care. However, a number of important special reports and studies of incomes and home ownership are more carefully compiled and more suitably tabulated for use in housing studies. Volume VI of the *Fifteenth Census of the United States* (1930) constitutes the most important document on both population and home ownership in this country. It is the one source of information upon which we must depend in developing a quantitative housing program for the 30,000,000 families which constitute the population of the United States.

In May, 1935, the Federal Housing Administration published a well conceived study, *The United States Housing Market*, which, in spite of its meager interpretative text, contains raw material for a series of monographs needed to clarify and elaborate our national housing policy. In August, 1938, the National Resources Committee published a study, *Consumer Incomes in the United States (Their Distribution in 1935-36)*, which further emphasized the economic factor in population distribution but not, however, in relation to housing. The housing costs being known, the housing market can be readily calculated with reasonable accuracy. For a clearer conception of the relation between housing costs and incomes, one might consult a rather dry but accurate computation of housing costs under various economic set-ups published in February, 1937, by the New York City Housing Authority under the title *Rent Tables*.

One of the outstanding public documents dealing with incomes and rents is a stenographic report of a hearing held before the United States Senate Committee on Education and Labor from June 4 to 7, 1935, on Senate Bill 2392, known as the Wagner Housing Act. The testimony of Milton Lowenthal is particularly valuable.

The material contained in the above-cited documents might gain added significance from a study of the following works: *The Chart of Plenty* (1935), by Harold Loeb and Associates; *Report of the National Survey of Potential Productive Capacity*, sponsored by the New York City Housing Authority and the Works Division of the Emergency Relief Bureau of the City of New York, under the direction of Harold Loeb, and the Brookings Institution's study *America's Capacity to Consume*. For a simple and graphic picture of our economic status, one should consult *Rich Man, Poor Man*, by Ryllis Alexander Goslin and Omar Pancoast Goslin, issued in 1935 by Harper and Brothers.

Surveys of Housing Conditions

The most important source of information regarding housing conditions in the United States is the *Real Property Inventory*, which has repeatedly been mentioned in this book. The *Financial Survey of Urban Housing*, published in 1937 by the United States Department of Commerce, is beyond a doubt the best analysis of sample housing conditions, and should be available whenever a study of urban housing is undertaken.

As regards other surveys, it would be quite out of the range of this work to list them all. There are, to my knowledge, about 450 such surveys, many of which have been mentioned, either in the exhaustive bibliographies of the *Housing Index Digest*, published by the Central Housing Committee of the Subcommittee on Research and Statistics of the United States Government, or in the numerous bibliographies on housing which are generally appended to books on the subject. One of the best of these bibliographical lists of surveys was published some years ago by the Russell Sage Foundation, in New York, and can be obtained on request. Volume VI of *The Regional Survey of New York City and Its Environs* is another important study dealing with housing conditions.

There is a good deal of material pertaining to the methods of carrying out housing surveys, some of which is of real value; but it must be remembered that each community has its own problems and needs its own approach. The present work contains what, in the writer's estimation, is fundamental to an adequate survey in this respect. Many guides have been published by various writers, but few have taken into account the newer aspects of housing study. Instead, they have confined their discussion to fact finding so far as it affects individual buildings, rather than the conditions that have created substandard housing.

Housing Legislation

There is no book of importance which gives a fully balanced picture of housing legislation. The various suggestions advanced have been fragmentary, and frequently have placed the emphasis upon some single type of law assumed to be essential in bringing about desired changes. Mr. Lawrence Veiller made the first attempt to outline a program of housing legislation which dealt with the physical improvement of buildings.

As far back as 1910, the German *Kaiserlicher Statisticher Amt* made an analysis of the various forms of housing activity in Germany, including the legislative enactments and their operation. It is a portentous volume of historical rather than practical value. Three years later, Dr. Otto Haase published an excellent little book entitled *Das Problem der Wohnungsgesetzgebung* which carried the discussion far beyond the matter of building control and laid down some important social, economic, and legal principles intended to guide cities and the national government in formulating housing legislation.

There are no books in the United States dealing with the subject from a similar point of view. Most of what has been written here has dealt with general social legislation. The reader may find Dr. Mary Stevenson Colcott's *Principles of Social Legislation* a helpful introduction, but it will not prove of great value as regards housing. It was this lack of adequate literature on the subject which prompted the rather long chapter on housing law contained in this book.

SUMMARY

To the above list of books I should like to add a number of general works which come under no special classification but which are important because they indicate the trend of thought in recent years on the subject of housing in the United States.

In May, 1931, the American Academy of Political and Social Science published a volume, *Zoning in the United States*, under the editorship of William L. Pollard. This volume gives a reasonably well rounded picture of zoning philosophy and zoning practice. The Academy published another volume in March, 1937, entitled *Current Developments in Housing*, edited by David T. Rowlands and Coleman Woodbury, which contains a well balanced assortment of articles by experienced writers familiar with the most recent activities and trends in housing. Prompted by the widespread interest in housing, the School of Law of Duke University issued, in March, 1934, a volume, *Low-Cost Housing and Slum Clearance*. This constitutes the second number of the periodical *Law and Contemporary Problems*. The legal aspect, however, was accorded scant space. Clarence Arthur Perry's "Housing for the Machine Age," published in May, 1939 by the Russell Sage Foundation is a very valuable work on housing with its main emphasis upon the neighborhood. In closing, I should like to cite the brilliant book by Henry Write, *Rehousing America*. This is a work which no one should overlook. It is steeped in practical experience and a sense of reality such as no other book on the subject has attained.

The reader should not assume that I have given a full list of the best books on the subject of housing. It is fair to assume that any student interested in pursuing the subject further will have no difficulty in finding vast stores of information even in the humblest of sociological libraries. There is, of course, a great deal of material to be found in periodicals and even newspapers which is often of great importance. All that I have attempted to do here is to afford the reader a general idea of the range of available reading matter. The serious student will have no difficulty in finding his way beyond my guidance, while the casual reader will find his time fully occupied in following the merest thread of any of the many lines of inquiry I have ventured to suggest.

Index

INDEX

Addams, Jane, 234
Adler, Felix, 234
Age groups, 262
Amenities, 26
American Public Health Association, 131
Architecture, 197
  control of, 15
Astoria, 6
Athens, xi

Bassett, Edward M., 151
Behrendt, Walter Curt, 207
Bellman, Sir Harold, 73
Belloc, Hilaire, 212
Benoist, Charles, 126
Bernouilli, Jacques, 227
Board of Transportation, New York, 181
Boards of appeal, 150
Boom, 24
Booth, Charles, 233
Booth, William, 233
Bossange, E. Raymond, 200
Brookings Institution, 97
Business cycles, 190
Byzantine Empire, xi

Chastellux, Chevalier de, 230
Chicago, 8
Citizens Association of New York, 201
City planning, 32
Cleveland, 8
Clinicians, 215
Columbia University Housing Study, 239
Community services, 16
Constantinople, xi
Council of Hygiene and Public Health, 231
Culture of cities, 175

De Forest, Robert W., 234
Detroit, 8
Dumb-bell tenements, 132
Dwelling House Act, New York, 132
Dwellings, old, 133
  standards, xiv
Dymoxian house, 198

Eberstadt, Rudolph, 33
Economic space, 260
Education, 211
Employment migrations, 190
England, xiv, 36
Equity, 109

Family, 52
  head of, 62
Federal Home Loan Bank Board, 67, 81, 114
Federal Housing Administration, 142
Federal Savings and Loan Insurance Corporation, 84
Financial Survey of Urban Housing, 71, 77, 78, 81, 83, 99, 100, 103-104
Finnish urban centers, 36
Forbes, Garrett, 231
Ford, James, 241
France, 78
Fuller, R. Buckminster, 179, 198

Geddes, Patrick, 229
Gemünd, W., 33
Germany, xiv, 36
Ghettos, economic, 187
Goods, 32
  overproduction of, 32
Government purchase, 27, 28
Graunt, John, 228
Griscom, John H., 231

Harrison, Shelby M., 235
Hegemann, Werner, 230
Holden, Arthur, 43
Holden plan, 42, 136
Home Owners Loan Corporation, 67, 77, 81, 83, 114
Home ownership, 61, 109
  standards of, 116
Housing, and earning capacity, 89
  changes, 120
  concentration, 27
  defined, xii
  market, 89, 118
  mobility, 91
  standards, 127
  subsidy, 27
Housing Act, United States, 109
Housing Authority, United States, 95, 102, 143
Hudnut, Joseph, 200
Human element, 261

Industries, decentralization of, 191
  fugitive, 190
  gypsying, 90
Interest rates, 78, 84, 102
Investment, 68
  large-scale, 73
  liquidated, 69

289

Investment— (*Continued*)
  long-term, 24
  productivity of, 70
  safety of, 72
Isolation, geographic, 246

Jefferson, Thomas, 230
Jocher, Katherine, 223

Kellogg, Paul U., 235
Kenngott, George F., 235
Klein, Alexander, 236
Koyl, George S., 200

Lagrange, J. L., 228
Land, acquisition of, 45
  agricultural, 88
  control, social, 34
    use, 34
  cost, 16, 27
  development, 18, 38
    economic, 23
  elasticity, 19
  expansion, 19
  exploitation, 30
  exploration, 19
  geographic relation, 5
  investment in, 20
  management of, 33
  needs of, 7
  ownership, 35, 38
  place of, 14
  policy, 30, 34
  price, 23
  raw, 4
  replanning of, 140
  restrictions, 15
  stability, 13
  subdivisions, 29, 144
    regulations of, 146
  taxation of, 38
  unit of ownership, 28
  urban, 25
Lansing, Catherine F., 263
Lasker, Loula D., 115
Laws, financing, 156
  housing, 125, 170
  planning, 127
  promotive, 128, 159
  protective, 128, 153
  restrictive, 128
  tariff, 171
  violations of, 154
Leadership, 216
Le Corbusier, 204
Leibnitz, Gottfried Wilhelm, 228
Le Play, Frédéric, 226
Levels, cultural, 247
  economic, 247

Leven, Moulton, Warberton, 98
Limited dividends, 160
"Living machine," 197
London, City of, 14
Los Angeles, 8
Lot-use restrictions, 142
Lowenthal, Milton, 95, 97, 99
Lynd, Helen Merrell, 236
Lynd, Robert S., 236

Management, 217
Marx, Karl, 228
Mauclaire, Camille, 199
Mayor's Committee on Planning, New York
  City, 150
McKenzie, R. D., 60
Megalopolis, 193
Metropolitan areas, 55
Metropolitan communities, 60
Metropolitanism, defined, 188
Middle Ages, 36
Middletown, 235
Milwaukee, City of, 46
Mitchell, Wesley C., 245
Modernization, 31
Money, 67
Moore, Harry Estill, 51
Moratorium, 134, 138
Mortgages, 70, 158
Mumford, Lewis, 187
Municipal boundaries, 192
  expansion of, 192
Municipal land ownership, 152

National Resources Committee, 37, 54
Neighborhood study plan, 252-259
Neighborhoods, 118
New Amsterdam, xi
"New Deal," xii

Obsolescence, 3, 118
  economic, 3
  physical, 31
  social, 3
  technological, 31
Obsolete districts, 135
Odum, Howard W., 51, 223
Outlook Tower, 229

Pascal, Blaise, 227
People, 51, 204
Perry, Clarence A., 43
Perry plan, 43-44, 142
Planning economy, 19
Plato, 226
Police power, 128
Political space, 230

Population, 54, 176, 177
  rural, 56
  urban, 56
Prefabrication, xiv
Property rights, 180
Public Relief Commission, 232
Public Services, 185
Public Works Administration, 84
Purchas, Samuel, 226

Qualitative analysis, 243
Quételet, 228

Rafalovitch, Arthur, 232
Reconstruction, 27
Regional planning, 187
Regionalism, 51
  defined, 188
Rehabilitation, 55
Relief and rent, 156
Rent tables, 79
Replanning, 31
Research, 223
Riis, Jacob, 233
Roosevelt, President F. D., xii
Russell Sage Foundation, 235

San Francisco, 8
Sinclair, Upton, 234
Slum clearance, xiv
Slum Clearance Committee of New York, 239
Social motive, 204
Spartans, xi
Stow, John, 226
Subdivision control, 46
Subsidies, capital, 162
  defined, 161
  improvement, 168
  interest, 163
  land, 168
  rent, 167
Sunnyside, 115
Supreme Court of California, 128
Surveys, 223-224
  analytical, 240
  descriptive, 240
  legal, 264

Surveys—(Continued)
  problem, 240
  project, 241
  propaganda, 241
  public agencies, 264
  statistical, 242
  test, 241
Sweden, xiv
Sydenstricker, Edgar, 53

Tax, 37
  delinquency, 45
  exemption, 157, 159, 160, 161
  occupancy, 164
  rolls, 36
  "single," 37
  values, 36
Technicians, 216
Technology, 178
Thucydides, xi
Transportation economy, 180

Uhl, Charles H., 79
Unemployment insurance, 157
"Unlike communities," 188
Unwin, Sir Raymond, 14
Urbanism, 175
  defined, 189
  lag, 189
  semi-, 189

Veiller, Lawrence, 234
Vienna, City of, 36
Vignola, 200
Vitruvius, 200

Wagner, Martin, 181
Washington, General, 230
Wickers, David L., 100
Wohnungspolitik, 127
Wood, Edith Elmer, 103
Wood, Robert A., 234
Woodbury, Coleman, 90, 101

Yonkers, 117

Zoning, 32, 149, 177